Damage Noted
BROWN STAIN
AT
WCLS

The Brooklyn Thrill-Kill Gang and the Great Comic Book Scare of the 1950s

The Brooklyn Thrill-Kill Gang and the Great Comic Book Scare of the 1950s

Mariah Adin

 PRAEGER

AN IMPRINT OF ABC-CLIO, LLC
Santa Barbara, California • Denver, Colorado • Oxford, England

Library of Congress Cataloging-in-Publication Data

Adin, Mariah.
  The Brooklyn thrill-kill gang and the great comic book scare of the 1950s / Mariah Adin.
     pages cm
  Includes bibliographical references and index.
  ISBN 978-1-4408-3372-4 (print : alk. paper) — ISBN 978-1-4408-3373-1 (e-book)
  1. Murder—New York (State)—New York—Case studies.   2. Juvenile delinquency—New York (State)—New York—Case studies.   3. Comic books and teenagers—United States—History—20th century.   4. Brooklyn (New York, N.Y.)—History—20th century.   I. Title.
  HV6534.N5A66   2015
  364.152'30974723—dc23   2014025946

ISBN: 978-1-4408-3372-4
EISBN: 978-1-4408-3373-1

19 18 17 16 15   1 2 3 4 5

This book is also available on the World Wide Web as an eBook.
Visit www.abc-clio.com for details.

Praeger
An Imprint of ABC-CLIO, LLC

ABC-CLIO, LLC
130 Cremona Drive, P.O. Box 1911
Santa Barbara, California 93116-1911

This book is printed on acid-free paper ∞

Manufactured in the United States of America

For Benjamin

Contents

Acknowledgments

Books are funny things: while there is only one name listed on the dust jacket, they can only come to fruition through the efforts of many. First and foremost, I would like to thank my advisor, Richard F. Hamm, whose insightful commentary, lightning-fast turn-around times, and overall support of this project made it a pleasure to write. I would also like to thank the other members of my committee: Frankie Bailey, Barry Trachtenberg, Carl Bon Tempo, and Laura Wittern-Keller, for their support, discerning edits, and assistance in the publication process. Further, both the history department and Judaic studies program at the University at Albany were extremely generous in the funding of this project, and a special thank you goes to Joseph E. Persico, Calvin and Patricia Zippin, and the family of Morris Altman for their generosity.

It is probably not a usual thing to thank archivists for saving one's life, but the 2011 earthquake in Washington DC was an exceptional event. After evacuating the National Archives, I realized I had left all my money, identification, and (most importantly) my diabetes medication in my locker. Dr. James Hutson and his staff—Patrick Kerwin, Jennifer Brathovde, Lewis Wyman, and Lia Kerwin—personally took up a collection to make sure I had the money to get to a hospital, my hotel, return to the archive the next day, and get a hot meal. I will never forget their charity in my time of need. I would also like to thank my intrepid research pals, Sarah Pacelli and Jennifer Thompson Burns, for cheerfully going on a several hours' tour of the local emergency room with me.

The research for this book could not have been completed without the help of Ri J. Turner, my excellent and dedicated Yiddish researcher and translator. A thank you also goes to Kem Crimmins for his efforts at the New York Municipal Archives, Jacqui McNulty for her assistance and good company at the National Archives, Justin Adin for his legal research, and Dianne Aimone for all of her help with interlibrary loans. Further, much of the style of this book is indebted to Elaine Forman Crane of Fordham University, who always contended that excellent history could be written without sacrificing the telling of a good story. I believe that she will see her influence all over this book, and I hope she is pleased by the result.

Many friends stood by me during the graduate school process and deserve my unending gratitude. Liz Hardman kept herself available through instant messaging for cheerleading, guidance, and general moral support during the entire writing process. Tracy Verteramo has always believed in me and my work, even when I had given up on myself, and for that I can't say "thank you" enough. And my cadre at the University at Albany—Christopher Daly, Josie Madison, Bryan Herman, Jackie Mirandola-Mullen, Minkyoung Park, and Tim Carelton—were probably the most supportive bunch of people I could ever have been blessed to be thrown together with in a graduate program.

But ultimately, my family were the ones who had to put up with this process the most, and to them I owe the deepest gratitude of all. From the very beginning of this endeavor, my mother has always been my greatest cheerleader, and I thank her for that. I also thank my father for all his sage advice and for instilling in me the love of good writing. My daughters—Azra and Ziva—helped me to keep this project in perspective, and Ziva's looming due date provided the firm deadline the book needed. But more than anyone, this book is indebted to my husband, Benjamin Greenwald, without whose support (financial, emotional, and otherwise) this book could never have been written.

Introduction

"Few cases have stirred the Nation or awakened its consciousness of juvenile delinquency as did the case of the Brooklyn 'thrill-killers.'"

—*Report of the New York State Joint Legislative Committee to Study the Publication of Comics, 1955*

Their crime spree came straight from the pages of comic books: Some victims they tested their strength on, turning them into human punching bags. Others were tortured, their arms or legs wrapped in kerosene-soaked rags before one of the boys would strike a match. Some nights the group sought out young women in public parks, groping their exposed breasts after they had been stripped and flogged—a "popular game for kids," the boys would joke. But their final crime that fateful summer of 1954, the one called the "supreme adventure" by the gang's leader, would result in the police's dredging up the body of a middle-aged black man from the murky depths of the East River. Self-identified as "Hitler-admirers" and "Jewish Nazis," these middle-class boys "from good homes" would execute a trail of assault and murder that appalled the nation and justified calls by anticomics crusaders for the censorship of the comic book industry.

By the summer of 1954, America was fed up with juvenile delinquency. The earlier months of the year had already seen public hearings broadcast on television, in which U.S. Senator Estes Kefauver and his Senate Subcommittee on Juvenile Delinquency probed the minds of psychiatrists, criminologists, police officers, social workers, school employees, and parents to try to determine the causes of—and solutions to—a wide variety of teen misbehavior, ranging from sexual promiscuity to underage drinking to gang violence and even murder. Focusing on the role of the mass media, on April 21, 1954, the committee famously faced off with comic book publisher William Gaines, who blustered over whether a comic book cover depicting a man holding up a woman's decapitated head was in "good taste."[1] At the local level, more meetings, committees, and hearings concerning juvenile delinquency were held by parents, schools, police, and religious and community organizations than ever before. Add to that the daily headlines about gang shootouts, stomp killings, and millions of dollars' worth of vandalism, and it becomes clear why, by the summer of 1954, America was not only obsessed with the issue of juvenile delinquency but weary of the government's impotence in stopping it.

At the same time, this era saw innovative theories among sociologists and criminologists that posited criminality and delinquency as being more nurture than nature. Departing from the biological interpretations of the eugenics movement that had reigned prior to the Second World War, these modern theories focused on poverty, lack of social mobility, broken homes, and abuse as causative factors in juvenile delinquency. Of course, in many ways, these theories were neither new nor modern, paying much homage to the earlier Progressive Era ideologies that had spawned the juvenile court system in the first place.[2] Nor was everyone in America willing to entirely dismiss the idea that some people are simply "born bad"—as demonstrated by the runaway success of William March's *The Bad Seed* in 1954. But overall, most experts and much of the American public in the early 1950s believed that juvenile delinquency was a problem that could, and should, be overcome through community activism.

However, when four middle-class boys—boys who came from "good," unbroken Jewish homes, who were college-bound and upwardly mobile—chose to inexplicably throw away their bright prospects in favor of beating up and killing decrepit old men, their actions could not be explained by the new sociological paradigms. Instead, activists looking for other plausible rationalizations for the boys' behavior would find an answer in the already mobilized anticomics movement. Within days of the arrest of the Brooklyn Thrill-Killers, New York State Legislator James A. Fitzpatrick called for stricter regulation of the comics industry, claiming in a press conference that comic books were the obvious "blue print" for the gang's crimes. By February of 1955, the famous psychiatrist (and anticomics "super-villain") Dr. Fredric Wertham would testify that the Brooklyn Thrill-Killers proved what he had been warning America about for years: that the contents of horror and crime comics had the potential to lead children down a path of deviant sexuality and delinquency. Even the *New York World-Telegram* ran the front-page headline "2 Thrill Killers Steeped in Horror Books," accompanied by a photo spread in which two of the defendants flanked a salacious cover of *Lorna, The Jungle Girl* the day following the verdict.[3]

For parents in 1954, regulating your child's access to the mass media was simply common sense. Unlike previous generations, when most children worked (be it in factories, on the family farm, or hawking on city streets), the sudden rise of an affluent middle-class and increasingly white-collar society meant that midcentury parents faced new standards of "good parenting" that went beyond their children's being alive, well-fed, and (relatively) clean. Instead, with an increased emphasis on scholastic achievement, personality development, and psychological well-being, psychologists and child experts warned parents that when it came to outside influences, a lack of extreme vigilance could mean the ruin of the child.[4] Quite reasonably, then, many parents and child experts became increasingly concerned over the influence of untested, brand-new mass media forms that were targeted at their children.

All too often, the historiography of comic books—and particularly of the Great Comic Book Scare—tends to dismiss the anticomics movement as a bunch of high-brow, sexually repressed elites upset over the popularization of American culture.[5] Modern sociologists, however, have made impressive inroads into understanding the fundamental causes of "moral panics" and the very rational reasons why people participate in them.[6] In particular, the work of sociologist Sean P. Hier argues that, in American society, individuals are expected to engage in responsible forms of "personal risk management." When our ability to manage risk comes into conflict with what Hier terms as "harmful others," the collective will often use defensive and coercive action in response to the perceived "threat" of those who refuse to act responsibly.[7] Many of these so-called moral panics have resulted in campaigns and legislation that the majority of modern Americans would consider to be helpful to society—such as campaigns to end drunk driving or the creation of sex-offender registries. Others, such as the Great Comic Book Scare, have not fared as well in public opinion.

The case of the Brooklyn Thrill-Killers brought many of these issues to the fore: ranging in age from fifteen to eighteen, the boys were held up as examples of the insidious nature of comic books, and the ill effect they had on the psychological well-being of children. Further, the four young men were scrutinized by the media and by parents as a cautionary tale, in which the good influence of adults could be so easily undermined by bad associations. Finally, through what modern criminologists call the "Iron Quadrangle" of the media, activists, governmental engagement, and the authoritative endorsement of "experts," the Brooklyn Thrill-Killers quickly became cultural symbols of public and parental fears that affluent, "bored" teenagers would stop at nothing to achieve ever-greater "thrills."[8]

While serving as a cautionary tale across the board, for the Jewish community, the case of the Brooklyn Thrill-Killers was also a story about assimilation and identity, about what it meant to be a Jew in America in a post-Holocaust world. For the larger public, the question of comic book censorship would take center stage. But quietly, in Yiddish newspapers where Jews across New

York City could safely discuss the trial among themselves, other questions emerged: questions like "Are we assimilating too much?" and "Are we losing our children to America?" More than just the usual immigrant story of generational flux, the recent decimation of European Jewry meant the fate of a five-thousand-year-old culture was at stake. For the Jews of New York, the case of the Brooklyn Thrill-Killers was not just a sad story of four boys gone bad. Instead, it was a frightening reminder that the future of world Jewry was now in the hands of young people who were more interested in horror comics and monster movies than in learning about the Jewish patriarchs or studying the Torah.

Beyond the social implications, this book is the unfortunate tale of four messed-up kids who threw away their lives by committing terrible crimes. It is also the biography of a deeply disturbed young man who was bullied for being different and whose sexual identity did not fit into a Lavender Scare world in which alternate sexualities were akin to treason. Finally, it is the account of how these boys would be used by the adults around them to further their own agendas: to gain money and public support for antidelinquency and anticomics campaigns; to argue for a more intensive "Jewish Education" of children (*Yiddishkeit*) in the Jewish community; and to make an impotent district attorney's office look tough in its war on juvenile crime. Much like today, all of these aims would be accomplished at the expense of the boys, who would find themselves railroaded through the criminal justice system; crucified by a press allowed unfettered access to staged confessions and posed depositions; and at the mercy of defense attorneys more interested in their Broadway careers than helping their clients.

It is perhaps shocking that this case—which made headlines throughout the nation, was used to vindicate the banning of horror comics in New York State, and ultimately led to the U.S. Supreme Court case *Kingsley Books v. Brown*—has been relegated to the dustbin of history. This book is the story of the Brooklyn Thrill-Killers, but it is more importantly a recounting of the climate that made them famous, the underbelly of America's Golden Age, a story of juvenile delinquency, the terrible price of assimilation, and the dystopia already present among American youth well before the 1960s.

The Crime

August 16, 1954
9:00 p.m.

It was the kind of night the newspapers decried as "soggy." The temperature had barely budged since the afternoon, and the humidity had only gotten worse. In the crowded Williamsburg section of Brooklyn, the none-too-sweet perfume of the East River clung to the air like rotten smog.[1]

Bobby and Jerry waited anxiously outside of Mel's house, a brownstone on tree-lined Ross Street in South Williamsburg. The three boys had just met up with Jack at the Marcy Avenue Station, when Mel inconveniently decided he needed to stop back home to change his shoes. The foursome obligingly trudged the half mile through the soupy air back to Mel's, and now the two younger boys waited on the front stoop. Once Mel and Jack finally emerged, the foursome made for the bridge. Jerry suggested they go into New York and have a good time—maybe go uptown to see a movie or cruise along East River Drive to see if they could meet some girls. After all, he, Bobby, and Mel had just gotten part-time usher jobs at the famous Roxy Theater that afternoon, and didn't that call for a celebration?

"No," Jack, the oldest boy, replied. "Let's go looking for bums."[2]

They all knew what that meant. The game had started in July with Mel and Jack. One of their first victims was a sixty-two-year-old homeless man named Felix Jaculowski. The old man was napping in the park on a drizzly afternoon when he suddenly awoke to find his leg had been wrapped in gasoline-soaked rags and set on fire. As he screamed from the pain—for the police—Jack ran. But the "big boy," Mel (210 pounds with a size 16 1/2 collar), went right over to the old man.

"You're the man we're looking for," he said. "Do you know me, you bum?"

When the frightened geriatric replied that he did not know the boy from Adam, Mel punched him in his face, breaking his nose, before casually strolling away.[3]

Just five days later, the pair struck again. That night, they beat up two men: One was a homeless man, who was later discovered lying unconscious in an empty lot near South Fourth Street and Bedford Avenue by a passing patrolman. The other was a sixty-year-old Hungarian basket weaver accosted as he tried to cool off outside his home. Pictures of the basket weaver revealed a face so smashed up that two weeks later it was still severely swollen and bruised, with a half-closed blackened eye. Jack would eventually claim they had beaten the man for a good three or four hours, kicking him in the face while he lay on the ground and burning him under his ear with cigarettes.

"It's fortunate for me," the scrawny eighteen-year-old with a Hitler-style mustache later joked, "that he doesn't speak English too well."[4]

But the climax was on August 6. That afternoon started innocently enough with a flick at the old Keap Street movie palace, The Republic, a special big-city movie theater popular in the earlier part of the century and originally designed for the vaudeville circuit. Built in 1921, The Republic's most distinguishing features were its lavish decorations and enormous size. Grand even for the era, the theater sat 3,100 guests and featured such "deluxe" amenities as a pipe organ, room for an orchestra, and velvet-covered seats. The ceilings were ornately carved, the chairs graded for maximum visual impact, and comfort and luxury oozed from its lounges. Outside, the open, covered vestibule extended over the sidewalk, giving patrons a place to dodge inclement weather while the cantilevered marquees, announcing new and ever-more-exotic spectacles, rose above their heads.[5]

By 1953, of course, the velvet was worn and shabby, and the spectacles announced by the (now electric) marquees were mostly B-grade horror flicks. On this particular occasion, the boys opted to see the mystery *Gorilla at Large*, a 3-D thriller that critics lambasted as a "straight scoop of melodramatic muck about murder and other odd distractions at an outdoor amusement park." But once the lights dimmed, the film was largely forgotten. Instead, the day's entertainment came from Mel as he regaled the two younger boys with tales of his and Jack's adventures. Of course, as Mel spun the yarn, the superhero-style trysts were merely a civic duty.

"They went around and got these bums," one of the younger boys later told the police, "and they beat them up to try to persuade them, as they put it, to get a job and stop drinking." Sitting there in the dark, among the carved columns and sparkling chandeliers, Jerry and Bobby found it all very hard to believe. They kept insisting that Mel was making the whole thing up.

For his part, Mel finally insisted the pair come along sometime and "see what it was all about." Before the credits rolled that afternoon, the three had made arrangements to meet up after dinner.[6]

They reconvened between 9:00 and 9:30 p.m. in front of Jerry's house—a six-room air-conditioned apartment filled with "expensive furniture of modern design" and conveniently located only a few doors down from the family's lucrative appliance store. From there, they walked the seven blocks to Triangle Park, in the shadow of the Williamsburg Bridge. But as there were no likely targets milling around, Mel suggested another nearby and more promising location. So the boys reversed their tracks on Broadway and meandered east until turning up Rodney Street.[7]

Once on Rodney, they paused to hide in the shadows of the immense Lutheran church, St. Paul's, with its attached vicarage and looming bell tower. Designed by the famous American architect J. C. Cady in 1884, the building was one of the most exceptional examples of the Romanesque Revival style, an architectural movement that combined Greek and Gothic elements and was considered, at the time, to represent an "authentically German" viewpoint. The style seemed particularly appropriate for St. Paul's, as its brick and terra-cotta bulk housed one of the first churches established by Williamsburg's German community. Further down the block, brick apartment buildings with art nouveau façades rambled one into the other.[8]

But what interested the boys was not the immense brick structure behind them; they had turned to face the remains of what had been the west side of Rodney Street. In 1952, the city acquired the west side of Rodney Street as part of the construction of the highly anticipated Brooklyn-Queens Expressway. At the moment, the portion between South Fifth and South Fourth Streets was in the process of demolition. In the meantime, the abandoned buildings served as temporary shelter for the local vagrant population. On the night of August 6, there were two men relaxing on the stoop in front of the second building.[9]

The boys crossed over and struck up a conversation, asking the men what their names were. The first man called himself "Tex," and the second said his name was "Whitey." Tex was a moving man who actually had a residence on South Fourth Street, although he liked to come by from time to time and drink with some of the fellows. Whitey's formal name was John Perrett. He was a fifty-two-year-old down-on-his-luck painter, described by both the police and newspapers as "a little, gray-haired vagrant." While they were chatting, a third man came downstairs, but he caught one look at the boys and hid behind a door. Tex finally managed to coax the reluctant squatter outside, but only by promising that they would go for a walk. The third man was Eddie Walsh, and he knew all too well why Mel was there. Eddie was the guy the police found unconscious in the South Fourth Street lot just a couple of nights ago, courtesy of Mel's fists.[10]

Now alone with Perrett, the scene turned ugly. One of the "smaller boys" (likely Bobby) ordered the elderly man to get up. Perrett swayed to his feet only to be smashed to the sidewalk by Mel's fist. The boys ordered him to get up again, but the decrepit little man could not move. Bobby started to pick him up, but finding the poor vagrant only semiconscious, he decided to slap him back awake first. Once he roused him, Bobby punched Perrett—followed by Jerry, followed by Mel—until the little, gray-haired vagrant finally "fell down, and this time he stayed down." According to Perrett's own testimony, the boys laughed at his struggle to get off the sidewalk while they abused him.

As the boys walked away toward the handball courts on South Fifth Street, they passed another drunk who had just stepped out of a bar at the end of the street. Forty-three-year-old Peter Rhinehold Ulrickson was a steeplejack and rigger by trade as well as part owner of a steeplejack company. He cut a tall, lean figure at nearly six feet tall and 170 pounds. On August 6, 1954, he had spent the day painting a stack at Atlantic and Grand Avenues and was expecting to get $55 for it. According to his business partner, he was a clean-living man and a hard worker. His mother later confided to the press that he was trying to save enough money to start a new business in New Jersey and that he often earned as much as $75 a day. But according to the little, gray-haired vagrant whom the boys had just left lying on the sidewalk, Ulrickson was a friend he affectionately called "Pinky" who came by to visit him after work—sometimes staying the night in the abandoned building if they had imbibed one too many. That he was mistaken by the boys as also being a vagrant likely had as much to do with his clothing as his drunkenness.

As his fellow steeplejack and business partner, Sam Ungarten, wryly noted, "When he works he wears old clothes; you don't paint smokestacks or flagpoles in your Sunday suit."[11]

As they passed Ulrickson, the boys taunted him. Bobby asked the man if he wanted to fight. The boys then turned and walked back to where Perrett was still lying on the ground, bleeding. They stood there and waited for the drunken steeplejack to stagger his way to the stoop.

When Ulrickson finally got close enough to see Perrett, he thought his friend was merely falling-down drunk and began to laugh at him. But when he crossed the street to help Perrett up, Ulrickson's expression changed. Meanwhile, the three boys stood behind the beaten old man and continued to mock his struggle to get off the sidewalk. Ulrickson asked Whitey whether he was drunk, and Perrett managed to moan out, "No, I've been struck." The drunken steeplejack looked at the boys and raised the bottle of beer in his hand.

Still laughing, Mel asked, "Why don't you help your friend who's on the sidewalk?"

Ulrickson waved the raised beer bottle menacingly. "Why don't *you* help him," he sneered at the teens. "You just finished beating him."

Bobby grabbed a rock, and the man taunted him, "Throw it at me. Hit me with it." But Bobby tossed the rock away.

In the meantime, Mel also grabbed a rock. The situation then escalated, with the man and boy circling each other in a momentary standoff, each threatening to pummel the other with their chosen weapon. Finally, Mel, becoming increasingly agitated, dropped the rock and simply punched Ulrickson flush in the jaw.[12]

The steeplejack crumpled to the sidewalk.

The boys sauntered off, down South Fifth Street toward the handball court again. They stopped at the Sunset Restaurant to wash the blood off their hands and enjoy a cool drink.

The next day, Bobby telephoned Mel. He had just read an article in the *Brooklyn Daily Eagle* that claimed a man who was beaten up at South Fifth and Rodney Streets was at Greenpoint Hospital in critical condition.

"I know," Mel replied. But what he did not know was that a week later Ulrickson would be dead, his brain having received its fatal traumatic injury when his skull hit the sidewalk's gutter and fractured.[13]

So when, on that hot, soggy night of August 16, Jack said, "Let's go looking for bums," the boys all knew what he meant and what was in store for that evening. On the walk back to Mel's house from the elevated-train station at Marcy Avenue, the three boys even bragged to Jack about what they had done on August 6. When they finished, Jack told fifteen-year-old Bobby, "Now you are a bum beater."[14]

*   *   *

There were no objections to Jack's suggestion to look for bums, so the boys headed in the direction of South Fifth and Rodney, back to the abandoned buildings. But when they went got to South Fifth, Jerry balked. The slender, 150-pound youth was frightened to return to the scene of their previous crimes. So Mel and Jack went ahead and saw that the coast was clear: the vagrants, it had turned out, were too scared to hang around there anymore. The group headed south toward Broadway and then turned in the direction of the East River.[15]

They converged on Triangle Park around 9:00 p.m. Lurking in the shadow of the Williamsburg Bridge on-ramp, the "park" was really just an euphemistic title for a triangular slab of concrete with a waist-high cement wall topped by a crumbling iron railing. Five low, stone benches lined the east side of the triangle, while seven more lined the west side, punctuated by a handful of ornamental lights. A kicked-in wire wastebasket slouched next to the park entrance, but litter seemed to congregate everywhere except in its recesses. The park was an afterthought, a useless scrap of land leftover from the juxtaposition of bridge construction and grid-like streets and avenues.[16]

"Let's go in and look for some bums," Jack said.

Two minutes later, they left the park disappointed. It was too early yet, and no one was hanging around. So the boys retreated to a candy store at the corner of Roebling and Broadway, where they purchased some sugary treats and bided their time.

At 9:30 p.m., they returned to the sad little park, and this time two bums were sitting on one of the benches. The boys approached the two men, and

Mel ordered them to kiss Jack's feet. One man, eyeing Mel's bulk, got on the ground and embraced Jack's shoes. The second man, however, made the mistake of objecting. The gang beat the old man until he consented to join his friend on the ground, kissing Jack's feet while the boys laughed at him.[17]

The boys decided to continue the "bum hunt" in McCarren Park and proceeded to swagger their way north up Driggs Avenue. Unlike Triangle Park, McCarren was true parkland. From its inception in 1905 as Greenpoint Park, it boasted two playgrounds soon followed by a quarter-mile track, a field that served as an ice rink in the winter, tennis courts, a dancing platform, and fields for baseball, football, and soccer. In 1936, the Works Progress Administration added a giant swimming pool, which quickly became a summertime social hub for the Greenpoint and Williamsburg neighborhoods.[18]

The four boys entered the park at the northwest corner of Driggs Avenue and North Twelfth Street. Not too far in from the entrance, Jerry spotted two girls sitting on a bench near the metal-slatted fence. He was still keen on his original idea of spending the evening cruising for girls, so he convinced the other fellows to go over. The girls, however, were not particularly interested.

Unbeknownst to Jerry, Mel had anticipated finding some girls that night. Hidden under his shirt was a black leather whip, one that Jack had won on a recent outing to Coney Island. While Jerry and Bobby waited downstairs, Mel and Jack decided to bring the whip along in case they came across any girls in the parks. It was not the first time the two had whipped young women out at night. They later confessed that they had overwhelmed and flogged girls in the streets or parks on at least five or six other occasions. Sometimes they forced them to kiss Jack's feet, and Mel often touched their breasts. Jack later characterized it as "a popular game for kids."[19]

They grabbed one girl, but the other one ran. Mel handed the whip to Jerry. They lashed the girl several times, before leaving her crying on the grass. On the way out of the park, they spotted two more girls who were chatting and necking with two boys on the lawn. As the four approached menacingly, the boys fled. They grabbed one of the girls, and Jack whipped her across the back.[20]

As they left McCarren Park, Jack suggested that they revisit the south side of the bridge to see whether there were any more bums milling around. The boys walked back down Driggs Avenue, a long eighteen-block promenade that returned them to Triangle Park. The bright full moon was nearly at its zenith.[21]

*   *   *

Arriving once again at the dirty, little concrete triangle, the boys found that their earlier victims had fled. They now saw two men at the bench immediately to their right engrossed in a game of either checkers or chess. On the bench next to them, about five feet away, another man was sleeping. He was curled up on his right side, and his knees, encased in blue slacks, were bent so that his bare feet rested just on the bench's edge. His head lay on his shoes, blue two-toned suede, with the socks curled up inside them. His tan-shirted chest rose and fell. He stunk of alcohol.

Jack spotted him and turned to the others. "Let's wake him up," he said.[22]

They quietly formed a semicircle around the sleeping figure. Jack went around to the drunk's feet, on the side of the bench farthest from the chess players. Next to him was Mel, followed by Jerry, and finally Bobby—the tallest of the boys at six feet—who stood at the man's head, obstructing the view from the other bench. Nothing was said. They were all waiting.[23]

The men at the next bench continued their game.

The drunk's left foot was bare. Jack lit a match and held it dangerously close to the outstretched limb, but it had no effect. So he reached into his pocket, took out a cigarette, and lit it. With glacial speed, Jack inched the cigarette to the instep of the sleeping man's foot, and the vagrant woke with a scream. At the trial, Bobby imitated the cry to a packed courtroom, splintering the air and ushering in a shuddering silence.

But on August 16, the howl was met with a command. "Get up and put on your shoes. Come with us."[24]

The stupefied man struggled into a sitting position and turned his head several times to see who was there. Mel, Jerry, and Bobby backed up a couple of steps. Jack joined the two younger boys at the opposite end of the bench near the chess players. Mel, the group's muscleman, moved in closer to the vagrant. Still soused, the bum slowly lifted his shoe from the bench. But after a moment's hesitation, he deliberately placed the shoe down again in exchange for a sock, which he struggled to slip on. He then painstakingly repeated the performance.[25]

In the meantime, Jack whispered to Jerry to take a swing. Jerry shook his head, and Jack derided him as a "chicken." He then turned to Bobby and whispered the same offer, "Go ahead, Trachtenberg; do you want to hit him?" But Bobby, too, declined. So Jack told the two younger boys to meet up with him and Mel later.

Relieved, Jerry turned to Bobby and said, "Bob, let's get out of here." Then he began dragging his younger friend out of the park. But Bobby, ever curious, hung back wanting to know where the two older boys planned to take the vagrant.

Jack turned his head slightly to the left, while glancing at Mel, and whispered to Bobby, "The waterfront." Then he abruptly snapped his head back to look directly at the younger boy and ordered, "Get lost," waving his hand in dismissal.

Turning back again to look at Mel, Jack whispered, "Go ahead; we will meet you boys later and tell you what happened."

Jerry and Bobby left the park as the man finished putting on his first shoe. Next to them, the chess players never even looked up. They just quietly continued their game. [26]

Jerry and Bobby left the park and walked down Broadway toward the waterfront. When they reached the gasoline station just off the driveway from the bridge, Jerry suggested they cross the street and figure out what they were going to do. So the two boys walked up Driggs Avenue and turned left in about half a block.

Feeling they were at a safe distance from Mel and Jack, Jerry informed Bobby that he had had enough and wanted to go home. "What do you want to do?" he asked his best friend.

Bobby thought about it for a minute and then finally replied that he wanted to follow the older boys to see where they were going. He later recalled the conversation: "I also told him that [Jack] Koslow told me that they were going to the waterfront, and I told him I was curious, and he said 'O.K.'" At that same moment, they saw Jack, Mel, and the inebriated man crossing Driggs Avenue and Broadway. Jerry and Bobby let the threesome get about a block ahead of them before they followed along on the opposite side of the street.[27]

*   *   *

It was a strange group that slowly perambulated down Broadway. On one side walked a lean, six-foot-tall redhead whose countenance was often described as "sallow." On the other, was a large, burly teen whose clothes bulged against muscles carefully cultivated at the Keap Street YMHA (Young Men's Hebrew Association). Both boys sported Hitler-style mustaches, scraggly with youth, one red and one dark. Flanked in-between was a tall, thin black man with curly dark hair for whom staying upright was proving a Herculean task.[28]

Along Broadway, they passed the Williamsburgh Savings Bank, a four-story Classical Revival building of limestone and marble. Bronze candelabra flanked the short flight of stairs that led up to the deeply recessed main entrance, framed by a two-story arch and paired Ionic pilasters. Across the street, a sign advertising Tydol gasoline competed with another announcing an upholstered furniture showroom. Beneath the signs, patrons entered and exited the famous Peter Luger Steakhouse. As they walked toward the waterfront, Jack asked the man questions. The boys learned the man's name was Willie Menter and that he worked making burlap bags. As they turned up Bedford Avenue, Jack continued his interrogation.

"Are you married?"

"Yes."

"Why aren't you home with your wife?"

"I don't give a damn," Menter muttered.

"Don't you have kids?"

"Yes."

"Don't you care whether they eat or starve?"

"I don't give a damn," Menter reiterated. "Let my brother worry about it."[29]

They continued on in silence.

*   *   *

Willard Menter was only thirty-four years old in 1954. Originally from Enterprise, Alabama—a small, rural city noteworthy only for its statue erected in gratitude of the boll weevil—Menter was one of the six million African Americans in the mid-twentieth century who chose an uncertain existence in the North over the brutal reality of the Jim Crow South.[30] In 1954, Willard worked for the New York Bag Company at 101 Grand Street, making burlap bags, and earned $1 an hour on a blowing machine crew.[31] Or at least he did when he was working. According to his brother, Charles, over the last three years, Willie had often found himself in a vicious cycle of being laid off and hired back, as suited the factory. Unfortunately, this was a common experience for African American men in the midcentury period, who often found that discrimination denied them access to steady work in the manufacturing economy. So like many black families of the era, the Menters were a two-income household.

Willard Menter's wife, Emma, a pretty woman with high cheekbones and a fashionable halo of dark curls, worked as a file clerk for a large Manhattan firm. Emma was part of a new wave of postwar black women who, for the first time in American history, had access to white-collar jobs and wages comparable to their white counterparts. With a steady job and consistent wages, Emma was the family breadwinner. Whether the economic disparity of the couple contributed to the breakdown of their marriage is uncertain, but after ten years and three children together, Emma Menter was definitely tired of her husband's drinking. Although his brother weakly tried to defend him ("Willie, he'd drink a little bit," he told the newspapers, "but he didn't start no fights.") Emma had already kicked Willard out of the house.[32]

On August 16, 1954, Menter had been staying at his brother's house at 131 Lewis Avenue, a three-story apartment building with carved rosettes over the windows in the Bedford-Stuyvesant neighborhood. Willie went into work on Monday around noon to ask his boss, Israel Schreibman, for a $2 advance on his pay. Schreibman asked what had happened to the $5 advance he had already given Menter on Friday. Willie told his boss he needed to go to the hospital. Schreibman gave him the advance. Willie then promptly left the factory and headed for the bar.[33]

*   *   *

When the trio got to Wythe Avenue and South Sixth Street, they turned under the bridge. Jerry and Bobby remained a half block behind on the opposite side of the street. They tagged along to South Sixth and watched as Jack, Mel, and the vagrant crossed Wythe Avenue and headed toward the waterfront.

The area by the East River in Williamsburg was home to an array of industries. Down Kent Avenue was the F. & M. Schaefer Brewery, established in 1916. In 1954, it was the sixth-largest brewing company in the United States and one of the largest industries in Williamsburg. In the area west of Bedford Avenue and north of the Brooklyn Navy Yard, the company had torn down entire blocks to erect garages, shops, and administrative buildings. To the north, between South Fifth and South Second Streets, the Domino Sugar refineries dominated the East River with their Romanesque Revival buildings and glowing neon signage that served as a kind of East River beacon. In the postwar period, as American demand for sugar rose to unprecedented levels, the brick waterfront factory became one of the largest employers in Williamsburg.[34]

The two younger boys waited about five minutes before taking after the trio. They turned right down Wythe Avenue to South Fifth Street and looked east. At the end of the block, they saw three people silhouetted against passing cars. Jerry and Bobby slowly walked toward the pier. The area was completely quiet except for the two-story brick building owned by the sanitation department, which was alive and humming with the evening shift. As the boys passed by the open rear-bay doors, they quickly glanced inside. A couple of sanitation workers and someone in a blue uniform, possibly a police officer, stood idly chatting.

Jerry began to get spooked again. He glanced at the obscuring darkness across the street. A bright security light streaming down from the top of the Domino Sugar factory created the last circle of illumination before the pitch-black pier. Jerry whispered to Bobby that he did not want to go any farther. Bobby headed toward the barricade alone.[35]

*   *   *

The threesome stood on the gloomy pier. Jack backed Menter up against the restraining fence and turned to Mel. "Vilstu klapn?" he asked softly in Yiddish. "You want a hit?"[36]

Mel replied, "Bring him over."

Jack motioned to Menter to approach. Mel took a swing. Menter put his hand up in a helpless gesture and doubled over.

"What was that for?!" he cried out.[37]

*   *   *

Just as Bobby reached the barricade, he heard someone whistling. Then, after a pause, he heard a voice emanate from the darkness. "Hey, Bob, come over here."

Bobby froze, and the eerie stillness returned. A few seconds later, the disembodied voice repeated the command.

"Hey, Bob, come over here."

Bobby remained motionless.

Mel stepped out of the darkness into the bright pool of light emanating from the Domino factory roof. "Hey, Bob, did you see what Koslow did? He pushed the man in the water."

"You're crazy."

Mel shrugged his shoulders and walked back into the shadows. Bobby scurried back to where Jerry was pacing, and the two boys retreated to the corner of South Fifth Street and Kent Avenue. After about five minutes, Mel returned. Jerry and Bobby stood in mute disbelief as Mel told them what happened. Then Mel returned to the pier. After about two more minutes, he came back to wait with Bobby and Jerry. No one said a word.

Five minutes later, Jack came up. "The man is in the water, boys," he announced.

Jerry was beginning to panic. "Come, on, Koslow, where's the guy? Where's the guy?"

"I just told you," Jack snapped. "And anyway, mind your own business!"

Jerry had had enough. All he had really wanted to do that evening was go cruising for some girls. He cursed Jack and asked him why he did it. Why had he brought the guy down there in the first place? Jack suggested they start walking.

As they headed down South Fifth Street, toward Wythe Avenue, Jerry continued his tirade. "You're crazy. You're kidding me. Are you crazy, doing something like that?"

Jack told him to shut up, and Bobby suggested they talk about something else. The four boys walked the next few blocks in silence.[38]

Under the bridge at Driggs Avenue, Jack stopped and turned to the other boys. He looked at them menacingly and told the younger boys to keep quiet about what had happened that night. He warned them that he could get the chair, Mel could get life, and that Bobby and Jerry could get "five years apiece."

"What for?" Bobby asked.

Jack informed the younger boy that because he and Jerry knew what had happened they were "accessories after the fact."

Jack looked all the boys in the eye. "Now we are all murderers," he intoned.

"Leave me out of it!" Bobby snarled at him. "I had nothing to do with it. Just remember that."[39]

The four boys split up. Bobby and Jerry headed home, but Jack and Mel headed to another park. After all, the night was still young.

* * *

A plainclothes detective walked out of the 90th Precinct Station at the corner of Lee and Division Avenues and into the muggy night air. He paused on the steps and looked out onto the small park across the street. Louis Sobel Park was dedicated to the memory of Private Louis Sobel, a Brooklyn native and veteran of the First World War who was killed at the Second Battle of the Marne on July 18, 1918. At the time of the park's dedication in 1938, it was the first public space in New York City to be named for a Jewish war hero. Across the way, he saw a tall, skinny redheaded kid standing under the streetlamp in front of the Jewish deli. He was smoking a cigarette. Next to him sat a big, dark-haired kid who was also smoking.[40]

Two vagrants on the left-hand side of the station-house steps were leaning up against the cool, white stone facade of the building. Detective John Burke walked down the six steps to the sidewalk and addressed the men. They seemed frightened. They told him that two kids had just worked over a man in the park. Burke recalled a case out of the 92nd Precinct in which an old derelict had been badly beaten up by two boys. He decided to take a stab in the dark.

"Does one of them have red hair?" he asked.

When the bums answered in the affirmative, he quickly crossed the street.

The Gang

In 1954, Jewish Williamsburg was a community in transition. Approximately fifty blocks in size and with a population of roughly 25,000 residents, it was one of the most densely packed neighborhoods in New York. Triangular in shape, it was bounded by Brooklyn's Broadway to the north, Heyward Street to the south, and the East River to the west. Traditionally a locus for assimilation-oriented Jewish immigrants, by midcentury it was a neighborhood broken. Ripped apart by the construction of the Brooklyn-Queens Expressway, the carcass of Williamsburg was slowly being picked over by a new, and increasingly insular, immigrant population while its former residents fled to the greener climes of Flatbush and Far Rockaway.[1]

It was not the first time, nor the last, that Williamsburg served as a backdrop of generational flux. Merged into the city of Brooklyn in 1855, Williamsburg of the late nineteenth century was filled with wealthy industrialists and professionals, their mansions and brownstones filling the shady, tree-lined side streets. Many were Jews of German extraction or from the Alsace-Lorraine region, who established their more liberal temples in the churches abandoned by Christian congregants. It was a time when Bedford Avenue was the seat of some of the most exclusive clubs in the borough, where the "top hats, tails and carriages" were "as plentiful as on Fifth Avenue." One observer gushed that the neighborhood was "like walking into a park, with trees and well-cared-for gardens on both sides of the street."[2]

A small announcement, published in an 1896 edition of *Engineering News*, heralded the end of the heyday of Old Williamsburg. Written by Leffert L. Buck, the newly appointed chief engineer, the article announced plans for the construction of the world's longest suspension bridge. Spanning the East River, the 7,200 foot bridge was intended to relieve the congestion already being felt on the recently constructed Brooklyn Bridge to the south. The problem was that at the proposed bargain price of $7 million (the Brooklyn Bridge had cost $15 million) the Williamsburg Bridge was designed for utility, not beauty. Destined to always suffer by comparison to its more beauteous neighbor, the Williamsburg Bridge was quickly lambasted by critics as an artless eyesore, driving down exclusive real estate prices. More importantly, in connecting Williamsburg with Manhattan's teeming Lower East Side, the neighborhood began to see a significant migration of middle- and working-class Jews from Eastern Europe, much to the dismay of the wealthy, liberal Jewish residents and their gentile neighbors.[3]

By the end of World War I, wealthier Jews had relocated to Flatbush and Crown Heights. In their stead, a significant number of Russian and Polish Jews began to take their place. These early groups represented a cross section of the immigrants who had been living in the tenements of the Lower East Side. Although they attended Orthodox synagogues, these first migrants to Williamsburg were moderate, upwardly mobile, and they embraced American middle-class lifestyles. By the 1920s, the district had turned into a typical low- to middle-class Jewish neighborhood, in which workers, employees, and small businessmen had fully replaced the wealthy former residents. Numerous synagogues sprouted up throughout the area, many in abandoned church buildings. Even the Reform Temple, Beth Elokim, the pride of the former Jewish community, was sold to the Orthodox rabbinate.[4]

As the population changed, so too did Williamsburg. Hebrew schools and organizations formed, and many of the exclusive clubhouses—beginning with the Hanover Club on Bedford Avenue—were taken over by Jewish organizations. Stores changed owners and began to carry Jewish foods and religious articles. Alongside these amenities of more traditional Jewish life, movie theaters also flourished, as well as pool rooms and dance halls for the young. As one old-timer put it, "It was a really fine Jewish life here in Williamsburg."[5]

But the neighborhood faced a third transition during the Second World War. Refugees from Eastern Europe, outrunning the Nazis as they swept through their homelands, arrived daily. After the war ended, the inmates of concentration camps, internment camps, and displaced persons camps flocked to America and, subsequently, Jewish Williamsburg.[6]

These survivors were different from the previous immigrants, who had been assimilation-oriented moderates pursuing the American Dream. Instead, these ultra-Orthodox Hasidim, as historian Arthur Hertzberg noted, were more akin to the Pilgrims or Puritans, coming "not in search of the American dream, but so that they could do what they had always done, in freedom, and without being persecuted—without being murdered by Hitler." Unlike the earlier immigrants, who often came with their families, many of the refugees arrived alone, with no family left or home to return to.

The handful of Hassidic leaders who survived alongside them—many of whom had suffered their own tragedies, such as the Klausenberger Rebbe, whose wife and eleven children had perished—became surrogate fathers to their surviving flocks, providing the newcomers assistance in finding apartments and jobs and arranging marriages in place of murdered parents. In turn, their adherents rebuilt their traditional communities, even at the expense of rejecting the many opportunities America had to offer.[7] The Hasidim soon realized that cultural survival meant creating an enclave in which they could take from America without being consumed by it. But this enclosure often put the new group into conflict with the established Jewish population in Williamsburg, who expected the refugees to pursue the familiar patterns of assimilation that they had followed.

In the meantime, the neighborhood was already suffering from the construction of the Brooklyn-Queens Expressway. Ten of the most populated blocks in the neighborhood were demolished, and nearly 5,000 residents were immediately displaced. The structure slashed through the business district on Broadway—an unhappy coincidence as manufacturing in the area was already on the decline. Over the next decade, the tracts located nearest to the "BQE" lost much of their population, and landlords stopped maintaining their properties as housing prices plummeted. The neighborhood that was considered the epicenter of a "really fine Jewish life" only a couple of decades earlier was quickly going to ruin. Jack and Mel, whose families were assimilation-oriented Jews who had migrated to the area from the Lower East Side, grew up in the remains of this decaying neighborhood that served as the backdrop for their crimes.[8]

* * *

Just to the north of Jewish Williamsburg, where today the border between South Side and North Side meet, were the homes of Jerome "Jerry" Lieberman and Robert "Bobby" Trachtenberg. Jerry Lieberman was seventeen years old in 1954, and he lived on Grand Street—the same block, in fact, where his parents had lived for nearly twenty-eight years. The family's most recent move, to a six-room, air-conditioned apartment at 335 Grand Street, was prompted by the Brooklyn-Queens Expressway demolition. Before then, they had lived down the block in an apartment located directly above the family's appliance store. Now, the Lieberman's radio and television shop occupied the first floor of 309 Grand Street—a low, two-story brick building with expansive storefront windows.

Jerry's father, Harry Lieberman, had immigrated to the United States from southwestern Poland in 1923.[9] Two years later, he met and married twenty-two-year-old Lillie Farkas, an immigrant from Hungary. By the age of twenty-nine, Harry was the head of a large immigrant household that consisted of his widowed mother-in-law, his own parents (Rabbi and Mrs. Leopold Lieberman), his twenty-five-year-old brother-in-law, a recently divorced sister-in-law, and his own wife and infant daughter. Originally working as a piano salesman, Harry soon picked up the more lucrative profession of radio repair, and by the time Jerry was born, he had opened his own radio and television store where he was known to have fair prices and a ready smile for customers.[10]

By 1954, Jerome Lieberman was an only child (his older sister was already married), living in a nice, air-conditioned apartment and attending Eastern District High School. Friends and neighbors described him as a kind, quiet, and scholarly boy.[11] Jerry was the smallest of the "gang," and his weak chin and round cheeks conferred upon him a baby-faced look. An accomplished pianist, he and his father spent time together playing duets, with Jerry on the piano and Harry on the violin. Harry, himself a composer, had hoped his son would become a great musician. As Jerry got older, however, he expressed an interest in science, which his father quickly encouraged. "Science is an amazing thing," Harry often told his son. He even provided Jerry with his own 17-inch television on which to watch science programs during those times the family's more luxurious 21-inch screen was otherwise engaged.[12]

As a child, Jerry attended a religious elementary school (the Talmud Torah of Beth Jacob Ohev Shalom) and continued to be a regular worshipper at the school's associated Orthodox temple through his teen years. He even studied Hebrew in high school, prompting his father to proudly boast that his son was "a real Jew." Like most boys from Brooklyn, Jerry was an avid Brooklyn Dodgers fan and played his fair share of baseball in the neighborhood streets. Other spare-time activities included poring through technical tracts and joining the high school science club. Even though he was only of average intelligence (according to the *Daily News* his IQ hovered around the 100 mark) and mostly a C student, Jerry was generally well-liked by his teachers and his classmates. He was known to be helpful to his father in the family store and considered overall to be a "good" boy with a ready smile and charming personality.[13]

In fact, not a single person could be found who had a bad word about Jerome Lieberman. The neighborhood women interviewed by the press all referred to him as their "sweetheart," and his upstairs neighbor, Mrs. Anna Portnoy, called him her "lovely boy." A local shopkeeper told the *Daily Mirror*, "Everyone around here admires the kid because he is such a fine piano player . . . such a fine family and a nice kid. . . . I can't speak too highly of him. He [is] a hard-working kid from a hard-working family."[14]

To his parents, Jerry was an ideal son. He was polite, helped out in the family store, and tried not to be a burden to his sickly mother. "He didn't want a lot," his father mused to a reporter from *Forverts*. "He helped in the store and I told him he could take whatever he wanted out of the cash register, without telling me, but he never did. When I offered him a dollar, he'd take only 40 cents." In exchange, his father claimed he was "ready to give him anything in the world."

"Perhaps," the reporter remarked, "you gave him too much?"

Visibly insulted, Harry snapped back, "How can a father give a son too much?" [15]

But during the summer of 1954, Jerry had been acting strangely. He began coming home late, and when his father asked what was wrong, Jerry uncharacteristically replied, "Dad, don't bother me." On the night of August 6, Harry particularly remembered Jerry coming home late and depressed. The father later claimed Jerry looked like he had been crying, and although Harry begged Jerry to tell him what was wrong, he only received the now familiar, "Don't bother me," by way of reply. Harry even took Jerry on a trip to the countryside, in the hopes he would relax and explain what was going on, but the boy simply continued his sullen and moody silence. [16]

*   *   *

Only two blocks away from the Lieberman home, Robert "Bobby" Trachtenberg lived in a three-story brick building, at 674 Driggs Avenue, that was owned by his maternal grandfather. The street was described by a resident as a "fairly well-contained neighborhood where nearly everybody knows everybody else. Kids are born and grow up and all the other kids and the adults know them." Bobby's immediate family lived in a four-room apartment on the third floor, while his grandfather (a retired carpenter) and grandmother lived on the floor below. [17]

Bobby was the youngest of three children. One older sister was a high school senior, while the other was a student at the local teacher's college. Bobby's father, Morris, peddled clothes, selling mostly to seamen along the Brooklyn waterfront. Big for his age, Bobby stood six feet tall and weighed nearly 170 pounds. [18] With his bushy dark hair and full features, he was one of those kids whose appearance belied that he was only fifteen. Like Jerome, he had attended Talmud Torah as a youngster (it is, in fact, where the two boys met) and often attended synagogue. [19] But unlike Jerry, Bobby was considered an exceptional student. In 1954, he attended the highly competitive Brooklyn Technical High School and was ranked in the upper half of the school's 6,500 student population. With a reported IQ of 135, Robert passed the school's rigid entrance examination with ease and went on to complete his first two years with grades that averaged in the 80s. He was hoping to someday become an engineer. [20]

Although known to be a bookworm (and usually spotted around the neighborhood with a book under his arm), he was also an avid Dodgers fan, liked swimming and playing baseball, and was a member of the Boy Scouts. [21] He also enjoyed movies and other entertainment, which he treated himself to with his generous $6-a-week allowance. [22] Overall, neighbors knew the boy as polite and studious. According to the *New York Times*, "His constant trips to and from the public library were as established in the neighborhood as his regular visits to the synagogue." [23] And while one neighbor reported to the

New York World Telegram that "with Robert it was always good morning and good evening and please excuse me," another confided that she encouraged her own son to play with Bobby as he was "such a nice boy."[24] Neighbors described Bobby as timid, polite, and quiet, a good boy, and a good student, from a good family who walked away from an argument before lifting hand to anyone, including the family dog, Spot.[25]

Bobby and his mother typically went to a seaside resort in the summer, but in 1954, Morris's business had not done as well as usual.[26] Instead, that summer, Bobby and Jerry were supposed to be working through August as camp counselors in upstate New York. But the two boys were sent home after only three weeks because they lacked the requisite "inspiration and enthusiasm" required of counselors (although the camp director assured their anxious parents that they were sufficiently intelligent, good, respectful, and religious for the position.)[27] It was unfortunate, neighbors remarked, that events had conspired to leave Bobby in Brooklyn that August. Even more unfortunate was that, as he convalesced from the flu after returning from camp, he should receive a visit from his good friend Melvin Mittman.[28]

*   *   *

Melvin "Mel" Mittman was a large, brutish-looking boy. At a muscular 210 pounds, he was known to be able to lift 170-pound weights over his head "without even trying" at the local Young Men's Hebrew Association (YMHA) where he frequently worked out. Even when he wore his tortoise-shell-rimmed glasses, he looked more like a prizefighter than a scholar. At the time of his arrest, in 1954, he sported the beginning of a small, toothbrush mustache—or at least, the scraggly teenage version of one. His mug shot is that of a pudgy kid with sunburn across his nose, wavy hair brushed back off his forehead, and piercing, light eyes that looked disdainfully at the camera.[29]

Although originally living only a couple of blocks away from Jerry and Bobby as a small child, Mel's family eventually moved to 98 Ross Street—the same brownstone where his grandparents, Abraham and Rose, lived. After many years as a broom maker in a factory, Abraham had saved up enough money to start a local grocery store where he and Mel's grandmother worked. Mel's father, Sam, who had started out as a cutter in a mill factory, had eventually moved up to management in a knitting factory and then worked as a cutter in the garment district. Mel was one of three children, with a younger brother, Calvin, and sister, Muriel. The family was well-off enough that Mel's mother, Sylvia Mittman—a well-formed woman with full lips and wavy hair—could stay at home.[30]

Mel was of average intelligence, with a reported IQ of 116. Much like Jerry, he was musically talented and played the piano in the school orchestra as well as several other instruments, including the banjo. He was hoping to ultimately go into show business. Like the other boys, Mel had an interest in baseball, and he was on a neighborhood handball team. He was also the locker-room custodian at the Young Men's Hebrew Association (YMHA), a position of trust and prestige.[31]

Unlike Jerry and Bobby, Mel already had a juvenile delinquency conviction under his belt. Occurring three years earlier, in 1951, the conviction could be easily overlooked as more mischief than malice: he and two other boys were caught breaking into Public School 16 to steal some ping-pong balls. Mel was brought in front of Brooklyn Children's Court, where he received a stern lecture and a suspended sentence.[32]

The incident was part of a deepening pattern of delinquency for Melvin. Although he held a good record in elementary school, both academically and behaviorally, Mel began a downward spiral in high school. His marks went from average to failing three subjects, and he took up smoking. Although previously commended for perfect attendance, in the year before his arrest, Mel skipped school often enough to attract the attention of the truant officer. When the officer confronted Mel's mother, she threw her hands up in futility. "What can I do?" she pleaded. "He doesn't want to go, no matter how much I beg him. He's been going around with bad friends." During the summer of 1954, Mel was supposed to be in summer school, making up the classes he had failed. He never bothered to register. His parents were notified, but they seemed unable to do anything to influence their son.[33]

Much of Mel's spare time was spent working out at the YMHA. One young woman who knew him from activities there characterized the hulking lad as being "not fresh or vulgar, he had a nice personality and he was very quiet."[34] Some neighbors also remarked on Melvin's kindness to his dog; that he was generally known to be a good, quiet, trustworthy boy; and that he never picked on anyone smaller than him.[35] But the neighborhood kids told the story a bit differently. In an interview with the *New York Journal American*, several neighborhood children confided that Mel exhibited his awesome strength among the younger boys, "throwing them to the ground and covering them with punches that brought tears to their eyes." They characterized Mel as a "terrible show-off" who battered younger boys to demonstrate his strength and told a reporter that "Mittman tried to laugh it off. But the kids didn't laugh it off. A lot of times, they were pretty badly hurt and had to be helped home."[36]

Another story, told to the *Daily Mirror* by a helpful Williamsburg resident, involved Mel's sister, Muriel. A couple of years earlier, community members complained that Muriel had been cutting the flowers out of their gardens. In an act of neighborly goodwill, "Her brother gave her a spanking," the woman recalled, "a brotherly spanking. And he went around and apologized to the neighbors for her." Following the arrest of the boys, however, the innocent story seemed sinister. It was Mel, after all, who commanded the whip, rendering lash after lash over the flanks of young women in the parks.[37]

Mel's parents knew something was wrong with their son, although they claimed not to have realized how serious it was. For her part, Mel's aunt believed the fault lay in his friendship with Jack Koslow, and said as much to a reporter for the *New York World Telegram.* Jack Koslow, she claimed, had stopped being welcome in the family's home.[38]

* * *

Of course, it was easy to blame Jack. The lean, six-foot-tall redhead, who looked suspiciously like a young Sig Arno, had never quite fit in.[39] As one neighbor told the *Daily Mirror,* "Some kids are good kids and some are bad, but Red was different. He was just plain mean, and he's been that way ever since he was four."[40]

Jack's family encapsulated the migration experience of Jewish New York. For the first few years of Jack's life, the Koslows lived in a crowded tenement on Lewis Street in the Lower East Side of Manhattan, just east of the Williamsburg Bridge. But as Sam Koslow's gasoline station and auto-repair shop became increasingly successful, the family sought the "fine Jewish life" in Williamsburg, moving to 110 Wilson Street. The $36-a-month apartment they rented in the nine-family building was a vast improvement from the crowded housing they had left on the Lower East Side. More importantly, the family was enviably located just steps away from the highly regarded Public School 16. From the very beginning, the Koslows prioritized the education of their extremely bright son. As Sam Koslow recalled years later, "Jack was too smart to go into business with me. He had the mind to be something wonderful. I didn't want him to be a mechanic." Jack's mother, Anna, an attractive, slightly plump blonde, seconded her husband, "We thought maybe a professional man. He was such a beautiful baby, and then he was so bright. People used to look at him and tell me 'Some day [*sic*] he'll be something big.'"[41]

At P.S. 16, Jack did not disappoint. With a measured IQ of 138, he was quickly placed in the gifted class, who Jack referred to as "all the other 'could-be geniuses.'" Jack later confided that he would rather have been placed "with the regular fellows," but overall, Jack did exceptionally well, coming in second place for the school's history medal and receiving high enough marks to gain entrance into the academically rigorous Boys' High School.[42] But the Koslows soon found that, as bright as Jack was, he had a great deal of difficulty fitting in with the other children. "He was different from other boys," his mother remembered. "He wasn't strong physically, and he didn't seem to coordinate well to play games with the other boys."[43] Always a small and sickly child, Jack was an attractive target for neighborhood bullies. One bully in particular, Jerome Forst, quickly took an interest in the newcomer. Whenever Jack tried to play on the street, Forst invariably showed up, stole Jack's ball, and then proceeded to beat the smaller boy. Eventually, Jack's exasperated mother came down and asked Forst why he was constantly torturing her son. In response, Forst simply spit at her and walked away.[44]

For the most part, Jack tried to avoid the fights. "Everytime [*sic*] I tried [to fight]," he later recalled, "I got beaten up and would finally run. I got yellow." Then, one day, things suddenly changed. In the middle of the fight, Forst bit the now thirteen-year-old Jack in the arm. According to Jack, "I saw red in front of my eyes and I nearly killed him. I hit him for hours until there was almost nothing left of him to hit."[45] Increasingly, it was Jack who started the fights. Once, while playing ball, Jack threw down his glove, hit the umpire in the face, and screamed, "Swine! Swine!"—all over a bad call.[46] One of Jack's elementary school teachers later told reporters that this was par for the course: "[He was] always hitting other children—sometimes openly, sometimes sneakily."[47] Another schoolmate recalled that Jack was always acting out in class, referring to him as a "crazy kid": "You never knew what he'd do next. He always was shouting and trying to take over."[48]

In one such memorable incident in the second grade, Jack suddenly jumped up in class, pointed at the teacher, and shouted, "Let's get her!" Another time, he gave the Nazi salute and shouted, "Heil Hitler!"[49] These incidents quickly landed Jack in the offices of the Bureau of Child Guidance, where social workers found the boy to be "emotionally disturbed." Recommending that Jack receive more extensive psychiatric testing, the bureau claimed the boy was "aggressive and subject to fantasies about killings." After only four sessions and an interview with the parents, however, Jack's mother became ill and took her son out of school for a month. When Jack returned, Mrs. Koslow declined to continue the psychiatric sessions.[50] "My mother did not want me to say that I was crazy," Jack later explained. "She did not want the stigma. So I did not tell [the psychiatrist] about the Nazi stuff. I did not dare to tell—on the outside I was a good American. He showed me these plates. . . . I did not say what I saw. I said they were all butterflies."[51] As the years went by, Mrs. Koslow became a frequent visitor to both Public School 16 and Boys' High School because of Jack's increasingly antisocial behavior. By 1952, Jack was finally turned over to the courts after he threatened a smaller boy with a knife. He was let off with a warning.[52]

Over the years, Jack became obsessed with the idea of leadership, and it quickly took the form of an openly expressed admiration of Adolf Hitler. His greatest ambition was to be a soldier, a great German militarist marching down Unter den Linden. At the age of twelve, he taught himself German, reading and rereading *Mein Kampf* as well as philosophical tracts by Spinoza, Nietzsche, and Kant. When he graduated from the academically rigorous Boys' High School at the age of fifteen, he won the school's medal for German.[53]

But Jack's cleverness did not always serve him well. Jack's father later admitted that his son had "bluffed his way through [math] in High School. He had a gift of gab second to nobody."[54] Jack also scammed his way out of gym class, buying off another student to "mark [him] off on the book" and instead sneaking outside to smoke. "You see, I ran my way through High School," Jack later admitted. "I was just interested in credits, not in marks. I didn't care how good I was in anything; [I] just wanted to get through."

Conflating kindness with weakness, Jack often tried to manipulate his teachers, seeing how far he could push them. He claimed that he had "something on everybody," imagining he could blackmail various teachers because they "did not run [their] class right" or "did not teach well." When one teacher took pity on Jack, allowing the boy to eat his lunch in a classroom rather than the school cafeteria (where the boy was often bullied), Jack repaid the kindness by describing the teacher as a pushover and illicitly smoking: "I did it because the teacher was very flexible. I could push him any way I liked to."[55]

While Jack may have figured out how to beat the system at Boys' High School, no one at New York University (where he enrolled the following fall) was particularly impressed. Jack quickly found himself in over his head. No longer able to bluff his way through, he dropped math in the second week, walked out of biology ("I didn't understand it and they didn't teach me anything"), and only passed his beloved German through "the good nature of the teacher."[56] In the meantime, the family migrated along a now-familiar route for Williamsburg Jews: they relocated from their rented apartment on Wilson Street to their own home in the more upscale neighborhood of Flatbush.[57]

Although he had originally enrolled in the pre-dental program to appease his mother, Jack soon tried to switch to teaching, but found his path blocked with red tape. When a counselor asked his reason for the change of major, Jack became agitated and ranted at the bewildered man about how he wished the Nazis had won the war because he "thought he would have fitted into their type of rule."[58] The counselor quickly referred Jack to Dr. Montague, a student psychiatrist at the Testing and Advisement Center, who promptly gave Jack a battery of psychiatric exams. Upon finding he was unable to complete the tests, Jack became increasingly angry. At first, he vociferously blamed his failure on the young woman who administered the tests, claiming she had failed to give him adequate instructions: "Before I knew it, half the time had passed. I had a maze of papers and I didn't know what to do with them." But Jack quickly turned his anger on the psychiatrist. "I was very antagonistic to Dr. Montague," he later admitted. "I did not believe in psychiatry. I was afraid I [would] come home a failure, a failing mark there would be friction at home."[59]

For his part, Dr. Montague diagnosed Jack as being in the early stages of schizophrenia (officially "dementia praecox with schizophrenic tendencies"). The psychiatrist sent a letter to the guidance department, strongly suggesting hospitalization, and referred Jack to Dr. Carl F. Sulzberger, a Freudian analyst and the clinical director of the New York University Neuropsychiatric Center at 321 E. Fifteenth Street, for further treatment.[60] Jack quickly realized that he needed to turn on the charm if he had any hope of returning to school. "I have never bulldozed anybody as I bulldozed Sulzberger," Jack later confessed. Sensing that Sulzberger liked him, Jack chatted amiably with the eminent psychiatrist for a few minutes before asking the good doctor to write him "a nice letter and get me back to college." After only a ten-minute interview, Sulzberger complied. His report stated that Jack was "of good intelligence, alert, well read, shows adequate responses and reactions" and that there was "no evidence whatsoever" of any psychiatric disturbance. That next week, Jack returned to the college and presented the letter to a shocked Dr. Montague. In Jack's words: "I made them eat crow."[61]

But Jack's triumph was short-lived. By the end of the term, he had failed out of ROTC, and his only passing grade, a B in composition, was in exchange for Jack's stopping his harassment of the professor, who refused to work with him any further. For his part, Jack claimed, "I got sick and disgusted with the college. It burned me all up in anger." Blaming the professors and Dr. Montague for conspiring to get him expelled, he later told a psychiatrist that he "would have had no compunction of killing [the professors] and Dr. Montague. They caused all the trouble." He started the next term but quickly dropped out.[62]

Jack's disappointed and frustrated mother finally gave the youth an ultimatum: get a job or get out. In the spring of 1953, Jack started a series of jobs, systematically losing each. He worked in a handbag factory, earning $40 a week, which he equated with being "a slave": "I had more intelligence than that kind of job. I worked with Spaniards and Porto Ricans [sic] I did not like them." The job lasted one week. Next, he spent a month as a cash clerk in a meatpacking factory. But the job's requirements of getting up at 5:00 a.m. and dealing with numbers and figures proved more than Jack could handle. After the meatpacking factory, there was a position as a gas-station attendant, a stock clerk in a clothing factory, a magazine salesman (he quit the second day), and finally a position as a clerk at Barclay's Bank. This last arrangement Jack considered the "best job" he'd had, and he managed to hold on to it for seven months, until June of 1954. But his difficulty with math eventually caught up with him. Described as an "indifferent employee," Jack was pressured to leave by the bank management.[63]

In the meantime, the family had relocated again, this time to 967 E. Tenth Street—a large, wood-sided two-family home on a shady tree-lined street in an even nicer section of Flatbush.[64] Jack was having little success in finding a new job, so Anna Koslow began pressuring Jack to return to college. But Jack was officially expelled from NYU, and starting at a new school was out of the question: Jack was petrified that he might run into someone from high school further advanced than him. According to Jack, he would then have to face being "a failure."[65]

In the summer of 1954, at the age of nineteen, Jack's behavior escalated to violence. According to the owner of a stationery store on Bedford Avenue, Jack and Mel came into the store one evening and pushed around a German refugee who had been minding his own business at the counter. Jack began to sing the *Horst Wessel*, and shouted at the thin little man about what a great leader Hitler had been. The refugee simply lowered his head in his hands and said nothing. Jack then proceeded to stand in front of the store and make a "Nazi speech." An aged Jewish man with a yarmulke came by, and Jack taunted him, telling the old man he should go back to Germany where he belonged. Finally, the shopkeeper had had enough: he told Jack that if he didn't beat it, he would "flatten him." Jack walked away. Mel, seemingly embarrassed by his friend's behavior, apologized to the storekeeper: "He said to me that Koslow was crazy and he was sorry about it."[66]

On July 19, Jack paid a visit to the family physician, Dr. Josef S. Smul, complaining of sleeplessness, vomiting, and a stomachache. Smul, who had attended Jack since birth, had been treating the boy for a "nervous disorder" for several years. But lately, he was beginning to suspect something much worse. After a long conversation with Jack, Smul independently came to the same conclusion that Dr. Montague came to two years earlier: dementia praecox and schizophrenia. Smul kept the diagnosis to himself but asked Jack to have his parents give him a call within the next three days. When they called, Smul planned to let Sam and Anna know that it was his professional opinion that Jack be institutionalized, preferably immediately. Jack never gave them the message.[67]

In the meantime, Jack took a trip to Rockaway Beach. At his hotel, Jack met Corinne Malin, twenty-two, a pretty brunette also spending a week at the seashore. According to Jack, he "fell in love at first sight" and quickly became the girl's constant companion, escorting her to swimming, dancing, and meals.[68] The young woman later told reporters that Jack was "a very nice boy, I thought, and we had many tastes in common." Jack bought Corinne several expensive gifts and flashed around his cash, once even paying for a meal with a $50 bill. He told Corinne he wanted to marry her in six months, when he turned nineteen and came into an inheritance of $11,000 from an aunt. Jack later told police that meeting the young woman was "the turning point in his life."[69] He quickly decided he would marry Corinne, enlist in the army, and then try his hand at a career in the police. "I was famished for love," he later explained. "I wanted security like. I wanted a girl. I have never been able to get one. I am generally repulsive to girls. I don't know why."[70]

Jack would never see Corinne again. Two weeks after their brief seaside affair, Jack was arrested for murder.[71]

A Dangerous Age

If there was ever a bad time for four wayward youths to start committing senseless acts of violence, the summer of 1954 was it. While in other times the unfortunate deaths of two vagrants and the senseless beatings of several others would have likely warranted a handful of articles in scattered local newspapers, the Brooklyn public in August of 1954 was both obsessed with delinquency as well as fed up with what seemed to be the impotence of city officials and civic leaders to do anything about it. Still reeling from the brutal "Stomp-Killing" of only a month prior and exasperated by the continuing crime waves and the shocking statistics reported by Police Commissioner Adams, an increasingly agitated public wanted justice and answers, and were receiving neither.

When the news broke on August 18, newspapers throughout the metropolitan area struggled to rationalize why the boys, quickly dubbed the "Thrill-for-Kill Gang," ended up on a path of mindless brutality that summer. Certainly teenage hoodlumism was nothing new to the average Brooklyn citizen. In the first few months of 1954 alone, readers of the *Brooklyn Daily Eagle* would have seen headlines such as "Teen Gangs Battle" and "Adams Wars on Hoods." Contemporaneous stories included the fifteen-year-old girl whose seventeen-year-old boyfriend brutally bludgeoned and then stabbed her mother to death when she caught the pair in bed and the case of a sixteen-year-old Brooklyn boy accused of attempting to kidnap the seven-year-old son of a city official for ransom. And according to an article published one month before the Thrill-Killers' arrests, Brooklyn teenagers and youths perpetrated four murders, five stabbings, one shooting, six assaults, three armed robberies, and seven "miscellaneous crimes" in the second half of June alone.[1]

But the obsession with juvenile delinquency did not start during the summer of 1954. According to historian James Gilbert, Gallup polls and *The Reader's Guide to Periodical Literature* both indicate a spike in the discussion about juvenile delinquency from 1953 to 1956.[2] This was partially because of the U.S. Senate Judiciary Committee's establishment of a special subcommittee to study the "youth problem" in the first half of 1953.[3] The bipartisan Subcommittee on Juvenile Delinquency, established on April 27, was originally charged with only three major tasks: examining the adequacy of existing laws in dealing with youthful offenders in the federal system, determining which types of sentences or other correctional actions were taken by the federal courts, and discerning the extent to which juveniles were violating federal narcotics laws.

But what began as a narrow inquiry soon became a far-reaching investigation. Over the next several years, the subcommittee questioned the effectiveness of the juvenile court system, youth institutions, and juvenile community control programs; explored teenage drug usage; questioned the exploitation of youth by black-market adoption and prostitution; held hearings on juvenile access to weapons and pornography; and, most famously, studied the relationship between juvenile crime and the mass media. Hearings opened on November 19, 1953, with the testimony of Dr. Martha M. Eliot, the chief of the Children's Bureau, who informed the senators that juvenile delinquency had risen 29 percent between 1948 and 1952, with over one million children running afoul of the law in 1952 alone. Even more shocking to those in attendance was the revelation that juvenile delinquency was not confined to inner-city slums. As Dr. Eliot noted, "Some of our most serious acts of delinquent behavior have been committed by children from so-called good families and good neighborhoods." A subsequent witness, Dr. George Gardner, the Director of the Judge Baker Clinic in Boston, was asked point-blank, "Do you find that this juvenile delinquency occurs only in the slum areas, or in the underprivileged groups?" Gardner responded,

> Juvenile Delinquency occurs in every socioeconomic group I know of . . . for every case where you can demonstrate a socioeconomic depression in the area where the child lives, we cannot only find a child comparable to that coming from the suburbs of your large cities who does the same act, who is surrounded not only by the necessities of child life, but surrounded by the luxuries of them.[4]

This observation concerning locale was particularly troublesome, as juvenile delinquency experts had long demonstrated a geographic pattern to delinquency, starting with the influential study *Delinquency Areas*, published by Clifford Shaw and Henry McKay in 1929.[5] The Chicago-based study concluded that delinquency followed specific geographic patterns in which the central area (usually populated by immigrants) was a zone of high criminality that receded as one traveled farther from this central hotspot. As historian James Gilbert observed, delinquency was understood as being a "by-product of immigration and Americanization" in that as immigrants moved from their ghettos into mainstream American neighborhoods, juvenile crime rates dramatically decreased. "Delinquency was sloughed off," he notes, "in the rough process of acculturation."[6]

While the "Chicago School" geospatial theory remained popular into the 1950s, competing theories emphasized individual psychological factors and inadequate families. The highly influential husband-and-wife team of Sheldon and Eleanor Glueck, Harvard-based criminologists, emphasized the importance of the familial dynamic in their first groundbreaking study, *One Thousand Juvenile Delinquents*, which was published in 1934. Their Boston-based survey contended that the vast majority of the delinquents came from homes that were broken or where the children were poorly supervised. Many came from homes where parents and other siblings had also had prior dealings with the criminal court system. And most were extremely poor: less than one-fourth had enough to maintain themselves in case of the unemployment of the breadwinner, and nearly two-fifths had mothers who needed to work outside the home to help make ends meet. The authors concluded, "On the whole we are dealing with parents and homes that in many respects must be characterized as unwholesome or under-privileged."[7]

By 1950, the Gluecks had completed what would become one of the most important studies in criminology history: *Unraveling Juvenile Delinquency* and the subsequent *Delinquents in the Making: Paths to Prevention*. The study carefully matched five hundred "persistently delinquent" boys to five hundred nondelinquents, accounting for age, race, ethnicity, general intelligence, socioeconomic status, and neighborhood. The purpose of the study was to find out why, when all these factors were accounted for, one boy became a delinquent and one walked the straight and narrow. What they discovered supported their original findings concerning the importance of family. The households from which the delinquent boys' parents originated were littered with mental retardation, psychiatric disorders, alcoholism, and criminal activity. When it came to economics, the families of delinquents were more likely to have reluctant breadwinners and fathers who had poor work habits. Delinquents also lived in homes with less effective household management and routine, and their parents were typically less self-respecting and lacked the ambition to improve either their social or economic status. The families of delinquents were also less likely to spend quality time together, and the children had both less supervision and few positive hobbies—defined as activities such as building model planes, raising pigeons, or collecting stamps.[8]

But one factor more than any other predicted juvenile delinquency and that was the "affectional relationship" between the boys and their parents. In case after case, the Gluecks found that the delinquent boys came from homes where their parents were openly indifferent or hostile toward the children and showed little warmth, sympathy, or affection. In return, only one-third of the delinquent boys reported having close, affectionate ties to their fathers.[9] Not surprisingly, far more nondelinquents reported feeling their father was the kind of man they wanted to emulate, that they had respect for their father's vocational or social standing, or that they had "some sort of common understanding with him" than the delinquent boys. The study also indicated that the delinquent boys were more likely to be deprived of affection by their parents and siblings and that, when it came to discipline, the parents of delinquents were more likely to erratically swing between laxity and being overly strict, with discipline inconsistent at best and typically physical in nature.

As Dr. Sheldon Glueck, a gray-haired professor with a boxer's face, described it to the senators on the second day of the delinquency hearings, the key was "consistency of discipline" that "isn't cruel but . . . firm and kindly." It was irrelevant, according to the psychologist, whether parents "hit [the boy] once in a while," as long as the child knew that he could "always count on his parents." What was damaging was "the father who is erratic, who one minute hits them and the next minute ignores them so that they never know where they are." According to Glueck, what made this second type of parenting style developmentally problematic was that child had "no chance to lay down a foundation inside of them of what are the rules of the game and what will happen if you do one thing or the other."[10]

Ultimately, what all this added up to was a child who was poorly conditioned to "obey legitimate authority"—a crucial component of successful adult male citizenship in the postwar period. While contemporaneous social critics (such as David Riesman) questioned whether the obeisance required by the new corporate masculinity constituted a feminizing crisis, several American sociologists posited the problem of male juvenile delinquency as simply being a hypermasculine version of this same corporate culture.[11] Consisting of traits such as teamwork, consensus building, and conciliation, delinquent boys, sociologists argued, typically possessed all of the crucial characteristics for a successful adjustment to good citizenry. For example, in an article published in the *American Sociological Review* in December of 1950, the authors considered that boys who participated in gangs were fundamentally extroverted youth who were highly successful at social peer adjustment and participating in consumer culture.[12]

That gang members could be recognized as possessing these social skills meant that the fundamental problem was not with the delinquent themselves as much as it was with society's inability to harness and redirect their talents into more appropriate channels. Some criminologists, such as the Gluecks, tacitly agreed. As Dr. Sheldon Glueck acknowledged in his testimony to the subcommittee, "Not all of these character and personality traits are necessarily undesirable." Glueck argued that many of the traits that gang members possessed, such as "adventurousness, vivaciousness, assertiveness, the quality of asserting one's will with regard to the environment, more extroversion;

that is, the going into action, and so on," were, in fact, the same characteristics found in very successful men in "legitimate enterprises." It was only when "directed toward antisocialism" that these potentially positive traits became "socially harmful."[13]

Further, certain crimes considered "white-collar" delinquency—such as automobile theft—were understood by sociologists to be the behavior of "well-socialized" young men.[14] A study from 1952 in the *American Journal of Sociology* found that this particular category of juvenile delinquent tended to come from more "favored" neighborhoods and had in common homes in which their parents expressed "broad and tolerant" moral views. These easygoing parents fostered an "adaptive" personality type, described as having high social intelligence and conforming easily to the expectations of whatever group they found themselves in.[15] Thus, if a boy's friends got pleasure from riding in automobiles, he might oblige them by "borrowing" a car. The problem, however, is that an adult with similar moral flexibility might commit white-collar offenses acceptable to his business peer group—such as bribery or insider trading. And, of course, if he had associates who did not balk at cruder or more dangerous crimes, he might be tempted to commit acts of burglary or physical assault as well.

The key, therefore, for this type of juvenile delinquent, to keep him from becoming a criminal, was to ensure that he had secure moral outside influences—such as religion, positive youth groups, and an association with peers whose parents had rigid moral codes. What was not in doubt, however, was whether these youths could be made into productive consumers and citizens. Just as the case with gang membership, car theft was considered a sign of adequate male social development that needed only to be more constructively redirected.[16]

Overall, what all of these theories shared was an emphasis on outside influences. A 1954 report in the *Congressional Digest* on the "Conditions Conducive to Youth Crime" listed "poor home conditions," including broken homes, poverty, neglect, and parental amorality, as the top causes for delinquency. Second to that was lack of religious education, followed by lack of youth groups, inadequate schools, salacious reading materials, and lack of public support for juvenile courts and stricter punishment. Only one brief line of the report mentioned the potential physical and mental defects on the part of the minor.[17] Other articles in the same issue debated whether TV standards for violence were strict enough and whether comic books promoted delinquency.[18] All of the digest articles echoed similar themes as most juvenile delinquency studies of the early 1950s, in which doubt was increasingly being cast on the idea that delinquency was the result of any physical or mental aberration as much as it was a product of learned behavior transmitted through the general culture.[19]

Not surprisingly, then, in the early 1950s, solutions to juvenile delinquency—whether following the model of the Gluecks and focusing on the family or of sociologists and focusing on the community—centered on remedies to correct the world outside of the male delinquent, rather than the teenager himself. An article in the *Journal of Educational Sociology*, for example, posited that reducing delinquency "is more a matter of building communities that understand, cherish and strengthen youth than it is of the biological nature of the youth."[20] Solutions to the problem were therefore typically community centered: creating more youth groups, reeducating parents and teachers, and improving the socioeconomic conditions of families. Further, unlike female delinquents for whom criminal behavior conflicted with normative feminine comportment, male delinquency had to be more carefully dealt with so as not to inhibit the aspects of the behavior that reflected positive masculine development. Coinciding with the Lavender Scare and worries concerning the survival of American masculinity in the face of corporate culture, the hypermasculine allure of gang culture and thrill seeking needed to be corralled but not crushed.[21]

*   *   *

How these theories played out in reality can be seen through a brief study of the variety of steps citizens in Brooklyn and greater New York City took to combat delinquency in the first eight months of 1954. In February, an exposé series by the *Brooklyn Daily Eagle* found nearly $500,000 in annual costs had been incurred by the board of education because of wanton teenage vandalism of school property. That same week, a group of three teenage boys invaded and robbed the home of a female physician. After binding and gagging her maid, the gang made off with nearly $25,000 in loot—but not before mercilessly strangling the family dog and hanging its lifeless body from a fence picket for her children to find. In response to these incidents, Bay Ridge assemblyman Frank J. McMullen (R) called on the New York State Legislature to create its own joint legislative committee to study the problem of juvenile delinquency. The New York Temporary Commission on Youth and Delinquency that was eventually created started its investigation in June of 1955.[22]

In the meantime, two public grade schools in crowded, low-income Bronx neighborhoods decided that an ounce of prevention was worth a pound of cure. Using the five-point criteria advocated by the Glueck study, the schools identified twenty first-grade boys as potential juvenile delinquents. The branded protodelinquents were quickly placed in group and individual therapy along with their parents. "The Youth Board will follow closely the progress of the boys," the *Brooklyn Daily Eagle* assured its readers, "so they can see just how helpful the treatment is in preventing delinquency." Results were predicted within the next three years.[23]

While the Bronx tried a controversial new identification system, Brooklyn spearheaded the crusade to ban deadly switchblade knives. Led by Special Sessions Justice John E. Cone Jr., the public was urged to "bombard" Governor

Dewey and lawmakers with demands that the sale of switchblades be halted. In the meantime, another Brooklynite, Assemblyman Thomas A. Dwyer of Flatbush (D) sponsored a bill to declare the possession of a switchblade illegal, placing the knife in the same category as blackjacks, brass knuckles, and slingshots. The latter proposal had the support of both the mayor's office and New York Police Commissioner Francis W. H. Adams.[24]

In March, Mayor Robert F. Wagner, declaring "we mean business," announced that eighty-one plainclothesmen assigned to the Juvenile Aid Bureau would be put back into uniform, with increased patrols in "trouble" areas. Additionally, police captains would start regularly meeting with school principals to "get a line on the troublemakers." Contemporaneously, a series in the *Brooklyn Daily Eagle* condemned the relaxation of discipline in schools that practiced "progressive education" ("Children are becoming bums," one irate father told the newspaper), prompting a flurry of responses from education specialists who turned the blame back on inadequate parenting and broken families. As the vice president of the Public Education Association informed the interviewer, "Neither the schools nor often-belabored progressive education created the growing number of narcotic addicts. They did not incubate the knife-wielders. They did not teach teenagers to disrupt and pollute schools with immorality and disorderly habits."[25]

While parents and schools exchanged blame, Councilman Philip Schupler urged the creation of special schools in each borough to rehabilitate juvenile delinquents and for a "dean of discipline" to be appointed to every city public school. The councilman further suggested the formation of a committee of noneducators to advise the board of education and superintendent on how best to devise a curriculum that may prove attractive to "groping youth."[26] Meanwhile, the New York Teacher's Guild penned a memo to both the mayor and Governor Dewey, stating, "The public must be informed that the schools alone cannot counteract the influences of broken homes, of poverty-stricken neighborhoods, of a world filled with destructive tensions"—although the remedies, according to the union, mostly involved increasing funding for schools.[27]

A week later, at the meeting of the Parents-Teacher Association of Abraham Lincoln High School, City Magistrate Charles Ramsgate placed the blame squarely on the shoulders of parents, proclaiming to the assembled crowd of six hundred that "Juvenile Delinquency is a misnomer. It should be called 'parental delinquency.'" Pointing out that of the 168 hours in a week a school only had a child for 25 (and a church, at best, for 1), he clearly lay the fault at the feet of those who were supposed to be supervising the other 132 hours. "From what I have seen during my thirty years of public service, I attribute ninety percent of the crime among our youth to broken homes, divorce or separation, and drunkenness of one of the parents or both."[28]

While Magistrate Ramsgate offered plenty of blame, but no solutions, across town, Chief Probation Officer Conrad Priatzlien of the Brooklyn

Federal Court told the Women's Federal Juror's Association that the city should set up a consulting service to which parents of unruly and delinquent children could appeal for advice. In the meantime, the officer explained the new Federal Youth Correction Law, which allowed for a youth charged with a federal crime and deemed unworthy of "deferred prosecution" (a process in which the U.S. attorney would agree to defer the prosecution of a first-time offender until or unless the youth committed a subsequent crime)—but not considered depraved enough to merit prison—the chance to be committed to a hospital, training school, or farm camp. The law, passed in 1950, was instituted in New York in September of 1954.[29]

The next night, however, columnist Michael O'Brien, speaking to the members of the Kings County Grand Juror's Association, claimed the old-fashioned rod was the cure for delinquency. Advising to place bull whips in the hands of parents, police, and school teachers, O'Brien argued, "I have never found the man or woman bent on crime that did not fear the so-called shellacking that the police gave the underworld via the nightstick. That also applies to the seat of the pants of youth." O'Brien faulted soft parents, particularly those who demanded assault charges be pressed against law enforcement officers instead of thanking them for "fanning the pants" of their unruly children.[30]

Whether the fault of parents or schools, and whether or not a good spanking could potentially solve the problem, the concern of Brooklyn citizens was further heightened when, two days later, two innocent passersby were killed during a teen gang battle in the Fort Greene neighborhood. In response, Brooklyn assemblymen served notice on the New York State Legislature that they would open the next year's session with a push to outlaw "zip guns"—homemade firearms that typically fired .22 caliber ammunition.[31] Before the weekend was out, a huge symposium on juvenile delinquency was held in Flatbush Court. With more than twenty-five speakers, including Assemblyman Max Turshen and Special Sessions Justice John Cone Jr., as well as jurists, public officials, educators, representatives of PTAs, and even several teenagers, the placement of blame for juvenile delinquency ranged from parents, to schools, television, pornography, and slums. By the end of the meeting, the 67th Precinct Coordinating Council voted to form a "Citizens Committee Against Juvenile Delinquency." The committee was tasked with tackling juvenile delinquency, and an organizational meeting was planned for the end of April. Rounding off the month of March, the Women's Division of Youth United, a social agency affiliated with various Brooklyn settlement houses, launched a research project to trace the "direct causes and reasons" for the rise of juvenile delinquency.[32]

April began with the Children's Day and Night Shelter at 130 Boerum Street reopening its doors to rehabilitate children well on the path to delinquency through intensive psychiatric treatment and "an environment of security and love." The next day, April 5, 1954, newspapers announced a $41 million plan, submitted to Mayor Wagner by the Welfare and Health Council of New York City, in which funds to combat juvenile delinquency would be allocated between the board of education and the Domestic Relations and Magistrates Courts. The seven-point plan recommended an increase in the Bureau of Child Guidance facilities, the proper staffing of educational-vocational guidance bureaus, English classes for non-English-speaking children, the establishment of additional playgrounds and youth centers, and the addition of recreational facilities in housing projects. Further monetary allocation would be made for adding psychiatric personnel for the courts; providing intensive services for families who were brought before the Home Term Court; adding psychologists, social workers, and counselors to the department of correction staff; and expanding mental hygiene clinics, detention quarters for boys under the age of sixteen, and temporary shelters for adolescents.[33]

A few days later, Assemblyman Frank S. Samansky told members of the West Midwood Community League that juvenile delinquency was a "community problem" that could only be remedied by strong training in civic-mindedness.[34] In another part of town, a crowd of four hundred listened to Justice John Cone rant about the "filth merchants" corrupting youth with "filthy and perverted films, books, cartoons, pamphlets and recordings." Calling for federal and state legislation to provide mandatory jail sentences, Cone argued that legislation was the only means to curb "this sale of gutter muck . . . aimed specifically at youth." A few weeks later, Cone repeated his speech, this time urging a crowd of over two thousand to demand the outright ban of crime, horror, and sex comics.[35]

The end of April into the beginning of May saw the opening of the Sports and Home Show—a 60,000-square-foot bazaar that boasted a wide range of sporting goods and home appliances. One-half of the gross admissions for the show would go to eleven settlement houses, community centers, and youth agencies focused on preventing juvenile delinquency by promoting organized activities for nearly 500,000 children.[36] In the meantime, the 67th Precinct Coordinating Council, bolstered by its recent success in lobbying the New York State Legislature to ban switchblade knives, formed a citizen's committee to combat juvenile delinquency in Brooklyn. Led, once again, by Justice John Cone, the committee's four-point attack on juvenile delinquency included persuading local politicians to allocate additional funding to schools, juvenile and adolescent courts, and correctional institutions; a campaign for more recreational facilities; a search for more effective means of combating vandalism; and the creation of an educational program to combat the conditions responsible for the high delinquency rates. Part and parcel, of course, was Cone's pet project to curb the sale of indecent comic books.[37]

At a panel in Flatbush, before a crowd of two hundred, six education and law enforcement officials declared that "the place to stop crime is in the cradle." Speakers ranging from Assistant District Attorney Joseph P. Hoey to the supervisor of the board of education's Attendance Division argued that "good or bad habits are formed in infancy" and that "children under the age of sixteen are first the responsibility of their parents. It is only later that they become, or should become, problems of the law."[38] Echoing this theme, a scathing editorial in the June 21 edition of the *Brooklyn Daily Eagle* (pertaining to a recent Chicago arson case in which an eleven-year-old whisky-drinking, cigarette-smoking boy set fire to a building, killing seven and injuring nine) called American parents "a nation of Milquetoasts, beaten to our knees by thoroughly wanton children." The author, citing several examples where delinquents were in need of corporal punishment, castigated local parents who had written letters of protest concerning the proposal by one of New York City's most prestigious private schools to restore the switch as a disciplinary measure.[39]

Although the panic concerning delinquency temporarily subsided during June, it was reignited in July by yet another brutal and shocking crime. On the night of July 10, Thomas Condon, a forty-year-old war veteran, father of four, and partner in the Air Conditioning Company of New York, was walking to his house on 614 Prospect Avenue while humming to himself. Meanwhile, three boys lounged across the street, drinking beer. One of the boys, seventeen-year-old Thomas Wysokowski, had nearly finished drinking six bottles and three quarts of the illegally obtained booze when the second boy, Ronald Loesch, age sixteen, suddenly yelled out, "Shut your mouth, or I'll shut it for you!" Annoyed by the man's continued humming, Loesch ran up to Condon and punched him twice, knocking him down. Wysokowski soon followed, kicking the prostrate man in the head. Two young women, who were walking home from the movies, shouted for the boys to stop and tried to pull Wysokowski off of the now-unconscious victim. It was already too late. Witnesses told police the former marine's last words were, "Oh my God! Oh my God! Not this!"[40]

Wysokowski's lawyer later argued that the boy was in a "semidrunken stupor" and had blacked out while committing the crime.[41] But an outraged Brooklyn public was not interested in excuses. Newspaper editorials demanded more leeway for police officers and emphasized the need for religious education.[42] In a special article published by the *Brooklyn Daily Eagle* on July 25, outraged community leaders spoke out concerning the "shortage of adult leadership" for youth. The Kiwanis Club of Brooklyn lamented the lack of adult volunteers, which limited the number of baseball teams they could run, while the president of the Flatbush Boys Club argued that parents needed to "take over rule in the home." "There are no delinquents," he quipped, "if parents are not delinquent in their responsibilities." He further advocated a 10:00 p.m. curfew for those under the age of eighteen.

Local churchgoers found themselves bombarded with sermons concerning the "Stomp-Killing" that Sunday morning, such as those in attendance at All Saints Protestant Episcopal Church in Park Slope. Other pastors, such as Father William Cullen of St. Peter Claver's in Bedford-Stuyvesant, argued for religious education as well as a curfew and for media restraint. Noting there was "too much publicity on teenagers in trouble," Father Cullen claimed it "spurs a sense of bravado, a silly sense of record making, a 'look-what-I've-done-attitude.'"[43]

Other religious leaders advocated the "spare the rod and spoil the child" approach, particularly the Rev. David Conwell of Grace Baptist Church in Sunset Park, who railed against progressive education. Rev. Conwell was joined by other Baptist leaders, such as the pastor of Bethany Baptist Church in Bedford-Stuyvesant, who claimed progressive education robbed parents of their "original authority." Nearly every church and synagogue polled indicated they were expanding their youth services to try to meet the needs of the crisis and to help provide youth with a much-needed moral center.[44]

Unfortunately, it all seemed to be too little, too late. On July 29, Mayor Wagner revealed that youth crime in the five boroughs had soared, jumping over 17.2 percent in the first six months of 1954 alone. In response, Brooklyn Assistant District Attorney Julius Helfland angrily called for (as the *Brooklyn Daily Eagle* put it) "Liberal use of the nightstick by 'two-fisted' cops in tough neighborhoods and less coddling of youthful offenders by softhearted judges." Appearing on WABD's popular television news broadcast *Between the Lines*, Helfland essentially advocated for an increase in what today would be considered police harassment and brutality as a remedy for juvenile crime: "Delinquency would decrease if two-fisted police captains were sent into tough neighborhoods to search out and harass juvenile criminals. More men should be put on police beats in these areas, if necessary using the nightstick."[45]

Appearing on the same program, Judge Samuel Leibowitz, currently assigned to the "Stomp-Killing" case, advocated for tougher sentences on the part of the judiciary to decrease the "contempt in which many young people now hold the forces of law and order."[46]

On August 2, Police Commissioner Adams responded to the crisis in a speech broadcast on both television and radio and reprinted in the next day's newspapers. Citing the "Stomp-Killing" case as an example of crimes that "are increasingly shocking," Adams went on to list brutal crime after brutal crime that had recently been committed by youth in the five boroughs before referring to scandalous statistics, including the FBI's claim that urban crimes were 39 percent higher than the pre–World War II average. "Conditions grow worse with each passing month," Adams intoned, "and now have reached a point where they must become a matter of the most serious concern for every citizen."[47]

Adams called for a massive hiring of new police personnel, claiming the NYPD was nearly 7,000 men short to meet the needs of the growing city. Blaming the expansion of social services for sapping vital monetary resources from hiring and pay raises for police officers, Adams argued for making law enforcement the dominant priority: "Unless these services can be enjoyed under conditions of law and order," he warned, "their value is lessened, if not destroyed."

Despite the limitations faced by the NYPD, Adams commended the overall clearance rates, with arrests in over a third of all felonies committed in the first half of 1954 and the most serious crimes—such as murder, rape, and manslaughter—averaging 75 percent and higher. The problem, however, was that the inadequate force meant manpower was being disproportionally spent on solving crime rather than preventing crime. Further complicating youth delinquency prevention was a "vicious new criminal element" that had "neither respect for nor fear of the law in this city." The only remedy, Adams repeated, was to "have enough policemen on the street to restore respect to the law."[48]

That night, Adams launched the first of multiple citywide crackdowns, with police raiding Times Square and arresting nearly a hundred hoodlums for charges that ranged from vagrancy and disorderly conduct, to prostitution, perversion, and unlicensed hawking. In an exclusive tip to the *Brooklyn Eagle*, Adams promised that "trouble spots" in Brooklyn would soon be receiving the same treatment.[49] But the raids could not come soon enough. The *Brooklyn Eagle* reported on Monday, August 9, that while the police continued their roundups in Times Square, Central Park, and Far Rockaway in Queens, Brooklyn continued to be in the grips of a "crime orgy," with eight violent crimes, including attempted rape, armed robbery, and a car chase involving gunfire and an attempt to run over a patrolman occurring over the course of one weekend.

In response, numerous civic groups and city officials banded together to demand $1,000 a year raises for police officers to alleviate what they called the "near collapse and demoralization of our police force." Down at City Hall, Mayor Wagner had all but consented to an increase in overtime for patrol and was even rumored to be considering the declaration of a crime "emergency," thereby allowing the city to borrow up to $10 million dollars against the following year's budget for additional police personnel. In his *Mayor's Conference*, broadcast on WOR-TV that Friday, Wagner made sure to point out to voters that "even before taking office I cited the need for more and better paid policemen." Calling for citizens to also consider the "long-range attack" on the causes of crime and juvenile delinquency, Wagner touted the various steps City Hall had already taken to combat the crisis: appropriating more than $600,000 to employ probationary and psychiatric personnel in the courts, enlarging the Domestic Relations Court, and expanding the Youth Board. But the mayor was quick to emphasize that while City Hall would "continue to attack [crime and juvenile delinquency] with every means at our command," what was desperately needed were more police, better housing, more playgrounds, and, most of all, a "greater sense of responsibility on the part of the public generally and parents in particular."[50]

Ultimately, the first eight months of 1954 saw a shotgun approach to juvenile delinquency, in which neither social theorists nor citizen reformers could agree on what caused juvenile delinquency or how best to solve it. Solutions ranged from corporal punishment to expanding youth services, from less progressive educational policies to legislative measures, from more playgrounds to more police officers. The one thing that everyone seemed to agree on, however, was that there were no "bad kids," just bad circumstances.[51] Whether it was inadequate homes, poor parenting, comic books, not enough recreational facilities, or any of the other myriad explanations for youth misbehavior, nearly every adult in the New York Metro area seemed to agree on this one simple fact: there was always a reason why juvenile delinquents acted the way they did and they could therefore be saved.

So when four boys who did not fit into any of the stereotypes, who had soberly assaulted and killed for absolutely no discernible reason, were arrested in the early hours of August 17, the public and the press went wild. Every last detail of their lives became fodder for public discussion. Psychiatrists and delinquency experts who had never met the boys weighed in with theories ranging from homosexuality to sexual sadism, from overprotective parenting to inadequate parental love. Neighbors, family members, teachers, and former classmates found themselves hounded by the press in the hopes of a revealing clue from the boys' pasts. All proved a desperate attempt to understand how four boys from "good, middle-class families" had defied every reigning sociological and psychological theory in their fall into depravity.[52]

Confessions

August 17, 1954
5:00 a.m.
Dawn was just breaking as the two weary detectives from the 92nd Squad rang the downstairs bell at 335 Grand Street.

After Jack Koslow and Melvin Mittman had been picked up outside of the 90th precinct, they were quickly transferred to the 92nd for questioning in the death of Rhinehold Ulrickson. By 3:00 a.m., the police focused their efforts on Mel, judging him the more likely of the two boys to talk. The hunch proved right: after only an hour of questioning, Mel gave up his accomplices, volunteering to take the police to their homes. By 5:00 a.m., the police had already picked up Bobby, and he was en route to an interrogation room.

The detectives standing outside of 335 Grand Street soon heard the buzzing sound of the lock being released and headed up to the second floor. A robed figure stood on the landing, waiting for them. Detective William Elliott and his partner, Detective Casimir Czarnowski, identified themselves to a bewildered Harry Lieberman. Within moments, a pajama-clad Jerry emerged from his room.[1]

"Are you Jerry Lieberman?" Detective Czarnowski barked.

"Yes."

"You will have to come with us to the police station. We want to question you."

The boy turned pale. His hands involuntarily thrust up to his face, fingers resting on his forehead in a gesture of grief.[2]

"The police? Oh my God. The river. I couldn't sleep all night."

As Detective Czarnowski later testified, they had no idea what Jerry was babbling about. Yet both detectives instinctively knew the case had broken wide open.[3]

*   *   *

Back at the precinct, Czarnowski told his superiors of the odd remark Jerry had made at his arrest, and it was quickly decided to interrogate the sobbing seventeen-year-old first.[4] Czarnowski began the interview with a few questions about the events of August 6, but after about fifteen minutes, he turned to Jerry's blurted confession and took a gamble.

"About the river," the detective began. "We know everything that has happened. Now we want to hear what you have got to say about it."

Jerry Lieberman proceeded to tell them everything. In fact, he not only told them everything, but he also consented to drive around with the officers for the next hour, showing them the exact route the boys had taken the evening before. The police quickly contacted the East River harbor patrol, and by 8:15 a.m., the tedious search for the body of Willard Menter began off of the South Fifth Street pier.[5]

Fueled with new evidence, the police returned to interrogating Jack Koslow. From the time of his arrest, Jack would ultimately be questioned over the course of nineteen hours by no less than fourteen different police officers, ranging in rank from detective to captain. Initially, the line of questioning concerning the death of Rhinehold Ulrickson went nowhere—Jack, after all, had not been present on the night of August 6. But his protestations about the events of August 16 would not last as long. At first, Jack denied being present at the crime scene: "I was not on the pier last night," he insisted. "I wasn't on any pier last night." But after another hour of questioning, Jack finally decided to talk.[6] Whether the change of heart was because of weariness, police brutality (as he would later allege at his trial), or a tactical change is hard to say. According to Jack's version of events, he was forced to stand against a wall and denied food and water until, between exhaustion and hunger, he collapsed on the floor and agreed to cooperate.[7]

Either way, it was Detective Raymond Duggan who caught the lucky break. Jack told the detective that on the evening of the August 16, he had been at home when he got the call from Mel Mittman to meet at Marcy Avenue and Broadway. Jack recounted the entire evening. He recalled the initial trip to Triangle Park for a "bum hunt," the subsequent walk to McCarren Park, and the return to Triangle Park. He described Willard Menter to Detective Duggan, down to the color of the man's shoes. He also described how he took a lit cigarette and touched it to the foot of the sleeping man.

"Why did you put the lit cigarette to the foot of the bum?" the shocked detective asked.[8]

"For a gag," Koslow coolly responded.

Next, Duggan took Koslow to the pier and asked the boy to point out where the man had gone into the river. After directing the detective to where the assault occurred (on the north side of the pier, about fifteen or twenty feet from the barrier), Koslow's expression suddenly changed. He abruptly paused and looked the detective dead in the eye. Mimicking the parlance of comic books, he gestured to the river and quipped, "That was the supreme adventure of them all."[9]

That afternoon, the police felt their case was strong enough to bring in the district attorney's office, who quickly sent over Assistant District Attorney Lewis D. Cohen and a department stenographer to take the boys' official statements. By 6:00 p.m., the airless meeting room was packed with police officers; three detectives, a deputy chief inspector, and a lieutenant all crowded into the small space to witness the statement of Jack Koslow. The room was sparsely decorated. On one wall, a dusty map was suspended next to a chain-link-covered window. The window, barely cracked open and the shade drawn down over it, did little to alleviate the oppressive heat, currently exacerbated by the press of bodies. Another wall of the tiny room was crammed with filing cabinets, which were used by curious detectives as spots to lean on.[10]

Cohen, a lean man with slicked-back, receding hair, wore a light summer suit with a white handkerchief peeking out of his breast pocket, which he occasionally used to remove the sweat from his brow in the suffocating space. Quickly concluding the standard biographical formalities, Cohen plunged into the interrogation.

"Last night, August 16, 1954, were you in the vicinity of McCarron Park at 11:00 p.m.?"

"Yes, sir."

"Will you tell me, please, what you were doing there?"

"I guess, looking for bums."

"For what purpose?"

"Either to abuse them in one manner or another."

"How would you abuse them?"

"Sometimes, I just curse them. Sometimes I look at them and walk away. Sometimes I'd even go so far as to hit them."

"Were you with Melvin Mittman last night?"

"Yes, sir, that's right."

"How would you categorize this method in which you went out looking for bums?"

"Just hit or miss. I'd find one. If he was particularly distasteful to either myself or the other boys, the person who he affected most would do what he pleased with him."

"What do you mean by 'distasteful'?"

"Just don't like him, that's all. Sometimes I see a drunken bum, very soused. He looks at you out of one eye. It's disgusting. It incites me to hit them. The two younger guys didn't have the hatred we did."[11]

Jack described the evening's activities: the bums forced to kiss Jack's feet, the girls whipped in McCarran Park, and the subsequent return to Triangle Park to find Willard Menter asleep on the bench.[12] He described to the ADA how he put the lit cigarette to the sleeping man's foot, how they had surrounded the man and ordered him to come with them, and how they brought Menter to the pier: "So we could bang him around in private."[13]

Finally, Jack gave his version of what happened on the pier.

"I backed him up against the fence. Melvin motioned to me to come over. He said, 'Bring him over.' I motioned to the bum to come forward. Melvin hit him. I don't know whether he connected or not. He bent his hand forward like a child. He doubled over. He fell sideways or laid sideways on the board. He was balancing on his kidney. I was going to get in front and punch into his face like this." Jack made a motion with his fist. "So he . . ." Jack put his arm up to protect his face from an imaginary blow.[14]

"He was just starting to rise. Then, just as I threw the punch—I did throw it—it went all the way around, it came from the floor—he was in the water either because he ducked the punch or because he fell into the water."

According to Jack, the man just floated in the water. In shock, he turned to Mel and said, "Let's fish him out."

"After this man fell in the water," Cohen carefully queried, "did you see him arise from the water?"

"No," Jack replied. "I just saw that belly float."[15]

*   *   *

As soon as they were done taking Jack's statement, the assistant district attorney summoned Mel. If he expected to get any better answers as to why the boys were going around violently attacking random strangers, he would not find them in Mel's curt replies.[16]

Once again proceeding efficiently through the biographical data, Cohen went directly to the events of August 16.

"What was your purpose in going to the park?" the ADA began.

"To look for bums."

"For what reason?"

"To beat them up."

"What was your purpose in doing this?"

"Just beat them up."

A frustrated Cohen tried again. "Why would you beat them up?"

"Just to see how hard we could punch."[17]

Mel's responses continued in this short, clipped vein. His accounting of events, although abbreviated, seemed to align with Jack's, with one important exception: when it came to the events on the pier, Mel told a very different story.

"I took a swing at him," Mel recalled. "Koslow took a swing at him. The guy ran for the ledge. He wanted to jump over. Koslow helped him over."

"What do you mean?" Cohen demanded.

"He pushed him over. He was going over, so he just—"

"Did you see Koslow push him over the pier?"

"Yes."[18]

After being held by the police and questioned for nearly nineteen hours, the boys were not arraigned on any charges until the following morning, August 18, when they were charged: Mel, Bobby, and Jerry with the murder of Rhinehold Ulrickson on August 6, and Jack for the assault of Joseph Kostyra. The body of Willard Menter still had not emerged from the depths of the East River. Although it was possible to charge the boys without a body, the district attorney was probably wary of trying such a circumstantial case in the media spotlight. The charges in the death of Willard Menter had to wait.

*   *   *

August 18, 1954
10:00 a.m.

Attorney and New York State assemblyman Edward S. Lentol stood up for the arraignment of Jerome Lieberman. The round-faced, balding politician with the jet-black mustache had long been an advocate for humane juvenile-delinquency solutions—even championing the creation of a community-based mental-health clinic in 1951. Although Lentol humbly credited the clinic to the influence of his first cousin, John Bianchi (then director of mental health services for Downstate Medical Center), others recalled the assemblyman as a tireless pioneer in the fight against the stigma of mental illness.[19]

For their part, the prosecution sent the big gun: the district attorney himself, Edward S. Silver. Silver was described as a prosecutor who "love[d] his fellow man" and believed in rehabilitation, particularly of youth offenders.[20] Long considered a "champion of better understanding and intelligent handling of juveniles," Silver helped organize the Brooklyn Association for Rehabilitation of Offenders in March of 1954—one of his first acts as district attorney. The group was charged with the study, treatment, and rehabilitation of young ex-convicts. "Our job," Silver told the *Brooklyn Daily Eagle*, "is to prevent these kids from becoming inmates of insane asylums or going back to prison."[21]

Silver's empathy with wayward youth came from his upbringing in grinding poverty in the tenement housing on the Lower East Side. Born on November 17, 1898, Silver was one of seven children of an Orthodox Jewish immigrant tailor who labored in the sweatshops of the garment district. The entire family lived in four dingy rooms before moving to Brownsville when Silver was a few years old. According to family myth, they had just moved into a new tenement on Christy Street when Silver's mother learned that a Jewish boy from the neighborhood had been put in prison for pickpocketing. Fearing for her children's morality, a determined Sarah Silver set out immediately to find new quarters for her family, relocating them to Brownsville within two days of learning of the incident.[22]

Entering City College in 1916, Silver worked after school to help his parents make ends meet. After graduation, he took an eighteen-month break from school to accumulate enough capital to enter Harvard Law School in the fall of 1921. The bright young man quickly made a name for himself as a legal scholar and eventually served as secretary to Professor Felix Frankfurter—soon to be a Supreme Court justice. After moving back to New York, Silver's big break came when Emory Buckner, a well-known corporation lawyer, was appointed U.S. attorney for the Southern District. A businessman with an eye for talent over politics, Buckner hired bright young lawyers without regard for religious or political affiliation. For Buckner, it mattered little that Silver was poor, Jewish, and a Democrat. What mattered to Buckner was Silver's shining brilliance and his armful of recommendation letters. He quickly offered the young man a position as an assistant U.S. attorney.[23]

After four years and becoming chief of the indictment bureau from 1927–1929, Silver retired to private practice until 1946, when Brooklyn District Attorney Miles F. McDonald recruited Silver to an appointment as the chief assistant district attorney. Silver held the position until 1953, when he ran for, and won, the position of Brooklyn's district attorney.[24]

With thick, dark hair, which he kept close-cropped, and heavy, expressive eyebrows, Silver looked every inch a force to be reckoned with. Both attorneys were self-consciously aware of the reporters who quietly filled the back rows of the courtroom. Silver began by highlighting the gang's activities for the magistrate, while the three boys—Mel, Jerry, and Bobby—shuffled silently at the defense table. As described by *New York World Telegram* reporter Norton Mockridge, "The three youths stood there during the exchange, seemingly unconcerned. Lieberman's nose and mouth twitched a bit but he stared into space, paying no attention to anybody. Mittman, burly and stolid, licked once or twice at his thin, sandy mustache, and the Trachtenberg boy, about six feet with bushy, black hair, kept his eyes toward the floor."[25] With dramatic flair, Silver referred to the whipping of the young women in McCarran Park as an "act of sexual sadism" and refuted the defense attorney's petition to have the case tried in Adolescent's Court. In response, Assemblyman Lentol attempted to shift the blame from his clients onto society, asking the same questions the newspapers had been for the last several months: "Are we going to build bigger jails?" he inquired of the court. "Or approach the problem of juvenile delinquency from the roots? Maybe we should lower the draft age to sixteen, to let the kids like this explode their extra steam. I don't know where the evil is, but we haven't done our job."[26]

"It may be," Lentol continued, "there should be other defendants here. I feel my guilt as well as any member of our society. We are reaping the results of our neglect of the problems of youth for the last twenty years."

"That's a pretty speech," Silver retorted sharply. "We are all doing what we can to meet the problem. But we can't rebuild or remake the past twenty years. Meanwhile, we have a serious situation that I have to deal with daily.

We have adolescents roaming the city, hell-bent on committing crimes. We have to deal with this—now."[27]

Turning back to the court, Silver asked, "What makes these kids go wild?"

But his musings were quickly interrupted by Lentol, who suggested that perhaps the district attorney had not, in fact, done "all he could" to curb delinquency. The infuriated Silver finally snapped at his fellow politician, "It's I who has organized a psychiatric clinic for these youngsters—not you."[28]

While reporters at the back of the room scrambled to get down every word of the verbal joust, Magistrate Cullen had had more than enough of the political grandstanding. Citing that "we have before us a case of murder," he refused to move the case to Adolescent's Court and denied the three boys bail.

* * *

August 19, 1954
11:30 a.m.

At 9:45 a.m., on August 19, Willard Menter's partially decayed corpse was located by grappling hooks and artlessly dragged onto the South Fifth Street pier from the leaden water. It was time to charge the four boys with murder.

Normally, the addition of further charges for an already arraigned suspect would take place rather unceremoniously at the Raymond Street Jail or the 92nd Precinct. However, with public anxieties over juvenile delinquency at a fever pitch and the case garnering national attention, the politically crafty district attorney had a much better publicity stunt in mind than a quiet fingerprinting at the jail.[29]

Which is why, at 11:30 a.m., on a particularly muggy Thursday, Arthur Drucker, the stenographer for the district attorney's office, arrived at the South Fifth Street pier while lugging his stenograph machine.[30] He was not alone. About fifty other men already milled on the pier, including television cameramen, motion picture camera operators, and dozens of newspapermen—all tipped off by the district attorney's office. In addition, two assistant district attorneys (David Epstein and Kenneth McCabe) and "a great many detectives present, too numerous to list down" loitered on the hot pier, mopping the sweat off their brows.[31] Jammed on the roofs of nearby barges and on the adjacent buildings and sheds of the American Sugar Refinery Company, a hundred or more men stopped their work to watch the scene in fascination.

In fact, the only people missing from the arena were the notably absent defense attorneys. The prosecutors later successfully defended this omission: as the boys had not been officially charged in the death of Willard Menter, the district attorney's office was not required to notify the boys' retained counsel. Of course, it was also 1954, and *Miranda v. Arizona* was twelve years away from obliging the district attorney to advise a defendant that his refusal or failure to answer questions may not be held against him or that he had the right to have his attorney present.[32]

Next to the pier, a crane with a magnetic lift loaded scrap metal into a barge, breaking the eerie silence. At the pier's end, three seagulls lazily circled, finally coming to rest on the steel post of a moored barge. Soon the boys arrived, each in a separate car and handcuffed to a detective. Under the shadow of grimy waterfront lofts, the boys, one by one, were made to identify the body of Willard Menter as the press captured every word and gesture.[33]

Jack, wearing a bright plaid sport shirt, was first. Led over to the corpse by ADA Epstein, he quickly recoiled when the elderly Lieutenant Parkinson dramatically drew away the blood-stained quilt.

"Is this the man?" Epstein barked.

Jack's voice failed him. His eyes flickered everywhere but on the body. He gulped, and then, in a shaking voice, answered, "Yes, that's the man."[34]

"Is this the man you beat up?" Epstein pressed.

"I didn't beat him up," Jack insisted. He paled and winced. "Take me away from here before I faint."

Epstein ignored him. "Is this the man you pushed in the water?"

"I didn't push him!" Jack cried. "As a matter of fact, I tried to keep him from falling in."[35]

Next in line was Mel, brought up by ADA McCabe, his great bulk straining the seams of a pair of blue dungarees and a dark blue polo shirt. Once again, the gray-haired lieutenant, a veteran Marine Division cop, obligingly lifted the canvas from the body's face.[36]

"Do you recognize this fellow?" McCabe asked.

Mel blinked back tears and averted his head. The question was repeated.

Looking scared and bewildered, Mel only managed to blurt out a feeble, "Yes."

"Is this the man? Point to him!" the assistant district attorney commanded.

Mel clenched his teeth, pointed at the body, and turned his head away in disgust.[37]

Then it was Jerry's turn. The slender boy wore a tan jacket slung over a white sport shirt with blaring horizontal stripes. Jerry's face was grim, his lower jaw grinding nervously against the upper. Yet unlike Jack and Mel, he seemed to have little fear of the body, cautiously looking directly at the dead man's face.

"Is this him?" McCabe queried.

"Yes."

"You sure of that?"

Jerry took another good look at the corpse. "It looks a lot like him," he mused. "When I saw him on the park bench I only saw the back of his head."[38]

Finally, the assistant district attorney signaled for the youngest of the boys to be brought over. Bobby appeared the most composed of all, bending down to take a good look into Willard Menter's sightless eyes.

"Take a look at him," McCabe spoke sharply. "Do you recognize him?"

"I'm not sure—it looks like him."

"Take a good look," the ADA pressed.

"I think he's the guy," Bobby mustered. "I think that's him; he had on a brown shirt."[39]

Next, the boys were led, one by one, to the stenographer, where official statements concerning the death of Willard Menter were taken. Tired of crouching on the pier floor, Drucker had moved his stenography equipment onto the track of the crane with the magnetic lift. The boys quietly gave their statements about the night of August 16 to ADA Epstein.

But the theatrics were not yet over. While the stenographer packed up his machine, the boys were brought back to the body. A large semicircle was formed around the corpse, including each boy flanked by plainclothes detectives, the two assistant district attorneys, and Lieutenant Parkinson, who once again obligingly uncovered the face of Willard Menter. Flashbulbs went off as photographers captured the dramatic staged scene, the boys once again instructed to look at and point to the body. The photograph, including the bloated victim's face, graced the front pages of the *New York World Telegram*, *The Daily Mirror*, and the *New York Journal American*. The *Brooklyn Eagle*, having gotten an exclusive first scoop on the story, published a photo taken much earlier in the day of the lifeless body with the Marine Division police.[40]

Of course, this was not the first time in this case that the press seemed to conveniently appear, snapping staged photographs of the defendants with members of the district attorney's office. When the story first broke of the boys' arrest on August 18, accompanying pictures showed the defendants sitting or standing in the interrogation room with Assistant District Attorney Cohen—courtesy of a photographer from the *Brooklyn Daily Eagle*.[41] Another photographer was on hand in the hospital room of Felix Jaculowski, as the injured man identified Jack Koslow as the person who had wrapped his foot in gasoline-soaked rags and set it ablaze. In the published print, ADA Cohen is seen hovering next to the hospital bed, carefully examining the man's injuries.[42] Later the same day, when Edward Walsh identified Jack as his abuser at the 92nd Precinct, the press was opportunely there to snap a picture of the elderly man pointing at Jack accusingly, while the district attorney's stenographer calmly sat between the two, taking notes.[43] Other newspapers, not quite as cozy with the Brooklyn DA's office as the *Eagle*, mostly ran police-provided mug shots of the three older boys and pictures snapped as they were taken in and out of courthouses.

But this intimate relationship with the press, although providing some temporary public goodwill, would ultimately hamstring the district attorney's office. The bold black headlines calling the boys "Thrill Killers" and the brutal photos of battered faces and dead bodies on piers all added up to one thing: if the district attorney's office did not want to appear "soft," then the boys would need to face the electric chair. The problem, however, was twofold: First, the death of Willard Menter was, at best, a manslaughter case. And second, to try all four boys as adults, the district attorney needed an indictment of no less than murder in the first degree.

* * *

In 1948, the New York State penal law was amended to redefine juvenile delinquency. Until 1948, there was no provision exempting children above the age of seven who committed capital offenses from facing the death penalty. But two sensational cases in the mid-1940s had pushed the public to demand legislative reform. The first was that of Edwin Codarre, thirteen, accused of raping and murdering a ten-year-old girl while at summer camp. Alternately labeling the child as a cold-blooded "killer" and "slayer," local newspapers enthusiastically demanded the boy's execution.[44] The Dutchess County district attorney, John R. Schwartz, agreed wholeheartedly. Schwartz stated that, as it appeared Codarre killed the little girl, he "[saw] no reason why [the defendant] should not be treated the same way."[45]

The second was the case of Jack Turk, fourteen, accused of drowning the three-year-old girl he was babysitting to stop her from crying. Unlike the Codarre case, the district attorney of Queens County was loathe to execute a minor and even refrained from asking for either the death penalty or life imprisonment at the trial.[46] But the fact that a boy of such tender years could potentially get the electric chair animated the public, and various community groups and state organizations began calling on the New York State Legislature to amend the definition of who was considered a juvenile under the law.[47]

Particularly troublesome was that the thirty-year-old provision had left the option available that a child as young as seven could face the electric chair in cases of murder, treason, or first-degree kidnapping. Originally drafted at the State Constitutional Convention of 1915, the progressive legislation had empowered state lawmakers to establish children's courts and domestic relations courts "to keep pace with modern theories of dealing with delinquent children."[48] But according to this early statute, any child between the age of seven and sixteen fell under the jurisdiction of the children's court, except when the crime they committed "if committed by an adult would be a crime punishable by death or life imprisonment."[49] The wording created a loophole that allowed children as young as the age of seven to be prosecuted as adults in instances of capital crimes.

Bowing to public pressure, in 1948, Governor Thomas E. Dewey signed into law five bills to amend the lower age limit of capital crimes to fifteen. "The time is well overdue," the governor wrote, "to state in law in no uncertain terms that a child under the age of fifteen has no criminal responsibility irrespective of the act involved."[50] For those who were fifteen, the new legislation "provides flexible procedures . . . an intermediate zone of responsibility and consequent punishment between persons just over sixteen years of age and those just under that age."[51]

* * *

What the new legislation meant in terms of prosecuting the Brooklyn Thrill-Killers was that for the district attorney to include fifteen-year-old Robert Trachtenberg in the indictment, he was extremely limited as to which charges he could seek. Charges such as manslaughter or assault would place Bobby in Children's Court. Further, a charge of felony murder required, in Bobby's case, proof that the boy committed a standalone felony that *independently* carried the weight of capital punishment or life imprisonment—such as first-degree kidnapping or first-degree robbery. If the district attorney could not get a first-degree murder indictment, Bobby's case would automatically be severed and placed in Adolescent's Court for treatment as a juvenile offender.

So on August 26 (Thursdays being "indictment day" in Brooklyn courts), after three long days of witness testimony, it was little surprise that first-degree murder was exactly the charge the district attorney asked the grand jury to indict the foursome on. As three of the boys intermittently read comic books in their jail cells and played checkers—calling the moves out to one another—the grand jury heard testimony from Emma and Charles Menter (the deceased's wife and brother, respectively), one of the boys' victims, and a variety of medical examiners and police officers. Of the four defendants, only Jack Koslow seemed to be particularly affected by the ordeal: a week earlier, his attorney moved to have Jack declared insane, claiming he was suffering from ulcers and colitis (both believed at the time to be triggered by severe anxiety) as well as dementia praecox.[52] "He is insane," the attorney informed the court, "has been insane for years."

For his part, Jack had a complete meltdown at the defense table. According to both the *Brooklyn Daily Eagle* and the *Daily News*, upon catching sight of his parents in the courtroom, Jack threw his manacled hands in the air and screamed, "Mama! Mama!" Then he slumped from his chair to the floor, weeping, gasping, and burying his head in his hands.[53]

Over the weekend of August 20, while the other boys reportedly ate well and caused little trouble, Jack refused food, complaining of nausea and severe stomach pain. The prison guards finally called in the doctor, who ordered an immediate series of gastrointestinal x-rays. For the remainder of the weekend, Jack appeared disconsolate and depressed, pacing back and forth in his cell and reading only sporadically. It was noted by newspapers that all four boys attended religious services on August 20 and were visited by the prison chaplain, Rabbi Sidney Honig, who spent an hour offering the boys much-needed spiritual advice.[54]

* * *

August 25, 1954
11:00 a.m.

Off the hallway of the fourth-floor grand jury offices in the Central Court Building at 120 Schermerhorn Street, Jerome Lieberman—sporting a gray sport shirt, tan slacks, and brown shoes—waited nervously in the grand jury anteroom while manacled to two detectives. The imposing structure, a blend of Renaissance Revival and Beaux-Arts styles, was considered the last of the great Renaissance Revival construction in Brooklyn. Steel-frame construction on top of a granite base, the building featured a gleaming façade of limestone and an upper-floor colonnade of Corinthian-style columns. Inside, the two-story marbled lobby with a coffered ceiling, boasted gleaming bronze elevators and railings. Created by the architecture firm of Collins & Collins at the price tag of $4 million, the building stood as an architectural vestige of better days—construction fortuitously having started right before the stock market crash of 1929.[55]

On Wednesday, August 25, fifteen minutes after Jerry's arrival, his parents, Harry and Lillie, were shown to a separate room. Denied access to their son, "upset and unnerved," the anxious parents begged the reporters skulking in the hallways to leave them alone.[56] When two photographers refused to do so, Mrs. Lieberman finally broke down, beating one photographer with her leather glove and smashing the other's camera.[57] The wait that day would be a long one for the Lieberman family: the new counselor hired for Jerry's defense was held up in court on another matter and would not arrive until later that afternoon. The attorney's name was James D. C. Murray.

*   *   *

At seventy-one years old, James D. C. Murray had been a criminal defense attorney for forty-seven years. Known for his inconspicuous dress, Murray was typically seen sporting horn-rimmed glasses and sedate neckties—always adorned with the same diamond-encrusted pin. Described as "quiet, shrewd, and fatherly," Murray had famously moved courtroom listeners to tears with his eloquence in numerous trials. The *New York Times* unabashedly described him as "[one] of the country's foremost criminal lawyers."[58]

Previous clients included the murderer George McManus—the killer of infamous mob boss Arnold Rothstein. Murray also had extensive experience defending youthful murderers, including Jack Turk, the previously discussed fourteen-year-old babysitter who drowned his three-year-old charge. It was, in fact, Murray's skillful defense of Turk that was solely credited for the boy's acquittal.[59]

At the time, Murray was defending John Francis Roche, who was accused of killing a seventeen-year-old waitress, an elderly widow, a thirteen-year-old schoolgirl, and a taxi cab driver, as well as the brutal beating and rape of a fourteen-year-old. Having confessed to all the crimes under what was likely coercive police interrogation (as the *New York Times* noted, Roche gave numerous incorrect details for the crimes, as well as confessing to a crime for which there was already a conviction), Roche was regarded as a mental case and a difficult defendant at best. He was also the first defendant in the history of the New York City courts to receive four first-degree murder indictments at once.[60]

But Murray enjoyed a challenge. So on Thursday, August 19, when Harry Lieberman walked into Murray's office accompanied by an unnamed "lawyer friend," James D. C. Murray quickly took the case. The veteran lawyer later told the press he was "much affected and commiserated with the father," despite what he called "a lack of a sufficient fee to justify defense in a murder case."[61]

When Murray finally arrived that Wednesday afternoon on August 25, there followed a series of conferences with Jerry, his parents, and the assistant district attorney, Albert V. DeMeo. But those who hoped that Jerry was going to roll on his pals were sorely disappointed. Asked whether Jerry was going to testify to the grand jury, Murray gave an emphatic, "No": "There was no absolute agreement he would, and in my judgment he shouldn't. There is a discussion about his appearing, and I determined against it. I do not believe he is guilty of any degree of homicide." Astute reporters at the scene, however, noted that when detectives left to take Jerry back to jail, they destroyed an order that would have moved the boy from the Raymond Street Jail to the local holding facility euphemistically known as "The Tombs." Whatever deal had previously been made with the district attorney's office on Lieberman's behalf, Murray walked away that day believing he could do better.[62]

*   *   *

But James D. C. Murray was not the only defense attorney who appeared at the grand jury offices that afternoon. Lloyd Paul Stryker, much like Murray, was a veteran trial lawyer of forty-five years, and he was at 120 Schermerhorn Street on this broiling hot day on behalf of Bobby Trachtenberg.[63] The heavy-set, blue-eyed sixty-nine-year-old was known as a "scholarly trial lawyer of the old school" and had even authored several well-received books in his spare time, including a biography of President Andrew Johnson.[64] Stryker had defended the infamous Alger Hiss at his first trial (resulting in a hung jury) as well as former Tammany leader James J. Hines and the scandalous ex-Brooklyn District Attorney William Geoghan—accused of corruption and of being in bed with the mob.[65] Although less experienced than Murray when it came to the defense of young criminals (in fact, he told the press he could not recall ever having defended a person so young), he was heralded by newspapers as a "well-known trial lawyer" and a "top-notch criminal lawyer."[66] When asked why he took on Bobby's defense, Stryker said he was moved by the boy's "extreme youth": "In our public policy and laws, a boy under 16 is not regarded as an adult. Ordinarily, this matter should be considered by the Children's Court and this fact interested me."[67]

On August 25, Stryker was seen conferencing with the assistant district attorney, and the rumors flew about Bobby's possible testimony against the other boys. If there was ever any loyalty among the foursome, it appeared to be quickly breaking down in the face of a potential grand jury indictment.

* * *

August 26, 1954

The four boys stood before County Judge Samuel S. Leibowitz. Sitting in the second row, Mrs. Sylvia Mittman was the only parent who came to hear the indictment read. Her husband, reporters were told, could not afford to lose a day's pay. In the hallway outside the courtroom, Melvin was dressed in a stained jacket, his unruly hair left uncombed. Next to him, Jack had shaved his wispy mustache but still wore the same bright green plaid shirt and baggy black pants as when he was arrested. Only Bobby appeared "jaunty" in his light checked sport coat.[68]

One by one, the boys were brought before the bench in front of the packed courtroom—first Jack, then Mel, Jerry, and finally Bobby—where the indictment for each was slowly read into the minutes. "The Grand Jury of the County of Kings, by this indictment, accuse the defendants of the crime of Murder in the First Degree."

Gasps of surprise came from a number of women spectators. Sylvia Mittman winced when the charges were leveled against her son. Melvin lowered his head, Jerry gulped compulsively, and Jack alternated between nervously fingering his newly clean-shaven upper lip and playing with the collar button at the throat of his shirt.[69]

The charge continued:

> The defendants, acting in concert and each aiding and abetting the other, on or about August 16, 1954, in the County of Kings, willfully, feloniously and of malice aforethought, did strike and beat Willard Menter with their fists and did push the said Willard Menter off a pier into a body of water, causing him to die of submersion on or about August 16, 1954.[70]

Mel and Jerry were further charged with second-degree manslaughter for the death of Rhinehold Ulrickson. As soon as he was led from the courtroom, Mel, the strongman who liked to use human beings as punching bags "just to see how hard we could punch," wept inconsolably in the hallway.[71]

It was official: all four boys were on trial for their lives.

Yiddishkeit

In the days following the arrest of the Brooklyn Thrill-Killers, a city already electrified by juvenile delinquency exploded. On August 20, the New York City Police Department responded to public outrage by intensifying efforts to corral juvenile delinquents. Over one hundred detectives joined the regular patrols, combing the area from Battery Park to South Ferry and arresting over 160 youths on a variety of largely misdemeanor charges in an effort to look tough on crime.[1] Meanwhile, the New York City Youth Board jumped on the publicity the case garnered to swiftly petition City Hall for an emergency appropriation of nearly half-a-million dollars to expand their outreach efforts to troubled youths.[2]

Within a couple of weeks of the arrests, the city council reaffirmed their commitment to creating additional recreational facilities for youths, arguing that if the "Four boys who committed the brutal slayings this month . . . had been able to work off their energies through boxing and other healthy athletic competition, they would not have chosen old men and young girls as the objects of their beating."[3] And in a speech to the Brownsville Boys' Club, Mayor Wagner avowed his continued commitment to "meet this twentieth-century plague which threatens our city," although he cautioned that the case of the Brooklyn Thrill-Killers might be beyond even City Hall's reach. "We know that of these essentials of a healthy boyhood—places for recreation, good friends, intelligent leadership, religious training—understanding parents and good home surroundings are of paramount importance," Wagner told the assembled crowd. "We know, too, through recent events, that some young men, despite good homes and loving parents, turn out to be evil. How? Why? No one has yet found the answers."[4]

But while for the larger New York community this was yet one more shocking example of the city's failure to protect its citizens from a youth gone wild, for the Jewish community, the Brooklyn Thrill-Killers brought underlying anxieties about losing Jewish children to America's mass culture to a boiling point.[5] The community's obsession with the case was swift and lasted for several months. As one journalist for the Yiddish newspaper *Forverts* noted, "Eight out of ten acquaintances that I have met since last Sunday, spoke with me about one theme—about the four Jewish boys from Brooklyn.[6] An editorial succinctly summed up the anxiety, fear, and shame that permeated Williamsburg after the Thrill-Killers' arrests:

> Not only the unlucky parents are ashamed . . . even complete strangers are ashamed. I am ashamed, you are ashamed. We each have the feeling that the odor of demoralization and decay . . . is in the air which we all breathe. The odor comes from outside through the open windows into our homes, into our institutions. But who knows, maybe it's the opposite: Maybe that very stink actually comes *out* from our homes and institutions and poisons the outdoors?[7]

Jewish parents were suddenly hit with the uncomfortable reality that their children, who seemed well-adjusted on the outside, could be hiding dark secrets. As one Brooklyn father described it, "Up until now I've been proud of my sixteen-year-old son: he plays piano and reads a lot, but now? Lieberman also played piano, you know, and you know Trachtenberg was also a bookworm."[8] Nor was discussion of the case limited to just local residents: representatives from Jewish agencies as far away as Minnesota and the Dakotas commented on the crime spree: "If such a thing could have happened with children from Jewish families . . . then all of America must hang its head and examine its heart by asking the question, 'Where are we headed? What kind of character is developing in the American people?'"[9]

In reality, the fears were unwarranted. The case of the Brooklyn Thrill-Killers notwithstanding, crime rates among Jewish children and adults—which traditionally made up a smaller percentage than other groups in the city—remained at an all-time low.[10] The percent of Jewish children appearing in children's court had even decreased to a third of what it was twenty years prior.[11] Additional statistics showed that among Jewish adults, the number of Jews accused of a serious crimes in Brooklyn was only 4.5 percent—even though Jews made up over 40 percent of the Brooklyn population. And throughout New York State, Jews represented only 3–4 percent of those incarcerated.[12]

But American Jews were as swept up in the panic over juvenile delinquency as their gentile counterparts, and facts about low crime rates in their community did little to reassure anxious parents that their own children would not follow down the same shocking path of delinquency as the Thrill-Kill Gang.

Instead, editorialists and readers yearned for simple answers for the boys' behavior and equally simple solutions to curb delinquency. For the next few months, within the privacy of the Yiddish-language press, the Jewish community debated how such degeneracy could be spawned in their backyard and what could be done to stop American mass culture from destroying their children.

* * *

In most ways, the conversation about the Brooklyn Thrill-Killers echoed similar themes being bandied about by the larger public: the need for more police, a far-too-lenient court system, issues with "modern" childrearing and education, and the corruptive role of the mass media. However, some of the issues and solutions were unique to the Jewish community: in particular, the lack of education in *Yiddishkeit* (Jewish values) and the lasting effect of the Holocaust on youth mentality.[13]

One of the first institutions that faced blame both inside and outside of the Jewish community was the adolescent and children's court systems. The charge was led by Kings County Court Judge Samuel Leibowitz. Leibowitz, a Jewish immigrant from Romania, was long considered one of the nation's top defense attorneys, famous for his zealous defense of the Scottsboro Boys.[14] Yet while Leibowitz's background was in criminal defense, once he crossed into the judiciary, he quickly obtained a reputation as a tough "hanging" judge who staunchly supported the death penalty.

In October of 1952, Leibowitz convened a grand jury accusing the Adolescent's Court of not being tough enough on crime. In an interview with the *Forverts*, Leibowitz claimed that the grand jury investigation was necessary because "some [adolescent and children's court] judges do a lot of damage by letting youths out on probation, even those who have been arrested for the second, third and fourth time." This laxity on the part of the children's and adolescent courts necessitated, according to Leibowitz, that he and other county court judges "make up for the shortcomings of the previous [Adolescent's Court] judges" by meting out extra-harsh sentences and penalties.[15]

After a two-year inquiry, the grand jury found that the Adolescent's Court was turning "a long parade" of crime-hardened youths loose on the community, resulting in "a menace to the public safety."[16] The presentment argued for the abolition of the Adolescent's Court's jurisdiction in any criminal matters and that the court should be limited to only youths whose behavior was not criminal, but "unamenable to the proper control" of parents, guardians, and other authorities.[17]

Having lambasted the Adolescent's Court, Leibowitz set his sights on the Children's Court next, accusing it of the same levels of leniency. Sitting on the bench at Brooklyn Children's Court was Justice Jacob Panken, also a Jewish immigrant (from the Ukraine) and a long-time political candidate for the Socialist Party of America. In addition, Panken was one of the most outspoken anti-Zionists on the Jewish left and was often in public dispute with Leibowitz on the issue.[18] Panken informed the *Brooklyn Eagle* that Leibowitz's convening of a grand jury in the matter was no more than a convenient publicity stunt in an election year. Proclaiming that children's court judges "have no power nor do they have the right to punish children," Panken reiterated that the job of the Children's Court was to "serve the welfare of the child."[19]

But critics both inside and outside the Jewish community worried that in cases such as the Brooklyn Thrill-Killers, compassion would fail to serve the needs of the public. An editorial in the *Brooklyn Daily Eagle* hoped that "no sentimental judge of Children's Court gets in the way of the march of this gang to the electric chair," while one in the *Forverts* contended that "part of the fault lies with the too-lenient treatment that young criminals receive in the courts." Both papers applauded Judge Leibowitz and endorsed his campaign for reelection as county court judge.[20]

Besides the accusations of judicial leniency, other issues that both the mainstream New York press[21] and the *Forverts* agreed on, and gave passing reference to, included the need for more police and underlying socioeconomic problems, such as poverty.[22] But when it came to the fundamental cause of the Thrill-Killers' crime spree, the mainstream newspapers and the *Forverts* diverged. For the conventional press, the answer was overwhelmingly found in psychology. In three separate editorials, the *New York Times* argued that the crimes were all "madness and bestiality," that the boys were merely "sadists," and that they lacked "normal emotional growth."[23] The *Brooklyn Daily Eagle* published the opinion of a "Park Avenue" doctor that the boys were "probably homosexual and victims of drives that have dethroned all inhibitions in the pursuit of the gratification of their passions."[24] Not to be outdone, the *New York World Telegram* called on the "world-famous psychiatrist and criminologist" Dr. Renatus Hartogs, who "despite the handicap of having only superficial personality sketches of the boys" laid their crimes on "sex fears and aggressive hate."[25] Various articles appeared throughout metro New York newspapers concerning the psychological state of Jack Koslow, in particular, ranging from predictions of an insanity defense to questions as to whether he was a sadist.[26]

Certainly, some editorialists and readers in the *Forverts* agreed that the issue was fundamentally a psychological one. An editorial in the August 20 edition of the *Forverts* argued that there was "no cause to fall into a panic" and that this was "not a criminal wave among youth, but rather . . . four mentally ill boys."[27] And the September 4 "Jewish Interests" column argued that the Thrill-Killers were no more than simple sadists, making this entire debacle a "human problem" and not, in fact, a Jewish one.[28] This sentiment was emphatically echoed by one *Forverts* reader, who wrote to the editor: "The youth are simply sick! Crazy! They should be treated medically!"[29]

But the vast majority of columnists and readers in the *Forverts* found the psychological explanations lacking. As one editorialist acerbically noted, "The psychoanalysts . . . find a theory for everything: father-hatred, mother-hatred, inferiority complexes, superiority complexes. Just now writing this article, I read a psychologist's opinion that the four killed the old people meaning to kill their fathers, and whipped the girls meaning to whip their mothers. What nonsense!"[30] Instead, the vast majority of the *Forverts* readers and writers placed the blame squarely on the shoulders of the boys' parents. One writer from the *Forverts* even openly accused the Thrill-Killers' parents of trying to give a false impression that their sons were normal boys who had received "quite a good Jewish education" when "it's clear that the parents did not want to reveal everything, or else they didn't know everything, about their boys." "Whether this is evidence of serious negligence," the editorial concluded, "we won't undertake to judge."[31] But if the columnist feared that his readers might be fooled by the families' protestations, he could be heartened by the numerous letters to the editor in which readers argued that it was "the parents of such children [who] are at fault."[32]

For some readers and writers, the main issue was that the boys' parents had done both "too much and too little." In an interview with Rabbi Honig, who had visited the four boys in the Raymond Street Jail, writer Dovid Liberzon surmised that "too much" was given in the forms of "too much freedom to come home late often and to have as much money as they want," while "too little" attention was paid to "their raising, their friends, their daily problems." "When children are allowed to come home after 11:00 p.m.," Rabbi Honig informed the *Forverts*, "or are given as much money as they want or need, then we are crossing a line, and we are also crossing a line in another way when children are allowed to wander around constantly without useful work."[33]

Forverts readers agreed. For example, Gedalia Kaplan of New York City wrote that "the parents . . . spoil them and don't take care to raise the children properly, with respect . . . and spoil the children in everything they might happen to desire." Another reader, Philip Cooper of Brooklyn, concurred: "The fault is certainly the parents', who believe that children must be given everything." "It's no surprise," Cooper concluded, "that . . . children become crazy from their perpetual holiday and look for some kind of 'excitement' in their monotonous lives."[34] One mother relayed her own personal experience, in which she took very seriously the biblical admonition "Protect your children as the pupil of your eye!"[35] "I have not let my child out of my sight even for even a minute," she wrote to the *Forverts*, including secretly following him when he was in high school "to see where he is and with whom he meets." The hard work paid off, she insisted, as now "he is married and has two children. . . . [E]ven now when he comes to our street, he is a welcome guest among the neighbors."[36]

A mother's vigilance was the theme of two "Women and the Home" columns in the *Forverts* dedicated to discussing the Thrill-Killers that September. Both columns warned that mothers needed to concern themselves their children's friends. The first, published on September 12, advised the following:

> From the moment of the child's very first step, it is necessary to keep an eye on whom the child becomes friends with. . . . we must protect the child from bad company, from street children. The task is very difficult. But there's no help for it. Let the mother go to the beauty parlor slightly less often, let her go to sleep a little earlier and wake up earlier. There is no shortcut. A good mother has not only a stomachache, but also a headache about how to raise the child.[37]

The second "Woman and the Home" column on the Thrill-Killers, published one week later, emphasized how making sure your children were selecting appropriate companions became both infinitely more difficult as well as more crucial once the child began attending school, where "he finds himself among a lot of other children from various parents, from various streets."[38] Other editorials followed suit. One, aptly titled "Tell Me Who Your Friends Are," employed Jerome Lieberman as the prime example of a good boy led astray by bad company. According to *Forverts* editor-in-chief, Hillel Rogoff: "He [Jerome Lieberman] befriended bad people, sick, brutal types, who dragged him into an underworld." "It is worth wishing," the editor mused, "that parents will apply the lesson that Jerome learned as they raise their children. Fathers and mothers need to take more interest in their sons' and daughters' friends."[39]

But supervising your children's choice in companions was not the only place where mothers needed to practice due diligence. The threat of a corrupting mass media was infiltrating the home. Mothers were admonished to keep a judicious eye on what their children were reading, watching, and hearing. One concerned reader wrote to the *Forverts* that on television, radio, and in the movies, "If there's no murder, no dice—limiting it to beatings and destruction is naturally out of the question." While another decried the "dirty, immoral books the children read, the so-called comics."[40] The "Woman and the Home" column called for concerned mothers to besiege congressmen and senators with petitions against the "murderous television shows" and "bandit movies," calling it "a matter of life and death for our children."[41] But yanking your child away from the television was not enough. In an article asking "What Does Your Child Do with His Free Time?," the *Forverts* helpfully supplied a list of Jewish youth groups, warning that "the dreadful deeds which were committed by the four Jewish teenagers from Williamsburg" meant that parents needed to be increasingly watchful of their children's after-school activities "so that such misfortunes would not happen with their [own] children."[42]

Other issues with modern parents included a complete and utter lack of authority. "I have seen families," one author complained, "where the parents are simply afraid to say a single word to the children. They're just doormats, provoking in their children mere contempt."[43] An interview with Dr. Harris

Peck, the chief psychiatrist from the New York Children's Court, concluded that many parents had "shrugged off certain duties . . . in the name of 'new parenting.'" "They have heard that one must give a child 'free expression,'" Dr. Peck told the *Forverts*. "So they have falsely interpreted this to mean that they must allow [children] anything, rather than exercising the authority of a father or mother when necessary."[44] Another editorialist also blamed modern parenting for the tragedy of the "four young boys." In a colorful vignette, the author told a story of a mother and child he observed on the boardwalk: "Suddenly I heard the sound of slaps, so I turned my head and saw how the child hit her mama." Upon observing the author, the young mother excused the child's behavior, explaining, "My daughter has personality; she has character." According to the column, the scene represented the worst of "modern parenting," in which parents "[talk] about how dangerous it is to 'suppress desires' in a child" while allowing for a complete inversion of familial authority. "She wants to have a normal child," the writer mused. "I think to myself now—who knows, perhaps the four Brooklyn boys are also the victims of such 'normalcy.'"[45]

Modern parents were further accused of giving "too much" materialistically. Judge Leibowitz warned the *Forverts* readers that mothers and fathers too often tried to curry favor with their children with "bigger gifts and concessions."[46] And writer Dovid Eynhorn accused parents of "giv[ing] children only money—money to satisfy all desires, whether good for the children or harmful."[47] Dr. Harris Peck lamented how many families chose material comfort over spending actual time with their children, arguing that establishing a "peaceful home" in which the parents have the time to "communicate with a growing[boy as they should" was infinitely more important than "hav[ing] enough money to send the children to camp and to buy a color television."[48]

But even worse than the lack of parental authority, inappropriate choices in companions, and material spoiling was the lack of religious education, or *Yiddishkeit*.[49] Within days of the arrest of the Brooklyn Thrill-Killers, it was quickly pointed out by the *Forverts* that the boys' parents had done a poor job in giving the youths a "true Jewish education."[50] An exclusive scoop from the prison chaplain charged that while all four boys had bar mitzvahs, two had attended Talmud Torah, and fifteen-year-old Bobby even went to synagogue from time to time, their Jewish education could only be described as "superficial" at best. What concerned the rabbi was that none of the boys seemed to have any understanding of *Yiddishkeit*, which he defined as "Jewish values." Honig implied that perhaps had the boys been given spiritual and moral heroes from Jewish tradition—"grand figures with high ideals"—they might not have turned to the "superman" ideology of Nietzsche (one of Jack's favorite authors). "There is no doubt that a good Jewish education can assist in strengthening ethics, in order to reduce the danger [that children] will slip off the path," Honig told the *Forverts*. Statistics appeared to be on the rabbi's side: according to the article, less than 2 percent of delinquent Jewish youths had a "substantial" Jewish education.[51]

Brooklyn District Attorney Edward Silver agreed. In an interview with the *Forverts* the following day, Silver argued that children who received a religious education were less likely to become delinquents than those who did not. Contending that the main thing children learn through a religious or Jewish education is "morality and human values," Silver recalled his own upbringing as one rich with *Yiddishkeit*: "There are sociologists who would say that my youth was characterized by need, by various shortages, but this is absolutely false. My parents gave me—spiritually speaking—millions." It was this upbringing, Silver assured the *Forverts* reporter, which kept him on "the straight path," and he, too, appeared to have the statistics to back up his claims that the religiously educated were less likely to become juvenile delinquents.[52]

Another editorialist, posing the question "Why are more crimes committed here than previously among Jews in the Old Country?," also determined it was because of a lack of "Jewish upbringing." In the Old Country, the writer argued, parents went out of their way to ensure that even the poorest child "should have a cheder, a Talmud Torah, in which to learn Yiddishkeit." Not only did parents make numerous sacrifices, "depriv[ing] themselves of bits of bread" to ensure that their children "were educated . . . in religious spirit, in moral discipline," but the parents' lives served as "the best and most beautiful example[s] for the children." For the children in these homes, *Yiddishkeit* gave them a foundation of ideals that for some stayed religious, and for others became political:

> [When] young men stopped spending time in the houses of learning and in yeshiva—where did the youth go then? Did they seek out empty entertainment, did they read foolish titillating literature; did they organize into gangs to play pranks, attack people, beat and torture them? Did they go down the path of crime? God forbid! The youth that left the houses of learning and the yeshivas joined movements that fought for national or social principles. They became Zionists, pioneers, Labor Zionists, socialists, Bundists. . . . they read serious literature, they engaged in dialogues about important questions and problems.[53]

Scholar and activist Abraham Menes agreed. In an editorial titled "The Education of Jewish Youth . . . What We Can Learn from the Tragic History with the Four Brooklyn Boys," Menes postulated that a Jewish education created a more restrained and responsible youth. While Menes recognized the need to live in a secular world and the necessity for children and parents to worry "early and often" about the child's future profession and educational needs, he argued that secular education only served to teach a child that "the whole world is set up to serve the child's every need." Only religious education, Menes declared, imparts on children the ideals of the social contract, in which the child is brought into the constraints and responsibilities of the community. Because the four boys were not properly indoctrinated into Jewish manhood, Menes reasoned, they sought instead to become "supermen."[54]

Various letters to the editor indicated that many community members agreed that the fundamental issue was a lack of *Yiddishkeit*. One *Forverts* reader complained, "Parents don't give children any religious Jewish education. The children know nothing about Jewish traditions or Jewish holidays. . . . They don't know what they are or who they are."[55] Another reader claimed that parents were failing to teach children ethical values, while a third even accused society of "corrupt[ing] the spiritual and moral aspect of [children's] lives."[56] The activist Rabbi Ben-Tsiyon Hoffman, writing under the pseudonym Tsivyon, even questioned whether the boys' lack of a Jewish education meant that this was not in fact a Jewish question at all, arguing that "aside from their birth they are just as much Gentiles as any other American child."[57] Other columnists lamented the "ideological emptiness" in the homes of children and decried that "a lot of our children live in a moral desert."[58]

Concerns about *Yiddishkeit* and the lack of an adequate "Jewish" education were reflective of a particularly vulnerable moment for the Jewish diaspora. From the beginning of Jewish immigration to America, there had remained a dependence on European Jewry for intellectual and cultural innovation, teachers, theology, and the preservation of traditional and cantorial music.[59] Decisions by American Jews on how much to assimilate into America's white mainstream were predicated on presumptions that European centers of Jewish learning and culture would always exist. The Holocaust, therefore, did more than simply kill a substantial number of Jews: it effectively destroyed the very heart of the Jewish world. With Israel in its infancy, American Jews suddenly found themselves thrust into a new leadership position for both the diaspora as well as the remnants of European Jewry. The various organizations and institutions that made up the infrastructure of American Jewish life struggled to rise to the challenge, while scholars, cultural critics, rabbis, and Jewish publications questioned whether American Jews were versed enough in *Yiddishkeit* to carry the mantle.[60] Debates quickly raged as to whether Jewish American children were becoming too "Americanized" and were no longer being adequately taught Jewish culture and values.

The central focus of this new anxiety—whether American Jews were worthy inheritors of the great Jewish cultural tradition—infused issues concerning Jewish youth and education. The 1950s in America saw a massive religious revival in American society, and Jews were certainly not immune to the trend.[61] The 1950s was, in fact, a "golden age" of institutional building and communal activity for American Jewry.[62] Congregations increased in membership, grander temples were built, and, most importantly, parents began to send their children to Jewish supplementary schools in record numbers.[63] Jewish summer camps and youth programs increased in popularity, and Jewish community centers with programs for both youths and adults multiplied in the suburbs.

Despite all this activity and growth, however, many worried that all this expansion was simply a form of "keeping up with the Goldbergs."

Commentators decried that the increases in temple membership were for social rather than spiritual reasons. And while Jewish children attended Jewish schools and programs at unprecedented levels, they seemed to know relatively little about Jewish religion and culture. Jewish learning was merely superficial, and the building of grand temples seemed little more than a vapid, materialistic enterprise. As historian Hasia Diner points out, this was hardly a new concern in American Jewish society—the issue of preserving Jewish identity and culture in the overly hospitable American climate had been debated since the first Jews arrived in the seventeenth century.[64] However, the Holocaust added a new layer of anxiety to the issue, as the children of American Jews unexpectedly became the future of Judaism. Suddenly, it was even more imperative that Jewish American children had a deeper *Yiddishkeit*, a true Jewish education.

The Brooklyn Thrill-Killers served as a frightening reminder that the fate of world Jewry was now in the hands of young people who were more interested in horror comics and monster movies than in learning about the Jewish patriarchs or studying the Torah. That their Jewish education was shallow, superficial, and incomplete only proved that the American Jewish community's neglect of *Yiddishkeit* was creating a youth that was both unworthy and unable to bear the heavy mantle of Jewish tradition. The lack of *Yiddishkeit* also served as a simplistic cause and solution for the *Forverts* readers and editorialists: Want to prevent your children from becoming like the Brooklyn Thrill-Killers? The answer could be found in Yeshivas, Talmud Torahs, youth groups, and Jewish day and summer camps. Unlike psychoanalysis, which meant years of self-centered introspection and no guaranteed results, *Yiddishkeit* was communal, immediate, and had the backing of both statistics and the Brooklyn district attorney.

The specter hiding in the background of all this was, of course, "Hitler's Catastrophe." Only a couple of editorials named the evil outright. Dr. Harris Peck of the Children's Court openly mused that "the murder of six million Jews while a world stood by indifferently . . . how can this fail to influence the mental condition of children and parents?" Dovid Eynhorn, in an editorial titled "Tragic Offender from a Confused Generation," blatantly compared the four boys to Hitler's *Sturmabteilung* (SA). Exchanging the homeless for Jews, Eynhorn reflected that if the four boys "had a chance to collaborate with a German Nazi, a Jew murderer," that they would likely feel a kinship rather than hatred. The Thrill-Killers, Eynhorn reasoned, were no more than sadists awaiting a great leader, another Hitler, to "organize these same young people into gangs, give them uniforms and badges, declare them to be great patriots, and give them weapons and the freedom to implement all this cruelty."[65] That the fundamental problem was a cultural zeitgeist in which "the person [has] lost his holy right to life" could be seen in the variety of national-social movements in which people were divided into "those who may live and those who may not."[66] Other authors used Koslow's admitted affinity for Nietzsche's "superman" philosophy as an oblique reference to Nazism and the Holocaust.[67]

It is interesting that while the mainstream press spent a great deal of time discussing Jack Koslow's predilections for imitating Hitler, obsession with Nazism, and frequent hate-filled speeches, the *Forverts* was largely silent on the matter. While publications such as *Inside Detective Magazine* ran headlines such as "Boy Hitler of Flatbush Ave.," Dovid Eynhorn was criticized by a *Forverts* reader for openly comparing "Jewish kids to Hitler Youth."[68] Instead, editorialists blatantly compared the boys to Leopold and Loeb—wealthy and depraved Jewish youths who had murdered for fun in the 1920s—while only vaguely referencing the boys' relationship to Nazism through indistinct allusions to Nietzsche.[69] Why was the *Forverts* so reluctant to engage with Jack Koslow's self-proclaimed fascism while the mainstream New York press made it a central feature of their coverage of the story?

Consensus scholarship concerning American Jewry's engagement with the Holocaust in the 1950s argues that American Jews—increasingly becoming assimilated into mainstream, middle-class American culture—chose to distance themselves from an event that so painfully differentiated them from other white, middle-class Americans at a time when the community wished to emphasize sameness.[70] Some scholars even posit that this silence was because of a reluctance to criticize America's newest Cold War ally (West Germany) in light of many Jews' previous affiliations with socialism and various communist parties, as well as a disinclination to call attention to Jewish victimization.[71]

While more recent scholarship argues that the American Jewish community was extremely active in addressing the Holocaust both commemoratively and educationally, it appears that when one of their own was actively identifying with Nazism and symbols of anti-Semitism, the *Forverts* community fell largely silent on the matter.[72] Was Jack's engagement with Nazism simply too shameful to address, even within the confines of a Yiddish newspaper limited to a Jewish audience? With the emphasis on *Yiddishkeit* as the solution to delinquency, it is surprising that Jack's Nazism was not engaged as an example of how a Jewish education was a means to counteract "feelings of inferiority" among Jewish children, bolstering their self-esteem as well as increased identity with Judaism.[73] Certainly, Jack's choice to emulate anti-Semites was a provocative foil to a child, steeped in *Yiddishkeit*, who would preferably identify with Jewish heroes.

This was also a period when American Jewry was anxious to express its loyalty and affinity to America and to emphasize the compatibility of Judaism with American ideals.[74] The Rosenberg trial, McCarthyism, and general anticommunism made it an imperative for midcentury Jews to distance themselves from earlier socialist activism and reaffirm their patriotism.[75] Further, stereotypes of Jewish men as being cowardly, noncombatant, and passive masked the fact that nearly 550,000 American Jewish men had participated in World War II—a reality addressed by groups such as the Jewish Welfare

Board, who publicized Jewish male war service and emphasized that Jewish men served less as Jews and more as Americans.[76]

The shock and outrage in the mainstream press concerning Jack Koslow's Nazism was certainly centered more around its unsavory, un-American aspects than Koslow's Jewishness. In one telling vignette from the *New York Journal American*, Jack's derivative behavior and cowardice is contrasted by a Jewish veteran's war service. The veteran in question, Sandor Schwartz, described his disgust at Koslow's pushing around an elderly refugee to the newspaper: "I'm Jewish and I was in the Army eight years and I couldn't take any more. I went out and told Koslow that if he didn't beat it I'd flatten him. He turned around and walked away. He was too yellow to fight."[77]

While New York newspapers highlighted Jack's un-American attitudes, cowardice, and (as discussed in the next chapter) possible homosexuality, the *Forverts* kept its focus on the boys' lack of *Yiddishkeit*, poor parental guidance, and bad choices in companions. Possibly overly sensitive to any accusations of anti-Americanism, the newspaper's editorialists and readers chose to overlook the more salacious aspects of Jack Koslow's behavior in favor of what they thought was a weightier larger picture.[78]

Regardless, it was obvious from the amount of newspaper space dedicated to the discussion of "the four boys" that the actions of the Thrill-Killers deeply shook the larger New York metro Jewish community. Readers and editorialists of the *Forverts* sought both to explain how four Jewish boys "from good homes" could have committed the crimes they were accused of and to find community-based solutions to prevent any more children from following down the same tragic path. Just like the Thrill-Killers were emblematic in the already raging moral panic over juvenile delinquency and, as we will see in subsequent chapters, the anti-comics movement, for the Jewish community, the foursome served as a lightning rod for the preexisting debate on whether Jewish American youths were becoming lost in the American mainstream.

Enter the Good Doctor

It was nearly five o'clock when the doctor arrived at the entrance to Raymond Street Jail. Shaped like a fortress, the foreboding Victorian-age holdover was a blend of Gothic castellation and rough stone, replete with turrets and arched windows. The bespectacled man with the slicked-back gray hair hurried up the concrete steps to the large white doors with the words "City Prison" emblazoned in the relief above. The early December day was seasonably cold, and he had little desire to dwell outside.[1]

After a wait in the anteroom (during which he perused a recent copy of the Catholic weekly *Our Sunday Visitor*), the doctor was ushered into a small interview room where a young man sat waiting for him.[2] On his person, he had an order signed by Judge Hyman Barshay that granted the psychiatrist unlimited access to the prisoner.[3] Over the course of the next three days, the pair discussed nearly every facet of the young man's life, from childhood memories to sexual predilections. At one point, the psychiatrist asked the boy whether he knew about the controversy concerning comic books and their role in juvenile delinquency.

"Yes," the youth replied. "There is a doctor who says they cause a lot of trouble. I know from my actual experience that this is true."

When the psychiatrist informed the prisoner he was that doctor, the boy appeared highly amused.[4]

*   *   *

Born Fredric Werthheimer on March 20, 1895, in Nuremberg, Germany, Dr. Fredric Wertham was one of five children in a middle-class, secular Jewish family. Raised in both Germany and England, he was studying medicine at King's College in London when World War I broke out, and he was briefly interred in a British concentration camp for German citizens. After the war, he concluded his studies in Germany, graduating with his medical degree in 1921. During medical school, he became interested in psychiatry and apprenticed in Vienna, London, and Paris before finally landing a position as an assistant to Emil Kraepelin, the world's leading authority on brain physiology and its relation to the study of psychopathology.

Considered the founder of modern psychiatry, Kraepelin's *Encyclopedia of Psychology* was the first work to claim that psychiatric disorders likely had a physical basis. In his later years, however, Kraepelin became increasingly convinced that the context of an individual's life—including culture and environment, as well as social and economic realities—were crucial to the treatment and understanding of a patient's psychology. While the more dominant Freudian school sought to help a patient to conform to society by only focusing on the neurosis of the individual, Kraepelin believed it was equally important to reform society to produce healthier individuals in the first place.[5] It is unsurprising that Kraepelin, therefore, believed that psychiatrists had a duty to be social activists, and Kraepelin himself campaigned against the horrendous conditions prevalent in asylums and advocated for the treatment of mentally ill criminals.

Wertham's own belief in social activism and the key role society played in fostering psychosis would soon be tested when he landed a position at the Phipps Psychiatric Clinic at Johns Hopkins University, located in the American Jim Crow South. Deeply upset by the realities of segregation, Wertham argued that the practice had long-lasting, harmful effects on the emotional well-being of African Americans.[6] Wertham quickly became known as one of the few psychiatrists willing to testify on behalf of indigent black defendants— a rarity in the psychiatric field in this era—earning Wertham the friendship of the famous defense attorney Clarence Darrow.[7]

Over the next several years, Wertham quickly moved up the ranks to being second-in-charge of the Mental Hygiene Clinic. Obtaining American citizenship in 1927, he also met and married a biology teacher and sculptor, Margaret Hesketh, who collaborated with him on some of his early medical publications. Wertham was the first psychiatrist to receive a National Research Council fellowship, which he then used to fund the completion of his manuscript, the highly regarded medical textbook *The Brain as an Organ*, published in 1934.

Wertham soon moved to New York and became the head of the Court of General Sessions Psychiatric Clinic, which was responsible for giving psychiatric examinations to every convicted felon in the city. This work placed Wertham at the forefront of the burgeoning field of forensic psychology—the subject of his next two books, *Dark Legend: A Study in Murder* (1941) and *The Show of Violence* (1949). Both studies combined Wertham's expertise in forensic psychology with wider social theory.[8] Wertham also worked at Bellevue Hospital as a senior psychiatrist in the alcoholic, children's, and prison wards and eventually became the director of Bellevue's Mental Hygiene Clinic in 1936. A few years later, he became director of psychiatric services at Queens Hospital Center, a job he held until his official retirement in 1952. Esteemed by his colleagues, Wertham was elected the coeditor of the *American Journal of Psychotherapy* and president of the Association for the Advancement of Psychotherapy, a national organization.[9]

Although Wertham's career had taken a turn into forensic psychology, he was still deeply committed to social activism, particularly racial inequality. Although initially hopeful that life would be substantially different for blacks in the American North, this optimism was quickly shattered by his experiences at Bellevue Hospital. Dubbed "a champion of the down-trodden" by critics, Wertham quickly petitioned City Hall, asking for the creation of a clinic in Harlem—a request that never came to fruition.[10] Instead, he shared his concerns with the acclaimed novelist and African American activist Richard Wright and the journalist (and aspiring politician) Earl Brown, who agreed that the oppressive forces of ghettoization and racism made the availability of psychiatric services in Harlem a necessity, not a luxury. In what one historian described as a "fateful discussion," the conversations ultimately led to the creation of the Lafargue Mental Hygiene Clinic in Central Harlem, under the auspices of St. Philip's parish.[11] Opened on March 8, 1946, the clinic offered psychotherapy to patients, regardless of race or ability to pay, on Tuesday and Thursday evenings from six to eight o'clock.

Although headed by two Jewish-American psychiatrists—Fredric Wertham and Hilde Moss—Lafargue was consciously staffed by an interracial mix of social workers and otherwise accredited volunteers, providing difficult-to-obtain clinical experience to many local black mental-health professionals. The main criteria for employment was a subscription to the idea of "universalism"—the novel assumption that the black psyche was the same as a white one. Further, Wertham's style of social psychiatry meant that little time was spent searching patients' personal histories for psychosexual conflicts. Instead, Wertham and the other clinicians sought to help patients cope with their immediate social surroundings, including the trauma of racism and segregation.[12]

Because of his work at the Lafargue clinic, as well as his previous experience testifying on behalf of indigent black defendants in segregated Southern courtrooms, Wertham was called upon in 1952 by the Wilmington branch of the NAACP to interview randomly selected children to determine the psychological effects of school segregation. The thirteen children—eight black and five white—were sent to the Lafargue clinic, where they were given a variety of psychological tests and interviews and participated in a highly revealing group therapy session.[13] In the subsequent trial, Wertham saliently testified that "most of the children we have examined interpret segregation in one way and only one way, and that is they interpret it as punishment."[14] The two Delaware cases the Lafargue study supported—*Belton v. Gebhart* and *Bulah v. Gebhart*—were eventually rolled into the historic *Brown v. Board of Education of Topeka* decision by the U.S. Supreme Court in 1954 that ended segregation in American schools.

Yet for all of his pioneering work concerning racial equality and criminal forensics, Wertham would be remembered by posterity as "the greatest villain of all time." Or, as one comic book fan claimed, "[He was] a prissy, cold Germanic elitist who wanted to deprive American kids of their entertaining reading material."[15] But Fredric Wertham was neither a prude nor a fan of censorship for its own sake. For example, not long before he wrote *Seduction of the Innocent*, Wertham had testified on behalf of a nudist colony that their photographic newsletter *Naturel Herald* was in no way obscene, arguing that the confiscation of the newsletter by the Post Office "constituted a dangerous restriction of civil liberties."[16]

Nor was Wertham the first (or only) voice speaking out against comic books. As historian Bart Beaty writes, the critique of comic books had been going on in America long before Wertham published *The Seduction of the Innocent*.[17] Further, Wertham never naively advocated that comic books were the actual cause of juvenile crime; instead, he explicitly stated on numerous occasions that comics were simply a contributing factor to juvenile delinquency and that "juvenile delinquency has only one cause: adults."[18] But well in-line with the ideals of his social-activist psychiatry, it was as imperative to Wertham for society to act on contributing factors as it was to act on the root cause.

With his awareness of social oppression—particularly racism—it is not surprising that what Wertham brought to the debate about comics was the exploration of both racist and misogynistic content prevalent in Golden-Age comics. In a closed-door hearing by the New York State Senate in December of 1950, Wertham pointed out that comic book heroes were always "a pure, American white man," while the villains were typically "foreign-born, Jews, Orientals, Slavs, Italians, and dark-skinned races."[19] In *Seduction of the Innocent*, he criticized so-called jungle books (comics set in exotic, tropical locales) with the observation that "while the white people in jungle books are blonde and athletic and shapely, the idea conveyed about the natives is that there are fleeting transitions between apes and humans."[20] The powerful combination of portraying nonwhites as "subhuman" while creating heroes who were "blond Nordic supermen" could only serve, Wertham argued, to further American racial division.[21]

In his studies with children, Wertham also found that the impressions the racial stereotypes made on the young were substantial and that already existing prejudices acquired at home were typically strengthened. Studies conducted at Lafargue showed that children familiar with the comic book trope could quickly identify the "good" characters (white, American) and the "bad" (dark-skinned, ethnic, foreign) based solely on appearance.[22] Comics also continued racist ideologies that nonwhites were amoral and therefore acceptable targets for violence and sexual victimization. For example, while the breasts of white women in comic books needed to be nominally covered up, it was completely acceptable to draw nonwhite women with their breasts fully exposed.[23]

Wertham argued that the racism in comic books was not only dangerous to American society but also had a devastating effect on America's Cold War image.[24] In *Seduction of the Innocent*, Wertham highlighted the hypocrisy in the U.S. government's spending millions of dollars "to persuade the world on the air and by other propaganda means that race hatred is not a part of American life" while simultaneously "millions of American comic books are exported all over the world which give the impression that the United States is instilling race hatred in young children."[25] In fact, an entire chapter of *Seduction of the Innocent* is dedicated to illustrating the black eye America was suffering from the international sale of comics. By 1953, concerns over the portrayal of violence in comics had led several European nations to ban or severely restrict their importation, and Mexico restricted the sale of American comic books that depicted racist portrayals of Asiatic peoples. In France, it was reported that children believed that America was a land of "gangsters and robbers where shooting, killing, and torturing were everyday occurrences."[26]

But it is the sexually sadistic element of many of the crime and horror comics that especially concerned Wertham. Some depicted routine types of domestic violence, such as a comic titled *First Love* in which a panel shows a muscular man viciously slapping a woman so hard that she is knocked off her feet captioned, "I'll teach you! I'll teach you to do as you're told!"[27] Others depicted women bound by ropes or chains being brutally beaten or tortured. While obscenity laws in the mid-twentieth century typically meant that adult magazines that featured images or descriptions of sexual flagellation were subject to confiscation by the U.S. Postal Service, scenes of scantily clad women being bound and whipped were routine in comic magazines.

At the hearing in which he defended the *Naturel Herald*, Wertham favorably compared the magazine's "realistic" portrayal of women to the misogynistic depictions found in comic books:

> I personally would much rather have a young boy and say, "Look at this [nudist magazine], this is how it is," instead of reading at night these pictures where girls are just in the poses of being tortured, torn apart, and it is only made good because at the last moment the hero comes and saves them, but before that there is all the excitement of reducing a girl to some kind of a tortured slave or somebody who has to give in for some reason or another.[28]

Wertham's main concern was that the portrayal of sexuality in comic books would severely affect psychosexual development in children, leading to sadistic or masochistic tendencies. "The sexualized brutality," Wertham wrote, "leads not infrequently to a connection between the thrill of suspense and that of sexual arousal."[29] But if Wertham needed a tailor-made case study for his theories, Jack Koslow was about to provide it.

* * *

They started with Jack's early childhood, a time filled with poor health and relentless bullying. Outside the home, the sickly boy was the target of neighborhood children who frequently beat him up. Inside the home, Jack recalled his constant fear of his father: "I was always afraid of my father as far as I can remember. When he got mad with me, he hit me. He shouted at me. Any time I did something I was afraid of him." Jack often juxtaposed his own physical weakness with his father's raw strength: "My father . . . is a powerful man, has good muscles, is very impulsive. My father has giant hands. When he says something to you, you can quake."[30]

The constant victimization—and perceived physical weakness—ultimately led Jack to embrace Nazism. A radio broadcast in 1942 left an indelible impression on the young Jack Koslow. Describing the Nazis as "the rolling German juggernaut invincible and indestructible,"[31] Jack quickly associated the Nazi regime with an enviable "power and strength" that was sorely lacking in the boy's own life. "During [the] war, [I] fell in love with Germany and Nazism. That solved the problem for me. It gave me a side. I had somebody on my side." Fantasizing that if he were in Nazi Germany he could "be something," Jack became avidly attached to anything German, teaching himself the language and then devouring Nietzsche, Kant, and particularly Hitler's *Mein Kampf.* More than Hitler, however, Jack preferred the generals, von Rundstedt and Rommel, in particular. "I used to listen on the radio how they marched and crushed everybody before them. You see, I was always weak, and I wanted to be strong. I was always weak, a runt." Jack's greatest ambition was to be a soldier, a "great German militarist." At school, he spent his time daydreaming of "marching down Unter der Linden."

It is unclear how Jack reconciled his Jewishness with this fantasy of being a high-ranking member of the Nazi regime, other than to argue that it was "bums," rather than Jews, who ought to be eliminated from the social order.[32] When asked whether he was a white supremacist, Jack replied, "I am a white supremacist all right; I was indoctrinated all my life, people, the people I lived with, the Negro is always made less than anybody, in comic books."[33]

Jack's answer was reflective of the relatively new "whiteness" American Jews were claiming, in a somewhat ambivalent manner, in the post–World War II period. The status of American Jews had always been ambiguous. Although Jews meshed well in the new suburban, industrial, capitalist order, they were also viewed suspiciously by white Americans for their somewhat voluntary ghettoization and preference for marrying within their own community.[34] Within the Jewish community itself, the claiming of "whiteness," which was necessarily infused with racial oppression, was problematic for a group whose self-identification hinged on narratives of subjugation—hence the ambivalency.[35] By the 1950s, Jews who sought to successfully "integrate" into white America tended to emphasize Jewish difference in purely religious terms and otherwise sought suburban, middle-class lifestyles that closely mirrored the prevailing Anglo-Saxon norm. Yet, at the same time, many Jews identified with African Americans, and they rejected white oppression and played prominent supporting roles in the 1960s Civil Rights Movement.[36]

Jack's self-identification as a "white supremacist" reflected a changing attitude among some young Jewish males who sought integration and assimilation into the dominant Anglo-Saxon community over continued ethnic affiliation.[37] In the postwar era, prominent Jewish intellectuals had developed a male-centered version of Jewishness that advocated the entitlement of Jewish men to white male structural privileges and upward mobility.[38] At the same time, such sociologists as Nathan Glazer began to use Jews as a "model minority"—juxtaposed against blacks, Puerto Ricans and Italians—as an example of an ethnic minority that was able to successfully assimilate into America's middle-class mainstream. Further, Glazer and other intellectuals argued for Jewish ethnicity as opposed to black race, a distinction that allowed Jews the privileges of whiteness while still being able to maintain and embrace ethnic traditions.[39]

In fact, it was the lack of recognition of Jack's "white" status that started the rampage in the summer of 1954. Roaming around Lewis Silver Park that July, Jack and Mel ran into two drunk vagrants, one black and one white. According to Jack, one of the men called him a "Jew bastard." It was unclear who started the fight, but according to Jack, "After I touched him, something changed. Something snapped in my head." After the initial confrontation, Jack then followed the man a half hour later and gave him another two "tremendous blows" and pursued the elderly man into the park to continue beating him.[40] While witnesses to other incidents recalled Jack's harassing African Americans with racial aspersions and fellow Jews with Nazi propaganda, when it came to himself, Jack would tolerate no questioning of his place at the top of the racial hierarchy.[41]

Besides his identification with Nazism and white supremacy, Jack also became fixated on portrayals of strength in movies and in comic books. Around the age of seven, he saw his first Frankenstein movie, which made a great impression on the boy: "He was so powerful, with one sweep of his hand he could destroy everything."[42] While his comic collection started out innocently enough with *Donald Duck*, Jack soon graduated to what he described as "weird horrors," particularly "the supernatural ones." Vampire comics fascinated Jack, who often imagined himself as a vampire with "long teeth and wings like a bat." Increasingly, Jack found that the comics "went to my head," and he often imagined that he was a vampire. He took to sleeping during the day and going out at night, as well as wearing a "vampire costume" of black leather pants and a black trench coat.[43]

But more than anything, what Jack liked the most about the comic books was the whipping. In his own words, "The only thing that excited me in the comic books is the whipping, there is an awful lot." Jack claimed that he started becoming sexually excited by scenes of whipping as early as the age of seven, and he began self-flagellating by the age of thirteen. He also collected whips—conveniently purchased from the back pages of the same comics—claiming he was only capable of sex after being hit in the buttocks with a strap or a whip. "The fantasy," according to Jack, "was that a woman would hit another woman. The older woman said nothing [other than] a command: 'Lift your skirt up.'" Jack would typically don women's clothing while self-flagellating, and he informed Wertham that were he ever with a woman, he would certainly prefer to be the sadist with the female playing the masochistic role.[44]

Further complicating the picture, Jack often engaged in homosexual trysts. When Jack was a sophomore, he had anal and oral sex with an African American boy of the same age. At seventeen, Jack met a much older man outside of a movie theater who invited Jack back to his apartment where they had sex both that evening as well as on several subsequent occasions. Over the last several years, Jack had often attended "queer parties" in Greenwich Village, but he found that his sexual advances were thwarted—most of the attendees were afraid of him, as he typically went in costume: "I was all black, black and kid leather gloves, women's gloves. I carried a big knife and a mixed-blade knife." The knives, expectedly, were mail-order purchases from comic book ads.[45]

Jack's sexuality had been widely speculated on and written about in the days following his arrest. An article in the *Daily Mirror* discussed the opinion of four "prominent psychiatrists" that the teenage quartet were "sexual deviates."[46] Without having interviewed any of the youths, one of the psychiatrists told the paper that the boys' "normal sexual development did not occur" and that therefore "the aggression usually manifested in higher forms of emotional and sexual life remain . . . on a primitive level."[47] The *Daily News* reported that Koslow had denied being a homosexual in repeated questioning by police, but the newspaper remained skeptical when it was revealed that Jack often took long walks through Greenwich Village, "handing out $1 bills to perverts because he 'felt sorry for them.'"[48] Newspapers also quoted the family physician, Dr. Josef Smul, as saying that "normal sex didn't interest [Jack]," excusing his infatuation with Corinne Malin (Jack's "seaside romance") as merely part of his mental illness.[49] Most damning was the Brooklyn interest column "Over the River" by Edward Zeltner who published this self-proclaimed "eyebrow-lifter": "A New York atty. [*sic*] who reportedly initiated Koslow into alleged acts of perversion is missing from his home and office—and a B'klyn [*sic*] business man who showed a peculiar interest in the youngster is hoping his name won't crop up in the upcoming trial of the teenagers."[50]

That Jack's sexuality was scrutinized by newspapers and psychiatrists is hardly surprising for the time. In 1954, the so-called Lavender Scare that ferreted out suspected homosexuals serving in the U.S. State Department was still in full swing. The idea that homosexual men and women were threats to national security was readily accepted by much of the American public, as homosexuals were placed in the same risk category as drunkards, criminals, and the financially corrupt.[51] America's obsession with the role of dangerous sexuality in society led some physicians to muse that so-called abnormal sexual behavior was "part and parcel of the Communist program to change American sexual mores, [resulting] in a breakdown of the family and the collapse of society as a whole, clearing the way for an easy Communist takeover."[52] In contrast, the monogamous, heterosexual couple and their children were heralded as the very symbol of American Cold War identity.

As historian Carolyn Lewis demonstrates, it was not enough for an individual to simply proclaim him- or herself a heterosexual. How he or she routinely performed that heterosexuality, both in and out of the bedroom, was the subject of medical, governmental, and public scrutiny.[53] Therefore, Jack's declarations that he was not, in fact, a homosexual paled in comparison to reports that he often interacted with known "perverts" in the Village. And while Jack may have had a recent romantic entanglement with a young woman, his long history of behavior that did not conform to proscribed heteronormative masculinity—such as not being able to hold down a job or his "effeminate" affect—made him suspect in the eyes of the public.[54]

Further complicating gender performance in the 1950s was a perceived crisis of masculinity in which it was feared that new patterns of consumption, a workforce that rewarded teams and consensus over rugged individuality, and a new emphasis on the domestic sphere all conspired to feminize America's most vital Cold War asset—the white male citizen. Historian James Gilbert argues that the increased interest in studying the American character (and American exceptionalism) brought new and significant attention to American men, who were the default object of these studies.[55] Part and parcel was the increasing importance of the new American virtue of consumption and the question of how men could stake a claim in a sphere already dominated by women.[56]

Ever since the publication of the Kinsey report on male sexuality in 1948, the performance of masculinity had become increasingly circumscribed to such heteronormative activities as marriage, childrearing, and being the family breadwinner. This is because the report shockingly suggested that nearly 40 percent of the men interviewed had engaged in homosexual activity and that "persons with homosexual histories are to be found in every age group, in every social level, in every conceivable occupation in cities and on farms, and in the most remote areas of the country."[57] The report shattered the stereotype of the effeminate homosexual and suggested that gay men were routinely passing for heterosexuals.[58] So while in another era men's participation in the domestic sphere and passive submission to corporate norms would have compromised their masculinity, in the 1950s, it suddenly defined it.[59]

This new, domesticated version of masculinity was still contested in the period, but the ways in which it could be circumscribed were also narrowly limited. Some men protested the rise of the "organization man" by joining motorcycle and other types of gangs. According to historian Robert Corber, these gangs allowed men to "recover forms of male homosocial bonding that were actively discouraged because they conflicted with the Fordist organization of production and consumption."[60] Others engaged in the new "swinging" lifestyle promoted by magazines such as *Playboy*, who advocated an urban lifestyle in which consumption was not associated with fatherhood or suburban home ownership.[61]

What linked all of these alternative lifestyles to heteronormativity, however, was the exploitation of women. In his study of youth gangs from this period, Eric Schneider found that gang members typically achieved manhood through fighting men and sexually dominating women, often in the form of "ritualized rapes."[62] And the new "swinging" or "Playboy" lifestyle was predicated on active womanizing: promoting homosocial bonding in locales in which women provided a sexualized backdrop and advocating the consumption of magazines (such as *Playboy*) in which women were routinely objectified. The problem, therefore, with the Brooklyn Thrill-Killers was that their gang was composed of four boys with suspect sexualities. Jerry Lieberman was reported to never have gone out with a girl, and when his father admonished him that he ought to start dating, the seventeen-year-old replied that he was "still too young." Neither Bobby nor Mel was known to have ever dated or shown a particular interest in girls, and both had reputations for extreme shyness. Only Jack, whose sexuality was already questionable, had any success with one momentary summer fling.[63]

That the quartet was sexually perverse, therefore, was exemplified by two of their recurrent acts: the first, that they chose to enact their aggressive tendencies on the bodies of homeless men, and the second, that when they chose to channel their sexual aggression onto the bodies of women, they did so in a nonnormative manner. While coercive heterosexual sex acts were considered proof of masculinity and an "alternate to economic success in validating manhood," even these forced sexual interactions were restricted to vaginal intercourse.[64] Date rape and even gang rape were considered acceptable types of heteronormative male behavior, while whipping young women in parks was not, nor was humiliating grown men by forcing them to kiss one's feet and grovel for mercy.

It was a new comic, *Nights of Horror*, that Jack claimed gave him the "impetus at last" to take his whipping fantasies to the streets. Jack began hitting women in 1951, although "never on bare back" out of fear of causing physical injury. The women ranged in age from sixteen to twenty-five and were typically assaulted in the streets or a park. Although for Jack the whipping was enough to cause an erection, on the occasions when Mel accompanied him on the outings, Jack reported that Mel typically touched the women's breasts subsequent to the beatings.[65]

Jack also admitted to Wertham that he felt sexual excitement when he watched Mel beating the vagrants. It would start with the boys playing a Superman role—sorting the bums into categories of good and bad: "Harassing the bums gives me a feeling of power. I enjoyed it. If he was nice and down on his luck, there was no end to which I would not help; one fellow I gave almost every cent I have. I had $7 and gave him $6.50, [and] that a colored man."[66] But woe to the vagrant who was deemed undeserving: "If a man answered back, if he lived for drink . . . or something like that, then I'd punch him, I'll have no control; I had no senses, I hit him till my hands were almost broken, in the face."[67]

The rules were simple: they could only hit one at a time, but it was acceptable to beat the men while they were already down on the ground. They never stole from their victims. Stealing, according to Jack, was too despicable a crime: "One thing I hate is theft. Can't stand it. Never did steal. That's one thing I couldn't do." Burning with cigarettes and matches happened on several occasions, although Jack insisted that the burning gave him no pleasure and that he did so to Willard Menter "only at the insistence of [Bobby] Trachtenberg," who Jack claimed lit the cigarette for him to use. When they went bum hunting, Jack always wore some part of his "vampire" outfit—most often the black leather pants—to heighten the association between his real and fictional selves and to increase the sexual stimulation. For Jack, the beatings had orgasmic climaxes, reporting that afterward he felt "limp like a wet rag."[68]

Ultimately, these excursions served several purposes for Jack: they reinforced his peculiar version of white male privilege by allowing him to bully an "other"; they granted him a modicum of sexual relief; and they mimicked male homosocial-bonding patterns that were an integral aspect of masculinity in 1950s' culture. Yet in all these ways, Jack failed, and his version of white American masculinity was viewed by outsiders as farcical. As a Jew, Jack was not acceptably white enough for his neo-Nazi rhetoric to be considered frightening or for his claims of white supremacy to be taken seriously. Labeled effeminate, his deviant means of sexual arousal could not be used to bolster his claim to heteronormative privilege. And that he used the bodies of old, decrepit, drunk men as the center of his homosocial-bonding rituals went against the era's self-conscious codes of masculinity.

* * *

After nearly ten hours of examination, Fredric Wertham spent the next week honing his testimony and diagnosis while awaiting the phone call from Mr. Morris Eisenstein—the attorney second-seating Jack's legal defense team—that it was time for Wertham to testify.[69] Although Wertham had diagnosed Jack as a "psychopathic personality of the schizoid type,"[70] his testimony could only serve to mitigate Jack's culpability, but not as a true insanity defense.[71] Wertham's testimony was highly anticipated. The press did not know of the famous psychiatrist's personal involvement, but various newspapers had been predicting a psychiatric defense since August.[72]

Finally, at 3:15 p.m. on December 10, the call came. It was answered by Mrs. Wertham, who handed her husband the following message:

> Mr Eisenstein: Mrs W? Haven't time to talk to Dr. W. at another no. just slipped out of courtroom and have to get right back. Just wanted to tell the dr. that the case has taken a totally different (good) turn—of the sort I discussed with the dr.—as possible—we will not be introducing any psychiatric testimony. So please give him that message. Will not need him tomorrow, therefore I will call him at home tonight—(Is this definite?) Yes. That is definite. No psychiatric testimony. Case has taken a completely different turn. It was nice talking to you. I will talk to him tonight about getting him paid, etc. (said nicely)[73]

Stiffed on his fee, Wertham never heard from Eisenstein again.[74] But the information he had collected from Jack Koslow would soon prove invaluable in his war against the comic book industry.

The Trial

November 15, 1954

The boys were seated one by one at the defense table. First was a clean-shaven Jack Koslow, wearing a conservative blue suit and a white dress shirt. He sat nervously, hands clasped "as if in prayer" with his knees occasionally knocking together. To his left was Melvin Mittman, wearing a lemon-yellow polo shirt and a shabby, maroon sport jacket. Described as being close to tears, Mel frequently rubbed his hands together nervously and brushed at his eyes. Next was Jerry Lieberman, looking "dandy" in a new blue gabardine suit (replete with starched white handkerchief sticking out of the breast pocket), suede shoes with tassels, and maroon socks embroidered with images of clocks. To the far left sat Bobby Trachtenberg in a beige suit, gray sport shirt, and four button cuffs, which the *Brooklyn Eagle* quickly pointed out as "fake."[1]

Next to the boys sat their defense attorneys: the illustrious James D. C. Murray for Jerry Lieberman and the veteran Lloyd Paul Stryker for Bobby Trachtenberg.[2] Representing Melvin Mittman was the highly respected former magistrate Leo Healy—a balding, portly man and a former Brooklyn assistant district attorney.

Born in 1894 on the 4th of July, Healy was considered a "spellbinding speaker" (in 1911, he beat out a competitor from Germany to win the title of "World Champion Intercollegiate Orator") and was in much demand at dinner parties. As a young attorney, Healy had represented the controversial Black Star Line, eventually serving as a key witness in the mail-fraud trial of Black Star Line president Marcus Garvey. In 1922, he was appointed as an assistant district attorney in Brooklyn, eventually becoming a judge of the Brooklyn Homicide Court in 1927. Resigning from the bench "for health reasons" in 1931,[3] Healy spent the rest of his career as a prominent criminal defense attorney. Unfortunately, Healy was also famous for his very public marital squabbles with his wife, (Anna) Gladys Cummings. One well-known incident took place at Thanksgiving, when a loud, public argument resulted in the turkey being thrown out the window where it landed squarely on Healy's head. And although he could hardly be called a "looker," Mrs. Healy's jealousy of her husband once led her to scale a fire escape on the Brooklyn Municipal Building in an attempt to catch Healy with his mistress at a district attorney's office retirement party.[4]

The newest member of the defense team, however, was State Senator Fred Moritt, who replaced Murray Cutler as the legal defender of "mastermind" Jack Koslow. Originally, Jack's parents had, on the advice of the Mittmans, sought to hire Judge Healy. But fearing a potential conflict between the two defendants, Healy had referred the Koslows to his associate, Murray Cutler. As the time of the trial neared, however, Jack's parents were increasingly underwhelmed with Cutler's defense and looked to find a brasher legal representative. So on October 19, 1954—less than one month before the trial's scheduled start date—Sam and Anna Koslow appeared at the offices of State Senator Fred G. Moritt and his partner, Morris Eisenstein.

It was hardly surprising that Moritt took the case. Besides being a lawyer and a state senator, Moritt was also a radio singer, a songwriter, and an aspiring Broadway playwright—in other words, he was known for being a bit of a publicity hound. The "singing barrister" of depression days, Moritt's tenor could be heard all over the New York theater venues in the early 1930s, earning him a weekly spot on the radio. Moritt copyrighted over sixty-one songs in his lifetime, including "Sing Everyone Sing," "Climb upon a Moonbeam," and "The Symptoms of Love." He was also credited as the principal songwriter on the 1956 musical *Cash on Delivery* (with Shelley Winters, also titled *To Dorothy a Son*), for which he received $50,000 from Warner Brothers Studios. Moritt subsequently authored an unpublished musical play, *The Third Kiss*, based on *The Barrets of Wimpole Street*; it was later reworked and retitled into the successful Broadway musical *Robert and Elizabeth*.[5] According to his father, a retired dealer of plumbing materials, Moritt was a success at everything he tried—except for getting married and providing his aged parents with grandchildren.[6]

Moritt's political career began with his election to the state assembly, representing Brooklyn's largely Jewish 17th District in 1937. In 1944, having fought in the legislature for the establishment of Brooklyn as an independent city as well as backing popular legislation calling for changes to judicial election procedures, Moritt was nominated as a candidate for the state senate. By 1953, he had become a ranking minority member of the powerful state judiciary committee.[7] Unfortunately, while Moritt's political and musical careers were somewhat illustrious, his legal career was less so. While experienced, he was hardly the veteran criminal defense attorney that Murray or Stryker was, and he further lacked the respectability of a Judge Healy. However, his quick wit and blustery ways won him the approval of his client, Jack Koslow, who glowingly stated, "My lawyer is oratorical; he is the personification of Adolf."[8] Veteran journalists, however, were less impressed, and they would describe Moritt's defense as "nervous, bumbling and inept." One reporter from the *Brooklyn Eagle* even went as far as accusing Moritt of being "so preoccupied with the campaign for his re-election to the State Senate" that "he was unable to give proper attention to preparation of the murder case."[9]

Proving the newspapers right, the trial opened on November 15, 1954, with Senator Moritt asking the court for a three-week adjournment. Moritt claimed the voluminous press coverage of the trial, in conjunction with having had only "thirteen working days" since his retainment by the Koslows, left him no time to read through the briefs of his co-counsel. On the bench, Judge Hyman Barshay balked at the request: "Let me tell you how much trouble I had in getting all these lawyers together to fix the date," he admonished Moritt, enumerating the various phone calls he had personally made to ensure all of the lawyers would be present at the November 15 start date.[10] Besides, Barshay continued, the code entitled a defendant to only two days for trial preparation, and as he had personally managed to read every single record within a period of two hours, "You can finish them," he assured Moritt, "within the same amount of time." But in a gesture of goodwill, Barshay allowed for a one-week adjournment—provided that one juror be seated so that the trial was considered started for official purposes.

The next two motions put forward by Moritt that day would set the tone of the trial. The first was a simple request that Jack be allowed to wear a tie in the courtroom—a privilege denied by the Raymond Street Jail warden out of fear that Koslow was a suicide risk. However, Moritt's poor choice of words was pounced on by the press: in addressing the court, Moritt asked to "allow my boy to wear a tie, because the newspaper reporters and the photographers are taking pictures, *and I do not want him to look like a bum.*"[11] While the request was granted, the unfortunate word choice only served to highlight Moritt's ineptitude and potentially further alienate public sympathy from his client.

The second motion made by Moritt was the first of many attempts to have the court rule on media involvement in the case. Moritt requested that the court "enjoin all the newspapers from using the words 'killer' or 'thrill killer'" in their reporting on the trial. Arguing that the continual media coverage labeling the boys as "killers" is "prejuding [*sic*] these boys and is prejudicial to them," Moritt contended that that the press should have "the right to refer to them as "killers" only postconviction. Barshay denied the motion, stating that the court "has no right or control over the press." It was the first of several motions on the matter throughout the trial, and a basis for later appeal.[12]

On this second matter, Moritt appeared prescient concerning the emerging divide between the legal system and the mass media. At the same moment that Moritt was petitioning Judge Barshay, halfway across the country in Cleveland, Ohio, a doctor named Sam Sheppard was on trial for the brutal slaying of his pregnant wife. Sheppard's subsequent appeals—which resulted in the U.S. Supreme Court ruling in *Sheppard v. Maxwell*—was based on the very same arguments Moritt was making in the Brooklyn courthouse: that the "carnival atmosphere" and prejudicial pretrial media attention resulted in the defendant's inability to "receive a fair trial consistent with the Due Process Clause of the Fourteenth Amendment."[13] In both cases, the newspapers published the names and addresses of jurors, inquests were held for the sake of the media, the jurors in the case were not sequestered, and newspapers ran virulent and incriminating stories concerning the defendants during the pretrial and trial period. The difference, however, was that unlike the presiding judge in the Sheppard trial, Hyman Barshay would not allow the press to take over the courtroom. He also cleverly paneled a blue-ribbon jury and prevented any trial events that held the potential to become a media circus, such as denying the prosecution's motion for the jurors be taken to the crime scene.[14]

Barshay's more sophisticated handling of the Thrill-Killers was likely because, unlike Judge Edward J. Blythin in Ohio, who was a career politician and bureaucrat, Barshay had been a career litigator and prominent criminal defense attorney. Although he started out in 1933 as an assistant district attorney, Barshay was catapulted to national prominence as the defense lawyer for infamous mobster Lepke Buchalter, the head of Murder, Inc. Described by opposing counsel as "a master . . . at the technique of lulling a witness with the velvet glove, then tearing him apart with the mailed fist underneath," Barshay skillfully defended Buchalter during the mobster's 1941 trial for the murder of former garment-industry trucker, Joseph Rosen. Barshay also made headlines across the nation in 1949 when he successfully defended Benjamin Feldman—a druggist accused of poisoning his pregnant wife.[15]

Although he was highly experienced in a courtroom, Barshay was quite new to the bench. He had been elected to county court in 1953 and assumed the judicial robes on January 1, 1954. That he was given the prominent Thrill-Kill trial only a few months into his first term was the result of luck. Trials in this period were assigned to judges at random, using a spinning drum with numbers—like a lottery or raffle. Because of the "great interest" in this case, County Judge Samuel Leibowitz arranged to hold this particular drawing in the presence of all five county judges. Barshay's name was drawn on September 3, 1954.[16]

While Moritt proved the more vocal advocate concerning media issues, on one occasion he was joined by his defense colleagues. Tuesday, November 23, 1954, opened with the staid Judge Healy requesting a conference in chambers to address an unsavory article that had appeared in the evening paper after court had adjourned the day before. The article, printed in the *Brooklyn Daily Eagle*, covered a speech made by a Brooklyn assistant district attorney, Ely Krammer, concerning the "object lesson" that teenagers should get out of the trial of the "four so-called 'thrill killers.'" Joining the objection, the venerable Murray informed the judge that while "I have never complained about newspaper publicity . . . recognizing that it is the function of a newspaper to provide material for their readers," he considered the statement of the assistant district attorney "scandalous and disgraceful" and "calculated . . . to deprive my client of a fair trial."[17]

Not surprisingly, Senator Moritt vociferously joined his colleagues. For his part, Assistant District Attorney McCabe argued back that the contents of the article were completely true and lacking in prejudice: "It is merely a statement to the effect that the trial itself should be a lesson to young people." "I think," McCabe continued, "that we all recognize that to be a fact . . . that you might land in court if you go around with fellows who do things that get them into trouble, or yourself into trouble, is a truism." McCabe then turned the tables on the defense attorneys, pointing out that while "much has been said" concerning the publicity the trial was receiving, he noted that last night's edition of the *Brooklyn Daily Eagle* carried on its front page a "posed picture of the three defendants and their three counsel, very prominent." Judge Barshay demurred to neither cite the offending prosecutor in contempt of court nor to enter the posed photograph of the defense into evidence, choosing to reprimand McCabe that "good ethics provide that no one speak about the trial."[18]

*   *   *

Besides grappling with the media issue, one of the first critical decisions Judge Barshay made was to order the selection of what was termed a "Blue-ribbon Jury." Blue-ribbon Juries were a legal phenomenon unique to New York State in the late nineteenth and early twentieth centuries, and were eliminated by the New York Legislature in 1965.[19] Most states that used England's "struck jury" model did not allow its use in capital cases.[20] But in New York, the law, passed in 1896, allowed special juries *only* in criminal cases to be used primarily *for* capital trials.[21] Qualifications for special jurors included education (at least a high school graduate), the ownership of at least $250 in real or personal property, and "general intelligence and character" as determined by a personal interview with jury commissioners.[22] Advocates of the system argued that the average person was often barely qualified to sit on a jury: many did not even understand such basic legal terms as "defendant" and "plaintiff."[23] Detractors believed that special juries were a violation of due process and a convenient way for prosecutors to stack juries with people less likely to respond to emotional arguments.[24]

It is not surprising, therefore, that in the case of the Brooklyn Thrill-Killers, the request for a Blue-ribbon panel was put forth by the district attorney's office and roundly objected to by the defense attorneys. On November 22, the first real day of jury selection, Moritt challenged the entire convened panel of 250 potential jurors, arguing that they were "illegally and unlawfully constituted" and in violation of the due process clause of the Fourteenth Amendment. "The jury panel from which a trial juror will be drawn," Moritt's associate, Morris Eisenstein, asserted, "is not a jury of the peers of the defendant Jack Koslow."[25] The law, however, was not on his side: as recently as 1947, the United States Supreme Court upheld in *Fay v. New York* that special juries did not violate the U.S. Constitution.[26] The motion was summarily denied.

A more unexpected challenge to the jury came from Mittman's attorney, Judge Healy. On the first formal day of jury selection, Robert Trachtenberg's case was severed, indicating that he was turning state's evidence. To spectators in the overcrowded courtroom, the separation between the boys was easily surmised: while Jack, Mel, and Jerry dressed uniformly in dark blue suits, white shirts, and blue neckties, Bobby stood out in a brown suit and a green necktie. And while Bobby sat at the same table as the other defendants, his body language isolated him. According to one reporter on the scene, "It was clear to everyone that 'something' was going on."[27] The visual appearance of the defendants in conjunction with the rumors reported in the press (based, in no small part, on Bobby's removal to Queens County Jail), meant that few were surprised when Assistant District Attorney J. Kenneth McCabe opened court that day asking for Robert Trachtenberg's case to be severed.[28]

In response, Healy moved for a dismissal of all of the assembled 250 potential jurors and the drawing of a new panel, arguing that the district attorney's motion in the presence of the jury panel was a violation of the defendant's constitutional rights. Healy's motion was quickly joined by the other remaining defense attorneys, but the motions of all three were overruled. A handcuffed Bobby Trachtenberg was led from the courtroom as the other boys reportedly "glared contemptuously at him."[29] Their one-time pal would now serve as the state's chief witness against them.

As the first prospective juror was called for Voir Dire, Moritt attempted several more fruitless defense motions, including once again demanding an adjournment of six months because of the "intemperate climate" caused by the media obsession with the case. Raising his voice, Moritt thundered, "I now ask the Court to take judicial notice of the articles in the newspapers and magazines, and the volumes of words that have been written, condemning the defendant before trial, so that this trial, the defendant claims, will be merely a legal gesture, and not the trial to which he is entitled."[30] Barshay denied the motion, pointing out that a motion for a change of venue could have been made at any time.[31] Morris Eisenstein, Moritt's law partner, then asked for dismissal of the indictment against Koslow on the ground his client "was never properly indicted" and that this was a case of "indictment by association." Eisenstein noted that the grand jury was presented with evidence for crimes in which Koslow was neither indicted on nor participated in (namely, the death of Rhinehold Ulrickson) to "load down this defendant with other acts of wrongdoing" and otherwise induce the grand jury to return an indictment of murder in the first degree. Barshay denied the motion, as well as the request by the defense to view the grand jury minutes. The indictment against Koslow stood, and the trial would proceed.[32]

The first prospective juror, Joseph R. Holahan, was finally voir dired. But as the press had already predicted when he was temporarily seated a week earlier, Holahan was summarily challenged and dismissed by the defense. That he would not remain on the jury required no crystal ball: the innocuous stockbroker of 250 Maple Street was the brother of OSS Major William Holahan—murdered in Italy during WWII during a "cloak and dagger" op by his own men. Joseph Holahan spent seven years sponsoring the search for his brother's murderers, who were then tried and convicted in absentia by Italian courts in 1953.[33]

The next person called was Mr. Sidney Daily, who was also soon dismissed when he revealed that he felt pity toward "young people who get sucked into crime" and was completely against the death penalty.[34] The next four jurors called were also summarily rejected, with the defense attorneys probing as to which newspapers the men read, what they had read about the accused, and whether they had read or heard about any media opinions concerning either the accused or their alleged crimes.[35] As juror after juror was challenged and dismissed, an increasingly frustrated Judge Barshay appealed to the lawyers to have "faith in the consciences" of their fellow citizens, but to little avail.[36] By the close of the first day of trial, only one juror had been seated.

By the end of the second futile day of jury selection, a frustrated Judge Barshay ordered a punishing night session to speed up the slow jury-picking process, giving the weary lawyers and jurors only a two-hour dinner break. Beginning at 8:00 p.m. and breaking up an hour and a half later, eleven men were questioned, six were challenged, and three others excused by the court. This time, it was the prosecution who did most of the challenging, rejecting any juror who did not believe in capital punishment, and sparking speculation that the district attorney's office would ask for the chair. By 9:25 p.m., when Judge Barshay finally called it a day at the request of weary defense counsel, only four more men had made it to the jury box.[37]

*   *   *

It may have been weariness, the lure of Thanksgiving recess, or simply a coincidence, but suddenly Wednesday morning, November 24, jury selection sped up exponentially, and the final six jurors were seated in time for the court to break early for the Thanksgiving holiday. Ultimately, fifty-five members of the select pool were peremptorily challenged, with twice that number challenged and dismissed for cause. One man had a sister mixed up in a criminal trial, another knew the relatives of the accused and had spoken to them about the events, a third had a relative by the name of Trachtenberg who was possibly related to the defendant, and so on it went. Most were dismissed because they informed the court they had already formed opinions on the case. The only two potential jurors who were black were quickly challenged and dismissed by the defense.

In the end, the blue-ribbon jury was a homogenous group of middle-class, white, male, white-collar workers. They ranged in trades from being an office sales manager for Kopper's Coke,[38] the archives custodian of the Bank of Manhattan Company, an assistant accountant of the commodity exchange, a purchasing agent for the Sayford Paper Company, an auditor of the New York Terminal Warehouse, an insurance underwriter for the General Insurance Company, a traffic clerk of the United States Steel Export Company, a hardware store owner, a bank clerk, a pharmacist, an aerospace engineer, and an insurance company clerk. Most were married with children—a design by the defense to create a more sympathetic panel that would be less likely to advocate for a teenager's death.

Noticeably absent from the panel, however, were Jews. With the exception of Samuel Levy, a hardware store owner and father of four sons, all of the other jurors and alternates were non-Jewish. Nor was this an oversight or a prosecutorial tactic. Instead, as reported by the *Forverts*, in a borough where over one million Jews were residing—nearly half the population—none of them seemed to show "any particular desire or will to sit on the jury."[39] Interviewed by the *Forverts* reporter, would-be Jewish jurors claimed they were "afraid to face the challenge, to find themselves in the tragic position of having to pronounce the terrible word: 'guilty.'" Instead, prospective Jewish jurors asked one by one to be excused, much to the chagrin of the defense counsel as well as Judge Hyman Barshay, who appeared "angry and ashamed" each time a Jewish candidate requested dismissal because he had a relative of the same surname as one of the accused or went to the same shul as one of the families.

The lack of Jewish jurors was troubling because, as noted by the *Forverts*, "the Jewish question hovers around this trial, whether we want it to or not."[40] "It is," the article byline boldly proclaimed, "unfortunately a Jewish trial."[41] Beyond the ethnicity of the four accused, the Jewish community was part and parcel of the continually unfolding story. The neighborhood where the crimes were committed was one "that contains a lot of synagogues and prayer-houses . . . and which overflows with Yiddishkeit and Torah, and with thousands of fine, upright, godfearing Jewish children."[42] The judge was known to allow his staff to leave work early to prepare for *shabbos*, and the elevator operator at the courthouse was famous for never having worked on the Sabbath once in over forty years.[43] Senator Moritt made sure to tell the *Forverts* (in perfect Yiddish) to call him "Fayvl," and the court stenographer was a son of an avid *Forverts* reader.[44] Even the choice of prosecutors was brought about by the district attorney declining to prosecute the case personally, as it would have interfered with a trip he was making to Israel. And day by day, filling the courtroom, the majority of the spectators came from the Jewish community.[45] Yet for all the "Jewishness" surrounding the trial, the fate of the "Four Jewish Boys" ultimately rested in the hands of non-Jews. The Jewish community chose to sit on the sidelines, judging the boys in press and pulpit but not from the jury box.

*   *   *

The three remaining boys were once again led one by one to the defense table. Mel and Jack dressed in the same sober navy blue suits as the day before, while Jerry wore a new suit of soft tan.[46] Several rows back, Jack's mother, Anna, quietly wept as her son walked in.[47] It was now a full two weeks from the official start date of the trial, and Assistant District Attorney J. Kenneth McCabe rose to give his opening.

Slim, thin-lipped, and with a youthful demeanor, the native Brooklynite joined the Kings County District Attorney's Office in 1940 after several years of appellate work. Quickly rising through the ranks, McCabe headed the misdemeanor branch by 1945 and the county court and homicide divisions soon thereafter. Appointed to the role of chief assistant district attorney by the newly elected Edward Silver in 1953, the Thrill-Kill case would be McCabe's first major trial in his new position. Outside of work, McCabe was a devout Catholic, the father of five, and reputed to be a fearsome bridge player.[48]

In an auspicious start to the trial, just as ADA McCabe rose to speak, Senator Moritt motioned the court "to instruct the jury at this time that the opening of the District Attorney shall not be considered by them as evidence in the case." Exasperated, Judge Barshay barked, "Mr. Moritt, please. Mr. Moritt, I will run this court without any suggestions. I will tell the jury at the proper time what the rules are. Now, please, that is not a motion."

"May I please the Court," Moritt cheekily replied, "I am reading from a motion made by your Honor when your Honor was an attorney." As the scene was later described by Barry Gray on his nightly radio broadcast on WMCA:

> Today Barshay, . . . is on the bench. Before him appears state Sen. Fred Moritt . . . [who] paid the judge high compliment by lifting verbatim the Barshay statement regarding the prosecutor's remarks and quoting exactly. And what does Barshay say, now wearing robes of office? He looks down at Moritt and coldly warns, "Don't try to run my court."[49]

Perhaps it was because Barshay had himself been, until his recent move to the bench, a well-respected defense attorney, that he found Moritt's theatrical tactics and attempts at pandering particularly distasteful. Whatever the reason, much of the drama of the trial was found in the exchanges between the lawyer and the judge. The next clash came only a few minutes later after the assistant district attorney gave his brief, skeletal opening. Turning to the defense, Moritt was called up to give his opening statement for Jack Koslow. Likely estimating that allowing the bumbling Moritt to open first would potentially alienate jurors from his own client, Healy quickly stood up and asked the court's permission to change the order in which the defense attorneys might open.[50] The request was denied.

Not content to let the ruling go and proceed with his opening, Moritt challenged the judge's discretion "vigorously protesting" the ruling. The two began to snap at each other, with Judge Barshay warning that Moritt had made his objection, that "there is no need to make a speech about it," and warning "let's not repeat that in the future." Moritt objected to the judge's use of the word "speech" in reference to his legal tactics: "I make no speeches," he huffed. "I am counsel for the defense."

A visibly annoyed Barshay enjoined, "You are doing that right now. Either you open, sir, or you waive."[51]

Moritt chose to open. However, he would not get very far. Within a minute of his opening remarks, McCabe objected to Moritt's use of the term "boys" to describe the defendants in light of an earlier ruling that they should be referred to only as "defendants." Acquiescing, Moritt proceeded to use the phrase as awkwardly as possible, emphasizing the word "defendant" to conflate it with "boy" in the jurors' minds:

> The usual discussion took place, "What are we going to do tonight?" . . . an occupational discussional [*sic*] and ambition of *defendants, young defendants.* . . . They talked about baseball, they talked about cars, they talked about automobiles, and they talked about the things that usually *defendants* speak about.[52]

The point having been made, Moritt then turned his statement toward outlining the actual defense. Claiming he was not interested in "gild[ing] the lily," Moritt argued that the boys went out that fateful night of August 16, looking for "mischief," but that "a mischief-maker is not a murderer." "That," Moritt argued, "is our defense."[53]

Moritt went further, describing how Koslow "looked for scraps, looked for brawls, looked for a fight, with vagrants." He described how, for Koslow, there were two very different kinds of bums, who deserved very different kinds of treatment:

> There was the vagrant . . . who was a down-and-outer on his luck, who through no fault of his own was down and out and . . . Koslow gave handouts, twenty-five cents or fifty cents for a night's lodging, if in his stupid opinion, in his self-righteous appointment as a committee of the do-gooder, that bum or loiterer was merely down and out on his luck. The road to hell is paved with good intentions. On the other hand, there was the bum that my client picked out, whom [*sic*] in his stupid way he thought beyond salvation. He was a bum with

a bottle in his hand, drunk, the kind that insulted women, the kind that used filthy and vile language, the kind that was no good to society.[54]

At the prosecutor's table, McCabe rolled his eyes and made a gesture with his hands. While it's impossible to know exactly what McCabe was thinking, one might surmise that he was overcome with disbelief; it was not often that a defense attorney would so badly impugn the character of his own client. Moritt turned to the judge, "I ask the Court to admonish the District Attorney not to make any motions with his hands while I am speaking, either of impatience or any other indication. I saw it with my own eyes." Moritt continued his opening, rebutting the district attorney's assertion that Menter was "ordered" around by the boys or that there was ever "any intention to murder" the victim. "Although a human being tragically lost his life," Moritt intoned, "that doesn't make it murder."[55]

Finally, Moritt laid out how mischief mistakenly became murder, and he laid the blame squarely at the feet of the district attorney's office: "The prosecutor and the police built this case up from mischief into murder by headlines, by giving out to the police and to the reporters, so that the headlines made it this monstrous thing."

The assistant district attorney jumped up to defend himself. "Now, if the court please, in view of that statement, I would like to register a personal objection, but beyond that, counsel at the present time is making a speech, completely unfounded in fact, and should he go over to the jury box on the left, he will learn by consulting with the press that they got no facts from Kenny McCabe."[56]

The judge sustained the objection, cutting Moritt off and ruling that "what [the district attorney] said to the press . . . is not a defense to this case." Moritt shrugged. "Your Honor is the boss." "No, please," Barshay retorted crisply, "I am not the boss and don't use that expression. I am a judge of this court."[57] Moritt refused to continue his opening, sitting down in protest and accusing the court that his "opening has been curtailed."[58] It was now left to a chagrined Judge Healy the unenviable task of opening for Melvin Mittman in the wake of Moritt's dramatics.

*   *   *

Whatever the strategy of the defense had been prior to Moritt's opening, both Judge Healy and James D. C. Murray needed to separate themselves and their clients from Moritt's escapades—and quickly. "I accept," Healy informed the jurors, "the opportunity that is presented to me, not to give you any evidence in the case, not to criticize anybody in the case, not to argue questions of law in the case, but to present a brief skeleton outline of Mittman's defense, so that you gentlemen will have more of an intelligent, intelligible appreciation of the defense of Melvin Mittman."[59] As expected,

Healy's opening was meant to calmly and rationally appeal to the venire-mens' sense of logic. Making it patently clear that he was not subscribing to Moritt's defense tactics, Healy declared, "Regardless of what my associate counsel may do, Mittman's defense will be tried on a proposition of law as well as one of fact."[60]

Healy began by reading the indictment to the jury and then proceeded to carefully, line by line, tear apart the accusations. First, Healy argued that "at no time did Melvin Mittman act in concert, did he aid or abet anyone else in striking and beating Willard Menter." Nor, according to Healy, did Mel push Menter into the East River, as the prosecution had claimed. Second, Healy asserted that the defense would prove that when Menter did go off the pier—of his own volition—he was alive and "swimming in the water" and that Mittman even went so far as to "le[ave] the pier to get help to try to save [Menter] from drowning." Finally, Healy professed that there was no point in time in which Melvin Mittman "willfully or feloniously or of malice aforethought" pushed Willard Menter off of the pier, thereby negating the charge of murder in the first degree.[61]

As Judge Healy sat down, James D. C. Murray stood up to open for Jerome Lieberman. He, too, quickly distanced himself from Moritt, declaring from the start, "What I am going to say to you I will say without frill or oratorical flourish."[62] Murray informed the jurors that the "facts we expect to prove" would serve to "exonerate" Lieberman fully, and further that they would likely "bring about a situation, as I hope, that you won't even have to deliberate on his innocence or his guilt."[63] As told by Murray, Jerry may have been in the park with Menter, but "at no time did he harass the deceased." Nor, according to the attorney, did he either speak to the victim nor "advise anyone as to any gesture toward the deceased." In an exceptionally brief opening, Murray simply reiterated the fact that at no time during any of the activities leading up to or occurring on the pier was Jerry Lieberman involved: he left the park before the others, was never on the same side of the street as Menter, had no idea where the other boys were going, and never even set foot on the pier itself. As Murray summarized, "Lieberman was never on the pier . . . was never in a position to see the untoward happening at the end of the pier, [and] that what had occurred on that pier was only hearsay so far as Lieberman was concerned." Raising his voice, the defense attorney concluded, "If this case does go to you gentlemen for your consid-eration, we shall expect an acquittal at your hands." Perhaps as a means to juxtapose himself against the overly verbose Moritt, Murray kept his entire opening statement to less than two minutes in length.[64]

* * *

The rest of the day was filled with a long line of straightforward wit-nesses: the civil engineer who drew up a map of the crime scene; the medical assistant, chief clerk, and stenographer for the medical examiner's office; a driver for the Department of Hospitals; and finally the deputy chief medical examiner. After the morning's dramatic session, the afternoon seemed almost boring, as witness after witness testified as to who marked the jars containing the deceased's organs and how those jars carefully made their way to the toxicologist at Bellevue Hospital. The only thing of note was that upon reading the autopsy report into the record, the careful listener would observe that there were no burn marks noted on the victim's feet.[65]

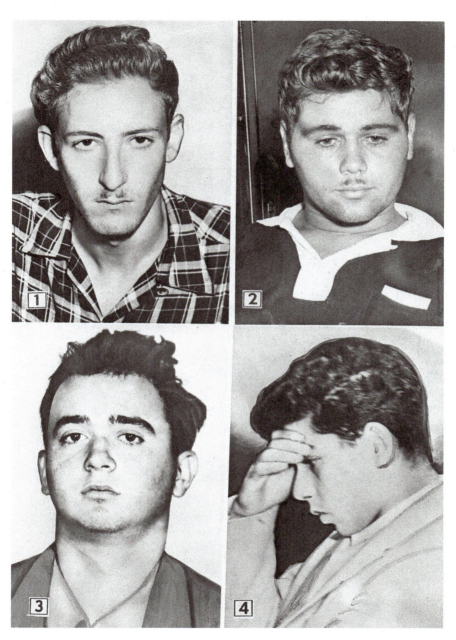

The members of the Thrill-Kill Gang: Jack Koslow (top left), Melvin Mittman (top right), Jerry Lieberman (bottom left), and Robert Trachtenberg (bottom right). Note Jack's and Mel's "Hitler"-style mustaches. (Corbis)

Edward Walsh literally "points the finger" at Jack Koslow while stenographer Arthur Monford looks on. This was one of the many posed photographs that Moritt would use to argue the impossibility of a fair trial. (Corbis)

Encircling the body of Willard Menter, the boys are made to point at the corpse while surrounded by police and members of the District Attorney's office. (Corbis)

Kill-for-Thrills suspects and their lawyers (from left): State Senator Fred Moritt, Jack Koslow, James D.C. Murray, Jerome Lieberman, Judge Leo Healy, and Melvin Mittman. (Corbis)

Guilty: A tearful Mel Mittman and sober Jack Koslow are led away from the courtroom after the verdict is pronounced. (Corbis)

New York State Assemblyman James A. Fitzpatrick reads from a comic book. (Corbis)

Four Little Bad Boys

The remainder of the trial provided significant fodder for the press. Replete with melodramatic fainting spells, shocking testimony, and strange doggerel-laden closing arguments, those in the courtroom gallery hoping for a spectacle were not disappointed. However, while the press and viewing public were enthralled by the dramatics, the defense landed quiet victories, exposing appellate issues and winning a dismissal for one of the defendants.

First, however, the defense needed to get through a few days that were proving strategically difficult. A series of police detectives were paraded to the witness stand to testify about the statements made by the four boys while in custody. Moritt spent nearly an entire hour grilling one detective, Raymond Duggan, accusing the veteran cop of beating and starving a confession out of Jack. Moritt also charged Duggan with violating due process by failing to arraign the boy on Tuesday morning, instead holding him another full twenty-four hours before making an appearance in Adolescent's Court. But any sympathy that Moritt's questions may have elicited from the jury were quickly erased by the dramatic revelation of Jack's quip that the murder was "the supreme adventure of them all" and Mel's casual admission, testified to by Detective William Elliot, that beating the old men "makes me feel big and strong. . . . We used [the bums] like punching bags to see how hard we can hit."[1]

Although the detectives' testimony was shocking, it was mere prelude to the main attraction. The most anticipated testimony came on the morning of December 3, when Robert Trachtenberg took the stand against his former friends as a witness for the prosecution. The "tall, darkly handsome" fifteen-year-old ascended the witness stand at 11:00 a.m. on the seasonably cool Friday morning.[2] Called as the twentieth witness by the state, he testified in a "calm, even voice"—often so quiet that he was frequently asked to repeat himself—as Assistant District Attorney Albert V. DeMeo carefully led the youth through the events of that fateful night.[3]

The first shocking revelation came as the ADA interrogated Bobby on his relationships with the other members of the "gang." The line of questioning revealed that—despite newspaper labeling otherwise—the four boys were hardly a gang, and barely even friends. Instead, it was a loose conglomeration—with Mel, not Jack, serving as the social nexus—that had set out to make "mischief" that fateful evening.

The longest relationship in the group was that of Bobby and Jerry, who had met nine years earlier in Hebrew school and had been best friends ever since. In 1952, Bobby first met Mel Mittman at the Keap Street Young Men's Hebrew Association and subsequently introduced Mel to Jerry. The three often met to work out together (as much as four to five times a week initially), although the budding friendship was primarily between Bobby and Mel, with Jerry sometimes tagging along. It was not until March of 1954 that Mel introduced Bobby and Jerry to his friend Jack. That evening, the four boys merely played pool together before going their separate ways. Three months later, Bobby, Mel, and Jack would spend another uneventful evening together.

Jerry Lieberman, less impressed with Jack, had left early that first night in March and declined to join the group at their second meeting. Therefore, according to the testimony of Bobby Trachtenberg, August 16 was only the second time all four boys had spent any length of time together as a group.[4] Further, although the previous day's testimony by Detective Elliott had placed the blame for the murder, according to Mel, squarely on Jack's shoulders, and despite that the media had already declared Jack to be the criminal "mastermind" behind the thrill-killings, it appeared to be Mel, not Jack, who assembled the group; Mel, not Jack, who served as the group's social nexus; and Mel, not Jack, who went out with Bobby and Jerry on the previous night of "bum-hunting," which resulted in the death of Rhinehold Ulrickson.

This latter fact was drawn out by the defense in the cross-examination of Bobby conducted by Senator Fred Moritt. Overall, Moritt's cross emphasized the handful of minor discrepancies in Bobby's testimony compared to his original statements to the district attorney back in August, in particular, that Bobby had told the police that, according to Mel, the man had fallen in the water and had not been touched by Jack Koslow.[5] But it was difficult for the defense to make much headway with courtroom spectators compared to Bobby's vivid testimony under direct examination. In what was one of the most dramatic moments of the trial, Bobby coolly and evenly recounted how the boys surrounded Menter on the bench and Jack touched a lit cigarette to the sleeping man's foot. When the district attorney asked what Menter said or did in response, the quiet, subdued fifteen-year-old suddenly let out a piercing scream that one spectator recalled "splintered the courtroom air and was followed by a shuddering silence."[6]

Following Robert Trachtenberg's testimony, the district attorney concluded his case by reading the boys' confessions into the record. Fought every inch of the way by Moritt, newspaper after newspaper quoted from Jack Koslow's statement: "Sometimes I see a drunken bum, very soused. He looks at you out of one eye. It's disgusting. It incites me to hit them."[7] Moritt spent the greater part of the next trial days attempting to discredit the statements as "fixed" by the district attorney's office—ironically based on the same newspaper coverage that Moritt had railed against for the duration of the trial.[8] Days earlier, in his cross-examination of the grieving Charles Menter—the victim's brother—Moritt had quizzed Menter on the number of television cameramen, newspaper reporters, and journalists present at the pier where the man had identified his brother's body. Charles acquiesced that there were, indeed, "hundreds of people around" on the pier and surrounding rooftops and that there were too many journalists, district attorneys, and policemen to count. However, Judge Barshay drew the line when Moritt asked whether Charles heard spectators chanting "Kill them now!" and the judge and advocate once again exchanged words concerning Moritt's courtroom demeanor.[9]

Having established the centrality of the press dockside through Charles Menter's testimony, Moritt was now able to argue that several newspapermen covering the boys' statements made at the pier on August 19 had recorded Jack's lament: "I didn't push him. As a matter of fact, I tried to keep him from falling in."[10] The statement, however, was noticeably absent from the stenographer's transcript of Jack's pier-side confession. Under cross-examination, the stenographer held firm, repeating over and over, "If he said it, it is in the record."[11] Moritt went so far as to bring in a rebuttal witness, an expert stenographer, in an attempt to prove the record was altered. Unfortunately, the expert's testimony only seemed to backfire against the defense: only nineteen minor transcription mistakes were found. Finally, Moritt's attempt to reopen the trial after the defense had rested to call the newspaper reporter, John Ferris, from the *New York World-Telegram* as a witness to Koslow's protestations of innocence on the pier was denied by the court—primarily because Moritt admitted that he "had not been able to locate" the reporter.[12]

* * *

Largely unnoticed by many in the courtroom, however, were two quiet defense victories: one that would prove to be minor and one that would prove to be important later on. The first concerned the testimony of Francis Sheridan, a barge captain whose grand jury evidence was considered crucial to securing the initial indictment against the four boys. After over an hour of examination, all of Sheridan's testimony was summarily struck by the court after it was revealed that he could not actually identify a single one of the defendants.[13] As defense attorney Moritt aptly described it later, "Captain Sheridan was the People's bomb, and legally Captain Sheridan's testimony was the worst dud I have seen in a courtroom in my whole lifetime."[14]

The second victory was found in the seemingly unimportant statement of an ordinary patrolman, Harold Neyer. Neyer, a veteran officer of twenty-three years whose beat included from Broadway and Roebling Street down to the East River, was at the pier when the body of Willard Menter was recovered. After testifying to the identification of the body on the morning of August 19, the prosecution led him through a series of questions intended to recreate for the jurors a crime-scene backdrop of a dark, lonely pier located in a quiet, isolated, industrial neighborhood. But cross-examination by the defense painted a dramatically different picture: one of a lively area, in which several stores, restaurants, and garages were open and packed with customers at the time Menter and the boys would have been walking past. The list included several candy stores that were open late, an all-night garage, an all-night diner, and no less than three bar and grilles, open until 4:00 a.m. Further, the department of sanitation building right before the pier had at least six night employees who worked with the bay doors open. Finally, along the seven or eight city-block route, Neyer testified that there were three fire alarm boxes and one police call box.[15] The significance of Neyer's testimony may have been lost on a press more interested in Detective Casimir Czarnowski's recounting of Jerome Lieberman's dramatic blurted confession: "Oh, my God, the river!" but it was eventually noticed by an appellate court charged with determining whether or not Willard Menter was feloniously kidnapped on the evening of August 16.[16]

Overshadowing these defense victories, however, were several dramatic scenes in the courtroom gallery. The first occurred during the testimony of Detective Casimir Czarnowski, as he recalled Jerome Lieberman's confession on the night of August 16. As the detective relayed the moment when Jack allegedly turned to Mel and intoned, "Now we're murderers," Sam Mittman, Mel's father, fainted. As the middle-aged man slumped forward in his seat, Judge Barshay quickly ordered the jury to leave the courtroom and instructed spectators to keep to their seats while court attendants "worked over" the unconscious man. After a suspenseful few minutes, the elder Mittman was revived and rose shakily to his feet. Accompanied by two court wardens and his wife, who had been sitting across the aisle from him when he collapsed, Mr. Mittman was quickly escorted to an open window in the corridor. Melvin burst into tears as he watched his parents unsteadily make their way from the courtroom.[17]

On December 9, a distraught Anna Koslow raced over to embrace her son, and then the plump, bespectacled blonde woman—wearing a somber black dress with a starched lace collar and a matching black coat and hat—promptly fainted into her husband's arms. As she was carried out of the courtroom by her husband and several court attendants, Jack reportedly "sobbed out loud" and then howled, "Leave her alone! Leave her alone!" at the photographers racing to capture an image of the ailing woman.[18]And if the fainting spells were not enough, minor celebrity sightings were causing "quite a stir and eye strain"—particularly the dark-haired beauty Barbara Brent who was covering the trial for the *Tex and Jinx Show*.[19] With all of the dramatics to report on, it is hardly surprising that not a single newspaper noticed that the defense had already built their case for appeal.

*   *   *

On Thursday, December 9, the prosecution rested. It was time for the defense lawyers to argue their motions for dismissal, maintaining that the prosecution had failed in its case to prove the defendants had "willfully, feloniously and of malice aforethought" murdered Willard Menter in the first degree. The first motion came from Judge Healy, on behalf of Melvin Mittman, which the court, expectedly, denied. The second, and more anticipated motion, was made by James D. C. Murray on behalf of Jerome Lieberman. Murray boldly asked the court for a directed verdict of acquittal, arguing that "there is no evidence in this case that the defendant Lieberman directly committed an overt act." Murray then began to systematically recount the events of August 16 from the perspective of his client, recalling for the court that "when a light was put to the feet of the victim," Jerry began to leave the park; that when an invitation was given for Lieberman to strike the victim, he demurred; and contending that Jerry successfully "disassociated" himself from the victim, as well as from Jack and Mel.[20] Ultimately, Murray insisted that there was "very powerful evidence that Lieberman did not know what was going to happen, and he did not know that a crime was being committed, and that he did not see what happened."[21]

Assistant District Attorney Aaron Nussbaum maintained Lieberman's guilt based on a theory of conspiracy, arguing that the conspiracy to commit crimes began at 9:00 p.m. on the night of August 16, when the boys set out "for the purpose of beating up bums," and only ended at midnight that same evening when Willard Menter "met his death by drowning in the East River."[22] However, two recent New York Court of Appeals cases complicated the prosecution's assertions: in the first, *People v. Ligouri and Panaro*, the court sustained that regardless that the codefendant was with the shooter prior to the incident, accompanied him to the place where the crime occurred, and fled with him afterward, it was insufficient to prove that that the codefendant "aided, abetted or otherwise participated in the homicide."[23] The second, *People v. Weiss*—in which two men were convicted as coconspirators in a murder committed by a third codefendant—the New York Court of Appeals determined that "the mere fact that Epstein and Weiss were at the scene of the crime" was insufficient proof that they "were engaged in a criminal conspiracy to kill."[24] The standard set by the *Weiss* case was that there needed to be direct evidence of a conspiracy. Because earlier rulings in the Thrill-Kill trial excluded any reference to the previous nights of bum hunting (or even any activities committed by the group earlier that evening exclusive of the death of Willard Menter), the district attorney was unable to argue that these earlier acts had created a standing conspiracy between the group.

Showing his hand, Judge Barshay proceeded to grill ADA Nussbaum, demanding he prove—after the initial surrounding of Menter in the park— "what act Mr. Lieberman did, what act you can advance was to be done, as an act to aid, abet, induced, counseled and advised [*sic*]." ADA Nussbaum futilely argued again for conspiracy. "I believe one thing must be certain here. . . . There was a conspiracy on the part of Lieberman with the other two defendants to commit this assault upon these bums. There was a conspiracy further that lasted to the moment that they marched this bum from the park to the pier. Surely," Nussbaum pleaded, "there can be no dispute that the conspiracy lasted to that point."

"Well," Barshay replied, "that is where we part company, at that second conclusion you draw."[25]

The case against Jerome Lieberman was unceremoniously dismissed by the court that afternoon.[26] While movie and television cameras set up in the corridor, a "pale and frightened" Jerry Lieberman was brought before the bench to hear the judge's decision. As the dismissal was granted, Jerry's parents wept, and even his codefendant, Jack Koslow, broke into a smile.[27] Jerry was led from the courtroom as Jack waved good-bye and was soon stammering out a statement for the television cameras and radio microphones: "I whole-heartedly thank my lawyer, Mr. Murray, for helping show my innocence; I thank Judge Barshay. . . ." It was as far as the boy could get before bursting into tears as his parents ran over to embrace him.[28]

Jerry's father, Harry Lieberman, told the assembled reporters that he had not only prayed for his own son, but for all the boys: "Can you imagine the suffering and torture my boy went through, knowing that he was innocent? They built up a case around him out of nothing."[29] Of course, the "innocent" Jerry was not exactly free just yet: he remained remanded to Raymond Street Jail to await his trial alongside Melvin Mittman for the fatal beating of Rhinehold Ulrickson. But that the boy no longer faced the electric chair was enough cause for celebration.

*   *   *

Neither defendant took the stand, and although he had enlisted the help of the illustrious Dr. Fredric Wertham, Moritt declined to present a psychiatric defense for his client. Keeping his eye toward potential appellate issues, Moritt called only one witness for the defense, Murray Cutler, Koslow's previous defense attorney, to establish that Koslow had been denied representation when he was interviewed by the district attorney's office at the pier.[30] Not a single witness was called by Judge Healy for the defense of Melvin Mittman.

Closing arguments began the following Monday, December 13. Moritt went first, giving an impassioned, two-hour summation. Keeping with his opening theme of making "mischief into murder," Moritt argued that Jack Koslow was no "brains" and he certainly was not a gang "leader." If anything, Moritt claimed, it was "the others," including his one remaining fellow defendant, who had egged Jack on, cajoling him into beating up Willard Menter. "The gang decided to go out for the evening . . . so they decide to call Jack Koslow. He is home in Flatbush. He is minding his own business that night. If they had left him alone," Moritt thundered, "he would never have been involved." The prosecution, he charged, had sought to create "a phony, outrageous" impression that Menter was murdered. Turning specifically to his own client, he asked, "How could you charge this defendant with murder by drowning if he didn't know whether the deceased could swim or not?" Moritt proceeded to argue that Menter was found 65 feet from the pier and that since the prosecution was unable to prove that he was brought there by the tide, "I tell you the deceased Menter on this hot August night swam those 65 feet." As he had stated in his opening, Moritt once again claimed that the state had sought to build "mischief into murder." Then he pleaded, "They still have souls. They are bad, bad boys, but they are children, not murderers. This isn't gangsters you are dealing with . . . the men with records as long as your arm. These are children, fools, stupid fools." Finally, lowering his voice to a confidential level, he once again reiterated to the jurors, "They went out on mischief that night."[31]

But it was Moritt's final words that struck the oddest note. For some of the last words the jury heard in defense of Jack Koslow's life was a rhyme of his own composing, unfortunately paraphrased from the once-popular minstrel tune "Ten Little Niggers" and recently repopularized as "Ten Little Indians" in the 1954 Agatha Christie film *And Then There Was None*:

Four little bad boys off on a spree,
One turned State's evidence, then there were three;
Three little bad boys, what did one do?
The Judge said, 'No proof,' and then there were two;
Two little bad boys, in court they must sit,
And pray to their jury, please, please acquit.

According to reporter Marya Mannes, no one in the courtroom smiled, except Moritt and Jack Koslow.[32]

Once again, Judge Healy was forced to defend his client in the wake of Senator Moritt's inappropriate dramatics. Striking a somber note, he began by admonishing the jurors that the "twelve of you, and you twelve alone out of the millions of people . . . will render a verdict, after which . . . Melvin Mittman will live or die."[33] As reported by the press, Healy went on to reprove his fellow defense counsel, "disowning Moritt's bid for poet laureate of County Court when he told the jury he would attempt to sum up the case 'like a lawyer.'"[34] "In determining this case," Healy intoned, "you will do so not by reciting doggerels of 'Four Little Indians' or four little boys; not by going back to our childhood or college days and reciting poetry."[35] After distancing himself from Moritt as much as possible, Healy proceeded to carefully tear apart the prosecution's legal case, contending that "the only proof against Mittman was that he may or he may not have attempted or did commit the crime of assault, for which he is not on trial."[36] To erase the implication of premeditation, Healy reminded the jury of Bobby Trachtenberg's testimony concerning the earlier part of that fateful day:

> Maybe you will say, "Well, perhaps he changed his mind after going to the Roxy. Perhaps he became a murderer all of a sudden. Perhaps God, in His divine providence, shot a bolt into his mind and made a murderer out of him later that night." Did he? What is the testimony: "Q. What did Mittman suggest?" . . . "A . . . going to pick up girls."[37]

Not so subtly, Healy placed the blame for the evening squarely at Jack's feet, asking, "Oh, I suppose it's easy enough to blame poor Melvin for everything. Melvin did this, and Melvin that. But . . . who was it who [asked] 'Villst Kloppen?'" Yet Healy was careful to point out that there was no evidence that Jack had done more than simple assault, either.[38] It was more reasonable to assume, Healy intoned to the jurors, the possibility that Willard Menter had fallen over the edge of the dock either "because of the condition of that pier or because of the physical condition of Mr. Menter."[39] Any of it, Healy warned, was enough to create reasonable doubt.

While Healy asked the jury to consider the case very narrowly, for his part, ADA McCabe used the age-old technique of directing the jury to consider the larger societal implications of their decision by instructing them to do precisely the opposite. "You gentlemen are not going into that jury room to decide any question of juvenile delinquency. . . . You are not here to go into the question of society in relationship to its teenagers."[40] Directly riffing Moritt's poem, McCabe also reminded the jury that there was another way the rhyme could go: "You are not going to try this case on a little doggerel based on 'Ten Little Indians,' because if we were, it could be paraphrased, if you started with three men out on a pier, and then there were two."[41] Arguing that the boys' intention in bringing Menter to the pier was murder, McCabe focused on two statements made by Jack Koslow: first, that he "was not concerned about the presence of police . . . if there happened to be police around," thereby negating the need to move Menter from Triangle Park merely for the purpose of beating him up, and, second, that what happened on the pier was the "supreme adventure of them all." "Was he talking about missing a man on the pier when he threw a punch at him?" McCabe incredulously asked the jury. "How could that be a supreme adventure? Would a punch in the jaw be a supreme adventure? Or," the ADA continued, "was it on account of something far more serious than a blow to the face, than the abuse of a bum?"[42] Jack's continually changing story, in the hands of the assistant district attorney, became the attempted cleverness of a killer trying to mitigate his own guilt: "If you want to believe him; that he swung at somebody and missed him, why deny your presence there, if that was all you were on the pier for? You missed him."[43] And as for Melvin, the ADA presented the jury with a simple analogy: just like it "takes nine men to win a ball game," whatever happened on the pier was equally the responsibility of both boys.

Ending his summation, however, McCabe went one step too far. In admonishing the jury to not consider the age of the defendants or to heed the "appeal to sympathy" made by defense's referral to Jack and Mel as "children" and "boys," McCabe asked the jurors to ask themselves where they were at the age of eighteen:

> Where was I when I was eighteen? Where was I when I was seventeen? Had I finished high school? Did I perhaps finish the first year of college and maybe the second? Was I already in the Army and wearing an award?[44]

Although both defense attorneys demanded a mistrial, Judge Barshay denied the motion, instructing the jury to "pay no attention" to where they might have been. Once asked, however, the questions were difficult to erase.

* * *

The jurors' deliberations lasted only two hours and fifty-five minutes. One week before the start of Hanukkah, the jury foreman, Walter Scott, slowly read the verdict for each defendant: guilty of murder in the first degree, as a felony murder, with the recommendation that the defendant be imprisoned for his natural life. Whether the judge would heed the jury's recommendation would be known in a month's time.

Jack's verdict was read first, and as the jury foreman intoned the word "guilty," the youth "cried out as if struck," bowing his head until it rested on the defense counsel table, sobbing. But when Mel's verdict was read, and the 200-pound "muscleman" burst into tears, Jack straightened up and threw a comforting arm around his friend's shoulders. By the time they left the courtroom, Jack had regained his composure completely. Photographs of the two boys being led away show Melvin with eyes downcast and face puffy from weeping, but Jack defiantly smiling at the camera. As he was led to the detention pen, Jack paused for the reporters, jerking a thumb to indicate himself, and jokingly intoned, "The would-be killer."[45]

In the meantime, barred from the courtroom, Sam Koslow and Sam and Sylvia Mittman wept in the corridor. "We did everything possible to save him," the elder Koslow told the newspaper reporters. "His mother and I thought we had done everything to make him a fine boy. We thought we had kept him out of trouble. Just think of them—pretending they were vigilantes. The mixed-up kids!" Shaking his head, the father lamented, "We nursed Jack through illnesses, we watched over him when he had an operation. . . . This is how it ends."

Sylvia Mittman was even more despondent. "I thought the trial would prove my boy innocent. The verdict is unbelievable, hopeless," she sobbed. And then, with the kind of blind refusal to acknowledge a child's wrongdoing that only a parent can muster, she cried, "He wasn't out to murder anyone. He was just curious, that's all. He went out on that pier to watch—and look what has happened to him."[46]

For an entire month, the boys waited to learn their fate. Although the jury had advocated for mercy, recent court rulings upheld the right of the trial judge to ignore the recommendation. In 1948, a jury had recommended life imprisonment for Samuel Tito Williams—convicted of murdering a girl in an attempted burglary. However, Kings County Court Judge Louis Goldstein, acting with information from the probation department that was unknown to the jurors, imposed a death sentence instead. Although Williams's conviction was ultimately overturned because of other legal challenges, the judge's discretion was upheld by both the Court of Appeals and the United States Supreme Court in *Williams v. New York*.[47] In response, the New York State Legislature passed a bill to compel a judge to accept a jury's recommendation of mercy, but the bill was quickly vetoed by Governor Thomas E. Dewey (although Dewey did agree to commute Williams's sentence to life in prison).[48]

On January 18, 1955, the two boys were brought to Kings County Supreme Court to learn the judge's decision. As he did on the day of the verdict, Judge Barshay barred the boys' families from the courtroom. The defense attorneys made one final appeal for leniency, and in a last-ditch effort to beg for mercy, Mel even penned a few lines for his attorney to read to the court:

I realize now that I have done wrong by assaulting these vagrants, but at the time I did not think I was doing anything really bad. I never tried to really hurt anybody, and I never expected or even dreamed it would come to this. I never had in mind the idea to kill or even kidnap anybody, and I am truly sorry that this happened. If I could have imagined beforehand what would and did happen, I would have never gone along and hit anybody.[49]

The judge appeared unmoved by the breast baring.[50] With little fanfare, Judge Barshay opted to accept the jury's recommendation. The two boys were sentenced to life without the possibility of parole. Jack and Mel reportedly took the pronouncement "stoically."[51] Because they were both under the age of twenty-one, they were removed from the courtroom to the Elmira Reception Center for assignment to a permanent place of incarceration.

*   *   *

For Bobby Trachtenberg, the wheels of justice followed a different track. On December 22, 1954, the first-degree murder indictment against Bobby was dismissed, and the now sixteen-year-old was taken to the Children's Court to face a juvenile delinquency charge in the assault on John Perrett—the little vagrant whom Rhinehold Ulrickson had valiantly tried to protect. Bobby was released on $500 bail—a steep price to pay for only one night of freedom. At his hearing the next day, the boy was quickly proclaimed a juvenile delinquent and remanded to Youth House for examination by the psychiatric staff.

Less than a month later, on January 18, 1955, Robert Trachtenberg was committed to a youth institution for an indefinite period. Although Bobby pleaded to be able to return to Brooklyn Technical High School so that he could become an engineer as "only in that way will I be able to repay my parents for all they've been through," Domestic Relations Court Justice Frederick Backer remanded the youth to Cedar Knolls, proclaiming it was up to the boy's own behavior as to whether he would spend "one month or four years" at the facility.

Particularly damning to Bobby's case was the testimony of the probation officer, George Banet, who informed the court that Bobby was an "emotionally disturbed" boy who "shows no sense of guilt or remorse for his crime." According to Banet, Bobby continued to deny his participation in the crimes, other than merely being present, although he clearly "enjoyed being a central figure in what was not right." Arguing that the boy's release would be harmful to the community, Banet concluded that Bobby was "in need of extensive therapy and if given treatment outside of his home he might have a chance." Perhaps proving the probation officer's assessment of his moral fiber correct, Bobby served all four years at Cedar Knolls, being released only when he aged-out of the reformatory system.[52]

*   *   *

Ultimately, the verdict and sentencing appeared to provide little catharsis for the public. As the *New York World-Telegram* noted, "The big questions behind the murder remain unanswered: what turned 'respectable' boys from religious, middle-income homes into cold-blooded killers?"[53] Max Lerner for the *New York Post* called the entire episode one that "began in blind and purposeless aggression" and now was "end[ing] in tragedy." Lerner lamented the lack of a Clarence Darrow, who might have placed a larger, sociological perspective on the trial, bemoaning that the "whole episode of the Brooklyn boys seems to have brought us not a step closer to such an understanding of the wider problem of guilt and responsibility, nor the problem of prevention and cure."[54]

Civic groups following the verdict attempted explanations. The Brownsville Labor Youth League promised to answer "What's Behind the 'Thrill Trial'?" at their symposium a few days after the verdict.[55] According to Isaac Fuhrman, a case supervisor in the Kings County Probation Department speaking at a Parents Association symposium titled "Are We Coddling Our

Youth," a crucial lesson of the trial was that problem youths needed appropriate psychiatric treatment. Furman pointed out that Koslow was recognized as a "problem" the first day he entered school and that his crimes may have been prevented had his parents not withheld psychiatric treatment out of shame.[56]

Others, however, knew exactly where the blame should be placed: the day the verdict was announced, the *New York World-Telegram* ran the headline "2 Thrill Killers Steeped in Horror Books," accompanied by photographs of Jack Koslow and Melvin Mittman flanking a comic book cover of *Lorna, The Jungle Girl*. The article claimed the two boys were "horror comic addicts" and "steeped in violent pornography." Disclosing that Jack Koslow had been visited by the esteemed psychiatrist and anticomics crusader Dr. Fredric Wertham while in Raymond Street Jail, Wertham revealed to the newspaper that Jack had a complete set of the sexually sadistic comic book *Nights of Horror*, which provided the "cues for whipping, beating, burning and torture" inherent in the boys' crimes.[57] In a second exclusive interview with the *New York World-Telegram* the following day, Wertham called horror comics "the invisible defendants" at the Thrill-Kill trial: "If these youths are to spend their lives in prison," he quipped, "I feel the publishers of horror comics should go to jail for at least one day."[58] The trial may have been over, but the public was not yet done with the Brooklyn Thrill-Killers. The gang was about to take on symbolic significance, a short hand for the nameless victims of the corruption and greed of the comic book industry.

The Fallout

The meeting would start sharply at 9:30 a.m. on an unseasonably warm February day that was turning the New York City sidewalks to slush.[1] Delegates, scurrying up the front steps of 42 West Forty-fourth Street, would soon find themselves entering one of the most beautiful buildings in Manhattan. The House of the New York City Bar Association, a six-storied neoclassical structure made from Indiana limestone, was hailed upon its completion in 1896 as "one of the most interesting and [architecturally] successful" buildings in New York.[2] Outside, the facade was a composite of classical architecture: Doric elements dominated the bottom three floors, while Ionic and Corinthian columns framed the building's upper portion. Upon entering, visitors were greeted by an elegant marble foyer, a curving staircase leading to a granite-lined reception hall, and a library of fifty thousand volumes presided over by a massive granite fireplace.

In the second-floor meeting hall, amid the mahogany-accented luxury, the New York State Joint Legislative Committee to Study the Publication of Comic Books assembled. The one-day meeting was to determine whether the committee would reinitiate its earlier attempts at legislative regulation of the comic book industry. Leading the proceedings this day was assemblyman and anticomics crusader James A. Fitzpatrick. With a clean-shaven choir-boy face and slicked-back hair, Fitzpatrick looked every inch the pious Catholic descendant of hard-working Irish immigrants. Born in Plattsburgh, New York, the assemblyman was the product of private religious schooling and a graduate of the Catholic University of America. After receiving his law degree from Columbia University in 1941, Fitzpatrick served in the navy during the

Second World War and turned to politics after his return in 1946. Wildly popular in his home district, the assemblyman would serve four terms, winning his 1952 election by such a landslide that he was unanimously endorsed by both the Republican and Democratic Parties in 1954.

During his time in the New York State Legislature, the father of five sponsored the bill that created the Adirondack Northway, connecting the northernmost parts of New York to the newly created interstate highway system. He also cosponsored the Feinberg-Fitzpatrick bill in 1949 that would have created a comic book division in the State Department of Education.[3] After the bill's failure in the assembly, the state senate created the Joint Legislative Committee to Study the Publication of Comics and appropriated $15,000 for the study of juvenile delinquency and its potential link to comic books.

Soon after its inception, the committee, then under the leadership of Assemblyman Joseph Carlino, conducted a broad survey asking for data on juvenile delinquency and whether comic books contributed to the statistics on juvenile crime. Polling county and Children's Court judges, state district attorneys, city clerks, and probation officers, the results of the survey were unfortunately inconclusive.[4]

It was subsequently decided to conduct hearings to allow experts to present evidence on both sides of the issue. At the initial hearing in June of 1950, the majority of witnesses—which included judges, assistant district attorneys, and child psychiatrists—favored state regulation of comic books in the crime and horror genres.[5] After the president of the Association of Comics Magazine Publishers (ACMP) asked for an opportunity to present a rebuttal, a second set of hearings took place in August of 1950 in which the comic book industry successfully argued its case for continued self-regulation.

The committee's first report, published in 1951, took a strong anticomic book stance, but it declined to propose any legislation.[6] Instead, it urged publishers to adopt a self-regulatory code, while warning that failure for the industry to do so might make future state regulation necessary. Despite the warning, however, the ACMP did nothing to either revamp its code or increase enforcement. When it became clear by 1952 that the comic book industry had no serious intentions of self-regulating, the committee recommended the passage of six laws that would serve to censor the publication of fictional accounts of crime, bloodshed, lust, or heinous acts. Vetoed by Governor Dewey in April of 1952, the committee's inability to pass any legislation killed its credibility and marginalized the group in the legislature. But in 1955, all that would change as new and spectacular evidence emerged that four middle-class boys went on a crime spree of assault, torture, and murder inspired by comic books.

*   *   *

Comic books had been under assault since the Second World War. It began with the Catholic Church, who railed against the genre from pulpit and publication, linking superhero comics in particular to both fascism and indecency.[7] In 1948, Detroit was the first city to crack down on comic books, seizing the publications from newsstands and examining them for objectionable material. The raids resulted in the legislative banning of thirty-six comic book series from the City of Detroit.[8] Within the next few months, over fifty municipalities followed suit, developing various laws to curb comic books sales.

Coincidentally, 1948's U.S. Supreme Court decision in *Winters v. New York* overturned the statute which outlawed publications "principally made up of criminal news, police reports, or accounts of criminal deeds, or pictures, or stories of deeds of bloodshed, lust or crime." While a strike against censorship, the majority decision ironically opened the door for legislation on comic books.[9] Although the Court considered the overturned New York statute "too uncertain and indefinite" to be enforceable, the majority opinion concurred that future legislation was possible, as long as the statutes were adequately specific. There was "no implication" in its decision, the Court wrote, that the state legislature "may not punish circulation of objectionable printed matter, assuming that it is not protected by the principles of the First Amendment, by the use of apt words to describe the prohibited publications."[10]

Interestingly, the increasing calls for comic book censorship went against the general trends for decreased censorship happening in the early 1950s. The beginning of the end of film censorship, judges in this era increasingly questioned the legality of prior restraint in favor of more expansive interpretations of First Amendment rights.[11] For example, the unanimous 1952 Supreme Court decision *Burstyn v. Wilson*, while not completely overturning censorship statutes, did specifically grant motion pictures the protection of the First and Fourteenth amendments. The majority decision also admonished censors that instead of cutting whatever they wanted, they henceforth had a "heavy burden" to prove that an individual film merited being banned or cut.[12] While, as noted by historian Laura Wittern-Keller, neither state courts nor the Supreme Court would "make good" on the enforcement of the burden shift until the 1960s, the case still provided significant legal precedent that would be used later.[13] At the very least, the legal and constitutional status of movies as censorable was starting to shift.

As for television, there were limited calls to censor the small screen. This was chiefly because of the fact that, unlike comic books and movies, which were mainly supported by sales, television was primarily supported by advertisers who cautiously shied away from being associated with any content that might be deemed controversial. Advertising, therefore, provided an internal control system for television content that did not apply to either comic books or films. Also, rattled by the U.S. Senate Subcommittee hearings on Juvenile Delinquency, the burgeoning industry quickly adopted its own code modeled on Hollywood's Production Code, signifying the small screen's willingness to self-regulate.

What made comic books distinctive from these other forms of mass media is that they were a genre whose audience (by and large) did not include adults. Even worse, unlike televisions, which typically sat in the family living room, or public movie theaters, comic books were cheaply accessible, easily hidden, and therefore often existed outside of parental purview. And finally, unlike the small screen, comic book publishers seemed unwilling or unable to self-regulate.

Some comic book publishers, seeing the writing on the wall, did attempt to implement a code of "minimum editorial standards" in July of 1948. But only fourteen out of thirty-five comics publishers were willing to sign on. Adapted from language in the motion picture industry's Production Code, the six principles included restrictions on publishing indecently exposed females, being overly sympathetic to crime and criminals, publishing scenes of sadistic torture, using vulgar and obscene language, representing divorce "humorously" or "glamorously," and ridiculing or attacking any particular racial group.[14] Comics submitted to editorial review by the newly created Association of Comics Magazine Publishers would bear the marks "Authorized A.C.M.P." and "Conforms to the Comics Code" on their covers. The main problem, however, was not only that a small minority of publishers had agreed to participate, but that the producers of the most violent crime comics (Fox Feature Syndicate and Harvey Thriller) refused to, essentially making the code useless.[15]

By 1949, the New York State Legislature opted to begin targeting the makers—rather than the sellers or readers—of crime comics. One proposed bill amended the wording of the original statute to "sordid bloodshed, lust or heinous acts," while the cosponsored Feinberg-Fitzpatrick bill would have established a new comic book division of the State Department of Education to go along with its preexisting Motion Picture Division. The new comic book wing, like its movie counterpart, would have held the authority to approve or reject comics prior to distribution. With a set fee of $3 per application, makers of comics that passed the division's approval would be granted a permit to publish. Those choosing to publish a rejected comic would be required to submit a sample of the book to the county district attorney thirty days in advance of its proposed sale date and carry a notice on the title page that a permit had been denied.[16]

The Feinberg-Fitzpatrick bill, deemed too expensive and too time-consuming, died in committee. But the proposal to amend the language of the original New York statute quickly passed the assembly and the state senate, the latter with a nearly unanimous vote of forty-nine to six. The new legislation was vigorously opposed by the comic book industry, and Henry Schultz, head of the ACMP, wrote to the governor that the bill was unconstitutional and suggested that the very premise that accounts of crime were harmful to children was not supported by any valid, scientific evidence.[17] Ultimately, Governor Thomas E. Dewey vetoed the legislation, declaring that simply adding the word "sordid" and substituting "heinous acts" for "crime" still created legislation that was too vague and therefore did not meet the *Winters v. New York* test.

Meanwhile, one of the opponents of the bill, State Senator Harold I. Panken, took up the industry's suggestion that the matter warranted scientific study. Suggesting that any further action be deferred until the matter of whether comic books really posed a public health threat could be adequately determined, on March 29, 1949, the state senate authorized the creation of the Joint Legislative Committee to Study the Publication of Comics. This committee would represent the very first legislative effort to study comic books and the comic book industry and would position New York as the epicenter of the legal battle over comic book censorship.

*   *   *

As historian David Hajdu notes in his study of the Great Comic Book Scare, the period between 1950 and 1951 saw the campaign against comics nearly fizzle out.[18] Tired of crime comics, many readers and publishers in 1950 began to emphasize sex, and so-called romance comics rose to prominence. With the decline of crime comics, the campaign against comic books may well have died out entirely had it not been for the introduction of a new genre: the horror comic. Horror comics soon became caught up in what Hajdu terms a "spiral of gruesomeness," in which one month might spotlight a man's neck being slashed, the next month might feature a full decapitation, and the third would depict the severed head being used as a bowling ball. As Hajdu describes it, "Publishers, unable to establish a following for a given title, had to compete for the attention of the same readers, month after month, and the game in this competition was shock."[19]

As public outrage over these new, more gruesome comic books mounted, the members of the New York State Joint Legislative Committee to Study the Publication of Comics became increasingly disillusioned with the industry's lack of progress toward self-regulation. So in 1952, the committee took another stab at regulating comic books, introducing six new acts and reviving the Feinberg-Fitzpatrick bill. This time, they changed the wording of the previous statute more significantly, prohibiting the publication of material "principally made up of pictures, whether or not accompanied by any written or printed matter, of fictional deeds of crime, bloodshed, lust or heinous acts, which tend to incite minors to violent or depraved or immoral acts."[20] The strategy worked, and on March 12, 1952, the New York State Assembly passed the act on the grounds that it specified fictional accounts and was intended to protect minors. But the amended statute was once again vetoed by Governor Dewey on account of vagueness.

The following year, 1953, saw another attempt at regulation of the industry. The set of bills that were introduced included raising the fine for displaying or selling "lewd, lascivious, filthy, indecent or disgusting" literature from

$50 to $250; a law that prevented distributors from doing "tie-in-sales" in which they forced dealers to accept comics by the lot rather than by the title; and a law allowing local sheriffs and police chiefs the authority to seize any comic or pocket book that might "incite minors" while granting local officials the right to seek injunctions against the sale, possession, or distribution of the same. Although Governor Dewey initially refused to sign the bills, mounting public pressure forced the governor to relent, and he signed the group into law when resubmitted a few months later, in April of 1954.[21]

Subsequently, the new laws allowed the mayor of New York City, Robert Wagner, to respond to the public outcry against juvenile delinquency during the summer of 1954 with an announcement on September 8 that the city would clean up bookstores of "publications teaching lust, violence, perverted sex attitudes, and disrespect for law and order."[22] Alluding to the case of the Brooklyn Thrill-Killers, the mayor declared, "Recent crimes committed by juveniles, clearly indicate that these publications are responsible in a great measure for the alarming upward trend in juvenile delinquency, particularly in the fields of violence and sex crimes."[23] Two days later, the mayor's legal arm, the Corporation Counsel of New York, filed a court motion asking for an injunction banning the sale of what was considered the most egregious of the comics found in recent police raids: *Nights of Horror*. Corporate Counsel Adrian P. Burke called *Nights of Horror* a "flagrant example" of the "obscene, lewd, lascivious, filthy, indecent, and disgusting 'literature' accessible to the youth of our City." And Police Commissioner Adams claimed that there was "a definite relationship" between "the types of crimes portrayed in *Nights of Horror* . . . and the crimes of sex and violence which beset the City of New York today."[24]

In the meantime, Assemblyman James A. Fitzpatrick, using the momentum created by the arrest of the Brooklyn Thrill-Killers, called a press conference to assure New Yorkers of a new statewide effort to crack down on the sale of horror comics. Labeling horror comics a "blue print" for juvenile crime, Fitzpatrick declared that the current crime wave "came as no surprise" to persons familiar with the type of printed matter "being fed" to teenagers by the "purveyors of horror, sadism, sex and lust," otherwise known as the comic book industry. "The newsstands of this country are covered," Fitzpatrick affirmed, "with material glamorizing and describing sadism, perversion and illicit sex. We can't constantly fill the minds of our young people with ideas of this type and thereafter express any honest surprise if their activities reflect practices that they have been led to believe are both common and acceptable." The assemblyman also claimed he had a number of comics, any one of which "could serve as a blue print" for the Brooklyn Thrill-Killers. In one, he said, "four teenage members of a city gang indulge in brutality after brutality, culminating in murder by drowning, as in the Brooklyn case."[25]

In the meantime, the comic book industry, faced with mounting public pressure and threat of further legislative action, finally began to take the idea of self-regulation seriously. Bill Gaines, head of EC Comics, initiated the final attempt to organize the industry and explore the possibility of self-censorship. The thirty-eight publishers, distributors, printers, and engravers who attended the meeting at the Biltmore Hotel in Manhattan on August 17, 1954, decided to call themselves the Comics Magazine Association of America (CMAA) and to establish a new code of standards as well as a system for enforcement by an independent overseer. To keep the enterprise above reproach, the group even voted to ask Dr. Fredric Wertham to be the first comics czar (whether he turned the position down or the association eventually changed their minds is unclear).[26] When the CMAA incorporated a few weeks later, its members included twenty-six publishers and nineteen companies involved in technical operations and distribution. Only two major publishers had declined to join: Dell, whose comic books were already considered "wholesome," and Gilbertson, whose *Classics Illustrated* were also adequately respectable.[27]

By the end of October 1954, the comics industry officially adopted their self-regulating code. Signed by twenty-nine out of thirty-one publishers in the comics field, eight national distributors, six engravers, twelve printers, and one matmaker, the new code would be enforced by the first "Comics Czar," Judge Charles F. Murphy—a former assistant corporation counsel of the City of New York, legal adviser to Mayor Laguardia, and former city magistrate. The code adopted by the association agreed not to glamorize crime or allow evil to triumph or go unpunished and to exclude scenes of excessive violence as well as "bloodshed, gory or gruesome crimes, depravity, lust, sadism, [and] masochism."[28] The code also placed limits on ridiculing or attacking any religious or racial group, prohibited nudity as well as "salacious illustration," demanded the portrayal of females to be "realisti[c] without exaggeration of any physical qualities," called for divorce neither to be "treated humorously nor represented as desirable," and restricted advertisements from liquor, tobacco, sexual literature, knives or realistic gun facsimiles, fireworks, gambling equipment, and medical/health or toiletry products of a "questionable nature."[29]

Ultimately, the CMAA Comics Code was more rigid than any current legislation, and it would cost the industry over $100,000 annually to enforce. To complete what he called a "time-consuming, back-breaking, ulcer-producing, artery-hardening job," Comic Czar Murphy assembled a staff of highly qualified reviewers whose varied backgrounds included a former assistant editor in the story department of Metro-Goldwyn-Mayer, a member of the English department of Hunter College, a librarian in public and commercial libraries, a former information specialist for the U.S. Department of Agriculture, and a social worker who dealt with juvenile delinquents.[30] Incidentally, all of the reviewers were women. "I took on women," Murphy told the New York State Legislative Committee, "because I felt they were more sensitive to the situation."[31]

All of which leads us back to that slushy day on February 4, 1955, at the beautiful House of the New York City Bar Association, because the one-day session of the New York Joint Legislative Committee to Study the Publication of Comics was really the day of reckoning for the CMAA's new code, the day when it would be determined whether the industry's efforts were simply too little, too late. Frustrated by years of the industry's refusal to self-regulate, a pessimistic Fitzpatrick (who had recently replaced Assemblyman Carlino as the head of the committee) had already testified to the U.S. Senate subcommittee that it was unlikely the industry would ever take self-regulation seriously:

> We tried that. We had these publishers in; we took their testimony; we issued a report. We said very plainly, "Gentlemen, we will give you an entire year to clean your own house. We feel the best regulation is self-regulation. You know this is bad. You clean it up and you will have no trouble from our legislative committee." We came back in a year, Senator. We called the same people before us. They had done nothing. They had attempted to do nothing.[32]

The assemblyman placed the issue in terms of morality. As he informed the senators, he had come to believe that "the people who publish this kind of thing, in my humble opinion, have no morals, and if they have no morals in distributing filth and breaking down the whole moral attitude of our youth, I don't think they care whether or not they have any standing."[33] It would fall to Comics Czar Charles F. Murphy, at this last-ditch meeting on February 4, 1955, to convince Fitzpatrick and the Legislative Committee that the industry was finally willing and able to clean up its act.

*   *   *

Called as the first witness to testify, the portly, middle-aged Comics Czar with the bulbous nose and receding hairline began defensively. Elaborating on his long experience as a city magistrate, which "brought me into contact with many youngsters who were in trouble," Murphy made it patently clear that it was his opinion that juvenile delinquency fell solely on the shoulders of negligent parents. "With respect to crime stories," Murphy authoritatively informed the committee, any bad ideas a child could get from them "is something that you could pick up any place, walking on the street or even at home."[34]

Murphy quickly moved on to extol the efforts of the CMAA while emphasizing that only a "small percentage of the publishers . . . put out this objectionable material," with a greater proportion publishing "good, clean, wholesome books."[35] Murphy also made it clear that it was the intention of the CMAA to pressure member publishers into "discontinu[ing]" horror and terror comics, with the ultimate goal being the genre's elimination. For now, however, Murphy assured the committee that he and his staff had diligently excised thousands of drawings, rejected hundreds of story lines as "unsuitable," and altered innumerable images to conform to the CMAA's rigid new standards. Murphy provided the committee with multiple examples of crime and horror comics that his office had reviewed and changed: a skeletal hand moving a pawn across a chessboard becomes a normal fleshy one; a story depicting a man shown strangling his wife and then pouring kerosene over her body has the rope removed as well as the panel where he pours kerosene over the corpse; and a story titled "Customer for a Coffin" was rejected entirely.[36] In another example, a western, a scene where a prone character is being kicked was removed, a knife was taken out of the hand of an Indian, and a scene showing an arrow going through a man was omitted.[37] Further, various advertisements for knives or that included women in negligees were also rejected by the reviewers.[38]

Committee Chairman Fitzpatrick began his rebuttal by praising Murphy's efforts: "You have done some fine work in several instances," the assemblyman admitted, "and we are particularly pleased with the types of ads you have eliminated."[39] Further recognizing that it was impossible to "completely face-lift the industry overnight," there was still, however, "significant concern" over the fact that "by and large" the comics on store shelves "still continu[e] to present themes of violence."[40]

The chairman then proceeded to lambast Murphy, exhibiting several comic books with the Code Administrator's approval that "in every instance there is violence portrayed."[41] In one, boldly bearing the stamp, scene after scene showed a man being kicked in the jaw, another being knocked to his feet, and yet another man being hit with a barrel. Other "approved" comics portrayed a dog being beaten with a whip, a man being thrown from the second-floor window and splattering on the sidewalk, and a man being trampled to death. Fitzpatrick continued to show example after example: men with hands being burned by acid; men electrocuted in the electric chair while crying, "No, you can't do that, I don't want to die"; men being shot; and a man without eyes violently taking the eyes of a convict.[42]

The Comics Czar defended himself, rearticulating that the goal was to eliminate comics in which there was "excessive violence" or violence was the "dominant theme," but "if you are going to point at every panel, because there is a little action as distinguished from violence, then I am saying to you, you will have no more comic books, no more TV, no more radio."[43] Further, Murphy reminded the committee that the ultimate goal of the new regulations should be to "re-educate the writers and editors and artists." One had to be careful, Murphy warned the legislators, not to "destroy an industry . . . which employs thousands and thousands of people."[44]

Fitzpatrick frankly asked the Comics Czar whether Murphy would support legislation in which the CMAA's regulations were legally codified, therefore giving the code administrator legal backing for enforcement. Murphy vigorously denounced the idea. "There are two ways of solv[ing] the problem," Murphy declared, "the right way and the wrong way. The right way . . . the

American way . . . is the effort that the industry is making at self-regulation." "Censorship," Murphy added, "has been found to be the wrong way, by the Supreme Court of the United States."

State Senator Stanley J. Bauer quickly castigated Murphy: "When the Chairman asks would you like to introduce bills based on parts of your Code, in my opinion at least I believe that would strengthen your position, and I think you are arguing against yourself. Right now," he reminded the Comics Czar, "you have no punitive powers under this code. To get [comic publishers] in line. . . . We want to help you put a club in your hand."

"As an American," Murphy crisply responded, "I do not favor that type of censorship."[45]

*   *   *

The ambush of Murphy had been carefully planned by Fitzpatrick, and it reflected the assemblyman's deep and personal disappointment in the industry's continuing failure to curb itself. When the two men first met in the autumn of 1954, Fitzpatrick walked away optimistic in his assessment that the Comics Czar and his team were the regulatory answer he had long been hoping for. As recently as December, Fitzpatrick wrote, "I have gone over the work that [Judge Murphy] is doing and have seen numerous examples of material that has been cut. . . . I came away with confidence that they were trying to do an honest job."[46] Yet by February of 1955, the assemblyman's belief in the CMAA was failing. In a letter dated a few days before the hearing, Fitzpatrick expressed his disillusionment: "Without any question," he wrote, "industry has failed to eliminate the dominate [sic] theme of brutality and terror. It is my intention to directly cross-examine Mr. Murphy and to bring this out."[47]

To this end, Fitzpatrick had enlisted some help. Testifying in the afternoon, by the assemblyman's personal invitation, was the effervescent anticomics crusader Dr. Fredric Wertham. With testimony sharply focused on the Brooklyn Thrill-Killers, Wertham's exclusive psychiatric interview with Jack Koslow would provide the evidence that Fitzpatrick and other anticomics legislators had been waiting for—a direct, causal link between comic books and juvenile delinquency.

This was not the first time that Wertham had testified before New York State Joint Legislative Committee to Study the Publication of Comic Books. He was first introduced to the committee in December of 1950, petitioning for public health laws to ban the sale of crime comics to children under the age of fifteen. A year later, Wertham appeared again, making a cogent argument for the futility of self-regulation and once more lobbying for public health laws against what he termed a "virus" that "psychological[ly] mutilat[es]" children.[48]

Wertham and Fitzpatrick had become friendly since that first meeting and maintained a regular correspondence. So it was no surprise that Fitzpatrick would contact Wertham in December of 1954 following the *New York World-Telegram*'s expose article "2 Thrill Killers Steeped in Horror Books," which spotlighted the psychiatrist's interview with Jack Koslow. As the assembly-man's office had been working closely with the corporation counsel in the *Nights of Horror* test case, Fitzpatrick was especially interested in hearing Wertham's opinion as to whether that comic in particular had influenced the gang's crime spree.[49]

For his part, Wertham had little use for either industry self-regulation or Judge Murphy. In his earlier testimony, Wertham had cautioned the commit-tee that harmless comic books do not sell and that the "crime comic book industry sees children as a market of child buyers and no more."[50] He had also privately written to U.S. Senator Estes Kefauver to express strong reser-vations about the CMAA's latest attempt to self-regulate. Calling the code a "new hoax," he lambasted Charles F. Murphy, claiming that the Comics Czar had "already made statements revealing that he either does not know or does not want to know the true situation." Wertham was particularly galled at the judge's professing firsthand experience to the media in having "never seen a single case where crime comic books had anything to do with juvenile delinquency." Calling the statement a "smokescreen to mislead the public," Wertham informed the senator that as Murphy was a magistrate of an adult—not a juvenile—court, he would have had almost no contact with juveniles during his legal career. "It is clear," Wertham exclaimed, "that we cannot teach adolescents respect for law and authority if a member of the judiciary lends himself to such a publicity stunt!"[51]

The February 4 hearing was Wertham's first opportunity to publicly denounce the Comics Czar and prove once and for all the ineffectiveness of industry self-regulation, and he would wield the case of the Brooklyn Thrill-Killers to accomplish both. Stressing that comic books were not the "sole factor," that Jack was an "abnormal personality," and that it was in no way his belief that "anybody reads a bad book and then goes out and commits a crime," Wertham's testimony meticulously detailed the disarming similarities between the comic books Jack read and the crimes Jack committed.[52] Call-ing it a "classical case," Wertham asserted that "Every detail, the drowning, the beating, the burning, all of them are described in detail and has been hammered into all of these children over and over again" by "innumerable comics books."[53]

Turning to the industry representatives in the audience, Wertham acknowl-edged, "I know that you as sellers are not interested in a doctor's opinion; you are more interested in what a doctor can prove." Wertham began by describing Jack's youthful fascination with vampires, cultivated by early horror comics: "Koslow . . . was particularly fascinated, overwhelmed . . . with all the vampire stories . . . that he imagined himself to be a vampire." Wertham reported that Koslow routinely went out at night in "vampire costume" and that on the night of the murder, he purposefully wore his "vampire" pants.[54] Wertham then went on to detail the various crimes committed by the Thrill-Killers, linking the instances to specific scenes from various comic books. Describing the whipping of girls in parks, for example, Wertham showed the committee a sample advertisement from a comic book for whips, similar to the one Koslow sent away for that was implicated in the crime spree. When Chairman Fitzpatrick interrupted Wertham to clarify that these are exactly the kinds of ads that Judge Murphy was rejecting in his role as Comics Czar, Wertham dramatically showed the committee a whip, purchased for $3.29, which he had received the day before in response to an advertisement from a comic book bearing the CMAA seal. Wertham also showed the committee a knife, recently ordered from the back of another comic book, that had passed the CMAA's muster.[55]

Opining that "the company of bad books is often more dangerous than the company of bad people, and I think that is one of the lessons of this Koslow case," Wertham submitted multiple comic books into evidence that depicted nearly identical crimes to the ones committed by the Brooklyn Thrill-Killers. One cover showed a piece of wood inserted between a man's toes with a hand about to light it, and others featured bums being beaten. Most damning were the copies of *Nights of Horror* that Wertham had taken with him when he visited Koslow in the Raymond Street Jail. Wertham testified to the committee that upon showing the illicit comics to Koslow, Jack stated, "Oh, I have a very much better edition; I have all fourteen volumes." According to Wertham, these particular sadistic and pornographic comics described in lurid detail "the burning, the torture with cigarettes, the whipping, the knife torture, the kicking and so on" as well as such degenerate acts as forcing the victim to kiss one's feet. As Wertham testified, "It is so much alike that one has the feeling that it is an actor performing according to script."[56]

The similarities finally prompted Fitzpatrick to ask Wertham directly whether it was his opinion "that the reading matter which was in the hands of Koslow and his associates was a contributing factor to the action which they thereafter committed?" Wertham gave the committee an unequivocal and resounding "yes":

> I will go so far as to say that it is absolutely clear that while I recognize the existence of other factors in this case, I will go so far as to say that had it not been for the crime comic books, the horror comic books, the *Nights of Horror*, and all these early indoctrinations of violence, these particular crimes would not have been committed.[57]

Wertham was also asked by the committee whether he felt there was any improvement in comic books since Judge Murphy had begun implementing the CMAA's code. As Murphy looked on, Wertham replied negatively. "None of the points that we have regarded as particularly harmful to children, as to none of them have we noted any real difference." Scoffing that the new code was no more than "history . . . repeating itself," Wertham recalled for the committee that in 1948 the comics industry had tried to self-regulate with a code and administrator, and that all it resulted in was "maybe a little girl's breast is covered a little more than before" but that "I don't think that girls are tortured any the less, even though their breasts are covered."[58]

For his part, a visibly annoyed Charles Murphy interrupted the testimony, demanding that the committee receive proof from Wertham that the various advertisements and comics he was citing had, in fact, gone through his review. Claiming that Wertham had "in his usual manner glossed over the fact when he was asked for specific references" while also noting that "Dr. Wertham has been in this field long enough to come prepared," Murphy challenged Wertham for not having made any effort to meet with the CMAA or assist the agency in any manner. Murphy also submitted one of Wertham's own books, *The Show of Violence*, calling it a "book which should be included on the 'How to Do It' shelf, how to commit murder . . . and this man is coming here and making statements about me, here. It's outrageous."[59]

But despite Murphy's protestations, Wertham had already provided the specific titles and dates of the reviewed comic books to Fitzpatrick in private correspondence, and the committee ultimately reported that no less than forty-seven comic books bearing the seal contained advertisements for illicit weapons—despite Judge Murphy's assurances otherwise.[60] In further condemnation of the industry, several other witnesses at the hearing earlier that day had also squared in on the Thrill-Killers' relationship to comic books. Some did so more obliquely, such as Police Commissioner Adams's testimony that there was a "direct relationship" between the "obscenity and lewdness that is published and juvenile crime" committed by middle-class teens. While others, such as Louis L. Roos, acting captain of the Police Department Legal Bureau, testified more directly that the sale of "strip-tease nudes" literature like *Nights of Horror* in predominantly middle-class areas provided a "direct effect and direct bearing" on the types of crimes being committed by middle-class juveniles, "such as the one Dr. Wertham stressed and referred to particularly."[61]

When it came to *Nights of Horror*, Milton Mollen, assistant corporation counsel, did not mince words: "I think they deal with every idea of sexual perversion known to man . . . placing hot coals against a female's breasts, placing hot irons against a female's armpits, pulling off a female's fingernails with a white-hot pincer, working a female's skin away from her flesh with a knife, . . . hanging by the thumbs, the torture rack, hair-pulling and skin burning, all described graphically and with pictures."[62] Mollen testified that once Governor Dewey had signed into law the bill empowering local officials to secure injunctions against the sale of any literature that was "lewd, lascivious, indecent, obscene, disgusting or filthy" as a "source of crime and a basic factor in impairing the moral and ethical development of minors, and a menace to the health, safety and morals of the People of the State of New York," the police and the corporation counsel quickly honed in on *Nights of Horror* as the most egregious of the lot, explaining, "We finally selected one which we felt was most indicative of all the things which were horrible and wrong, and not only from the viewpoint of obscenity, but from the possible impact upon the immature and juvenile mind."[63]

Besides the graphic, and pornographic, depictions of torture, the blatant masochism in the publications added an even more dangerous layer of misogyny. "The parties upon whom these practices were practiced, enjoy it," Mollen testified. "They intimate very clearly, that those who have not had the 'pleasure' of having these means of torture inflicted upon them, have missed something in life." Quickly picking up on the potential implications, Fitzpatrick directly asked, "Like the thrill killers?" To which Mollen quickly responded with a resounding, "Yes." The chairman then catalogued the Thrill-Killers' specific crimes, as reported to the committee by Dr. Wertham, asking whether Mollen remembered their appearing in these particular publications. Were there people in vampire costumes beating other people with whips? Yes. Torture of the feet? "Common." Victims forced to grovel at the feet of the torturers? Yes. "As I have said," Mollen assured the committee, "this series is a lethal weapon in the hands of an immature or unbalanced individual. It tends to provoke and, through this provocation, it supplies the perverted ideas which often are the impetus to the perpetuation of crimes and sexual degradation."[64]

The only solution, according to Mollen, was for the New York State Legislature to pass a law banning the sale of these books. Currently, the law allowed the city to obtain an injunction title by title, but "as we take action against one, they come up with another title."[65] Overall, the aggregate of the day's testimony led to the same conclusion: only blanket legislation banning the sales of the indecent books could prevent crimes like those of the Brooklyn Thrill-Killers from continuing to plague the good citizens of New York.

*   *   *

On March 14, 1955, the New York State Joint Legislative Committee to Study the Publication of Comic Books submitted its report to the New York State Legislature. That the case of the Brooklyn Thrill-Killers was considered such conclusive proof of the corruptive influence of comic books was evidenced by its being the very first, and most prominent, subject of the report. The report declared:

> Few cases have stirred the Nation or awakened its consciousness of juvenile delinquency as did the case of the Brooklyn "thrill-killers" . . . An analysis of the reading material of these boys should serve for all time as a perfect example of the contribution made to delinquency, by those who place in the hands of youth cheap, sordid, perverted and obscene blueprints for the crimes they commit.[66]

Detailing the reading habits of Jack Koslow, including his obsession with Nietzsche (decried as "the cornerstone of all that is tyrannical, racist and cruelly violent in the regime of Adolph Hitler"), the report focused on Jack's collection of *Nights of Horror*—"paper bound books selling for and portraying all types of brutality, illicit sex and perversion."[67] After having reviewed this particular comic series, the committee believed the comics contained "repeated descriptions of every foul deed committed by Koslow and his associates," as well as the "'feeling of power' [Koslow] described and the 'thrill' of brutality, whipping and killing."[68] The condemning report closed: "we have every reason to conclude that these books played a most important part in leading these boys down the road to disaster."[69]

Principal to the committee's recommendations was the testimony of Dr. Wertham, whose written statement was included in the report in full. According to Wertham, "In the course of my examination I analyzed in detail the different factors operative in this case. *Paramount as a direct, causative, contributing factor in these acts of violence was what [Jack Koslow] read*" (emphasis Wertham's).[70] Wertham detailed Koslow's "graduation" from crime and Superman comic books to horror comics, "his mind becoming filled with all the thrill of violence, murder and cruelty described in them." Wertham presented as "objective evidence" the fact that Koslow had imitated one of the stock characters of crime comic books: the vampire, going out in black costume and roaming the streets at night.[71] Further, Wertham enumerated the various ways in which the activities of the Thrill-Killers closely paralleled the text and pictures in *Nights of Horror*.

Declaring Koslow to merely be "the weakest link," Wertham's written statement determined that the only viable solution was to abolish the sale of such books as *Nights of Horror* to children completely. Referring to Mittman, Trachtenberg, and Lieberman, Wertham wrote, "Even if it is possible to keep some children away from comic books and 'Nights of Horror,' . . . it is not possible to keep them away from other children who are influenced by this type of literature." "If we want to protect any children," he warned, "we must protect all children."[72]

Ultimately, the committee concluded that while comic books were "but one of many factors" when it came to juvenile delinquency, they were "among the most important" contributing directly to the "lack of a sense of moral responsibility among the young, without which we cannot hope for the preservation of decency."[73] Throughout the remainder of the report, in which example after example of brutal violence was presented, the committee continually linked the depravity in the examples to the Brooklyn Thrill-Killers, although it also acknowledged that the odious *Nights of Horror* was on the radar of the New York Corporation Counsel "long before it was known . . . [the comic] was in the hands of Koslow and companions."[74] But citing a "'thrill kill' philosophy of comics," the committee also warned how the attendant media attention of the case inspired copycat crimes, including one where three young boys attacked another youth in Brooklyn, beating the victim savagely. The leader of the group purportedly rushed into the attack screaming, "I am Koslow, the Thrill-Killer!"[75]

As for the work of Charles Murphy and the code authority, the committee had little confidence in the Comic Czar's ability to curtail the industry. According to the report, "Comic books currently upon the stands and bearing the authority's Seal of Approval contain an abundance of the same type of material termed objectionable by the authority and purportedly eliminated."[76] The evidence against the code authority was damning: in one "approved" comic, for example, the committee noted that in eight of the nine pages of the story "someone is either shot, slugged, slapped or otherwise subjected to physical violence and brutality."[77] Further, the report revealed that Dr. Wertham was indeed correct in his assertion that the code authority had not completely eradicated the advertisement of whips and knives from the comic books bearing their seals: not only had Wertham apparently provided the committee with both the comic books and the weapons he had purchased, but according to the report, "Judge Murphy has since revealed that advertisements for . . . weapons of the type described were found in forty-seven books bearing the seal."[78]

With the ineffectiveness of the code authority proved, the second concern was with the structure of the industry itself. As the report noted, "The comic book field is one frequently invaded by the irresponsible 'fly-by-night' operators who will belong to no organization and will adhere to no voluntary code." The only remedy was to enact a statute completely prohibiting the publication or distribution of any comic books that were "devoted to, or principally made up of pictures and accounts of methods of crime, of illicit sex, horror, terror, physical torture, brutality or physical violence."[79] The proposed legislation, therefore, included Article 49, in which these types of comic books were declared a "contributing factor in impairing the ethical and moral development of our youth" and were therefore a "clear and present danger to the people of the state."[80]

Article 49 proposed banning the publication or sale of horror, crime, sex, or terror comics; banning the use of the words "crime," "terror," "horror," or "sex" in comic book titles; and prohibiting the sale of these comics to minors under the threat of misdemeanor charges. Violators would be punished with up to one year in jail or a $500 fine, or possibly both. The article was passed in its entirety on March 22, 1955, by a unanimous vote of the state assembly. It was then signed into law by Governor Averell Harriman on May 2, amending New York State penal law and taking effect July 1, 1955.[81]

The new law was a paralyzing blow to the comic book industry. According to David Hajdu, over eighty comics suddenly became illegal because of their titles alone. Further, the bans on account of "methods of crime" or "physical violence" were potentially applicable to every western, superhero, war, and detective comic on the market. By the end of 1956, the number of comic book titles published in the United States had dropped from about 650 to 250, as state after state followed New York's lead and enacted similarly restrictive legislation.[82] Whether the Brooklyn Thrill-Kill case was a deciding factor for the various state senators and assemblymen who voted for the legislation cannot be determined, but the case was certainly featured prominently in the report of the New York State Joint Legislative Committee and heralded as the one direct, causal example of the degenerative effects of comic books on the nation's children.

Epilogue

In May of 1958, Jack Koslow and Melvin Mittman won their appeals, overturning their convictions and granting them new trials. The money having run out long before, they had exchanged their illustrious counsel for free, court-appointed attorneys. The fundamental appellate issue was that the underlying crime of felony kidnapping, the basis for their first-degree murder convictions, was never successfully proved.[1] Crucial to the appeal was the testimony of Patrolman Harold Neyer, who had reluctantly, on cross-examination, painted a picture of a lively neighborhood, in which several stores, restaurants, and garages were open and packed with customers at the time Menter and the boys would have been walking past. Citing the lack of physical force or violence during the walk, or any threat made with a weapon, the judges in the appellate division of the New York Supreme Court found that the walk with Menter "bears no resemblance to what has always been understood to be kidnapping." In a 3–2 decision, the court determined that Menter's drunkenness was not enough to prove that, had he tried to run away from the defendants, he would have been "detained against his will," and therefore, the conviction was overturned and a new trial ordered. On July 1, 1958, both Mel and Jack pled guilty to charges of manslaughter in the first degree, a felony that carried a term of ten to twenty years in prison. The plea deal included a provision for the three years, four months, and eight days the boys had already served.[2]

While Mel and Jack went to jail and Bobby spent the next several years in a reform school, the wheels of justice would turn differently for Jerry Lieberman. After his acquittal for first-degree murder in the death of Willard Menter, Jerry's old public high school refused to readmit him. Further, the stress of the trial had landed his already fragile mother in an insane asylum. Jerry's father enrolled the boy in a private school, where he "made a fine record" and was subsequently accepted to attend the University of Arizona.

In a faraway place where press coverage of the trial had been minimal, Jerry was able to get a clean start and excel in college.[3]

However, this new life was still under the shadow of the jailhouse. While the charges against Jerry were dismissed in the Willard Menter case, he still faced a manslaughter charge in the death of Rhinehold Ulrickson. Unlike the other boys, Jerry's attorney, James D. C. Murray, stood by his client, continuing on with Jerry's defense at a highly reduced rate. As Murray told the court, "Knowing this boy Lieberman, as I know him now, this case is very close and dear to my heart."[4] On February 24, 1956, Judge Hyman Barshay dismissed the charge of manslaughter in the second degree against Jerry, citing lack of evidence that a conspiracy existed between Jerry and Mel to kill Ulrickson. Barshay further admonished the district attorney for trying to prove a tenuous conspiracy theory rather than having pursued a simple assault charge for the one crime Jerry did actually commit: slapping John Perrett.

The district attorney's office quickly appealed the dismissal. After the appellate division of the New York Supreme Court upheld Barshay's decision, the district attorney took the case up to the New York Court of Appeals, which found that "the defendant not only set out with the others to 'beat up tramps and vagrants' but that he participated in such beatings and made no effort to withdraw prior to the assault upon Ulrickson."[5] On January 24, 1958, the charges against Jerome Lieberman were reinstated.

The case being kicked back to Judge Hyman Barshay, who had dismissed the charges outright two years earlier, James D. C. Murray shrewdly asked for a bench trial.[6] Jerry returned for the trial from Arizona, where he had just graduated from college with honors and was planning to attend law school in the fall.[7] After only two days of testimony from prosecution witnesses, Barshay granted the defense motion for acquittal, finding Jerry not guilty of manslaughter and closing the case permanently.[8]

*   *   *

On June 13, 1955, Judge Matthew M. Levy of the New York Supreme Court rendered his decision in the corporation counsel's case against Kingsley Books et al. for distributing obscene materials. Opining that "Sex relationships can be and normally are beautiful, profound, inspiring and healthy," the judge held that *Nights of Horror* "was the perfect example" of what the legislature was seeking to curb. After explicitly cataloguing the numerous gruesome tortures illustrated in the work, Levy was particularly disgusted at *Nights of Horror*'s valorization of torture, rape and misogyny:

> The volumes expressed a philosophy of man's omnipotent physical power over the female of the species. On occasion, the young woman is said to have gained satisfaction from the brutal beatings and horrible tortures. If she did not enjoy them, she received the beatings and tortures anyway—until she submitted to

the sex acts desired by her tormentor. These brutalities were "my supreme pleasure" to the male, and resulted in "I'll be your slave" to the female.[9]

Acknowledging that he did not "consider censorship generally in the best
public interest," Levy found in favor of the corporation counsel, effectively
banning *Nights of Horror.* Describing the publication as "dirt for dirt's sake,"
the judge made it clear that had the work "indicated the slightest effort
to contribute to our culture or knowledge" he would have gladly "[held]
my nose with one hand" while "upholding with the other the right of free
speech."[10]

Upheld in a unanimous decision by the New York Court of Appeals, the
case was quickly taken up by the U.S. Supreme Court in 1957. By this point,
the lawyers for the booksellers had conceded the obscenity of *Nights of Horror* and instead challenged the constitutionality of the statute under the Due
Process Clause of the Fourteenth Amendment. Pointing out that the Constitution protects the distribution as well as the publication of printed materials,
Emanuel Redfield argued that the New York statute violated the booksellers'
rights by not allowing for a criminal trial before imposing an injunction and
destroying the obscene materials and that the statute effectively constituted
"prior restraint." The majority opinion, written by Justice Frankfurter, found
that "prior restraint" did not apply in this case as the injunction did not
"enjoin the dissemination of future issues of [*Nights of Horror*] because its
past issues had been found offensive." Adding that it was the future restriction that the Court considered "the essence of censorship," the U.S. Supreme
Court upheld both the New York statute and the lower courts' decision.

*   *   *

Like most trials notorious in their day, the case of the Brooklyn Thrill-Killers quickly faded in the public memory.[11] By 1958, when Mel and Jack won
their appeals, not even the local newspaper—the *Brooklyn Daily Eagle*—could
be bothered to report on it. Only a small, Associated Press blurb appeared
in a handful of upstate New York newspapers on May 20, 1958, announcing
that Koslow and Mittman had been granted new trials.[12] There is a decided
irony to the media silence: his dramatics notwithstanding, Fred Moritt was
right in asserting that the charges against the four boys were trumped up and
that the inherent media attention had prevented a fair trial. As law professor Abraham Abramovsky astutely notes, in sensationalized cases, "plea bar-
gaining is out, maximum penalties are in."[13] Such was certainly the case for
the Brooklyn Thrill-Killers. In a media-saturated environment, manslaughter
became murder, reformatories the electric chair. Of the four boys, the case
of Jerome Lieberman probably exemplifies this point the best: although on
trial for his life, the only actual crime Jerry had committed was slapping John
Perrett.[14]

Notes

ABBREVIATIONS

BE—*Brooklyn Daily Eagle*

DN—*New York Daily News*

Ex. G—*People of the State of New York v. Jack Koslow, Melvin Mittman* (N.Y. App. Div. 1958) (Ex. G)

Interview notes—Interview notes, interview with Jack Koslow, December 3 and 4, 1954, Fredric Wertham papers, box 22, folder 11, Library of Congress

Juvenile Delinquency Hearings—*Juvenile Delinquency (National, Federal, and Youth-Serving Agencies): Hearings before the Subcommittee to Investigate Juvenile Delinquency of the Committee on the Judiciary United States Senate, Eighty-third Congress, First Session, Pursuant to S. Res. 89 Investigation of Juvenile Delinquency in the United States.*

NYDM—*New York Daily Mirror*

NYHT—*New York Herald-Tribune*

NYJA—*New York Journal American*

NYSLC, transcript—The New York State Legislative Committee to Study the Publication of Comic Books, *Transcript of the Proceedings* (New York: Municipal Stenographic Service, 1955) in *Senate Judiciary Committee: Subcommittee to Investigate Juvenile Delinquency, 1953–61*, the National Archives, box 211, "Comic Books."

NYT—*The New York Times*

NYWT—*New York World-Telegram and Sun*

People v. Koslow—*People of the State of New York v. Jack Koslow, Melvin Mittman* (N.Y. App. Div. 1958)

People v. Mittman—*People of the State of New York v. Melvin Mittman and Jerome Lieberman* (N.Y. App. Div. 1958)

Wertham papers—Fredric Wertham papers, box 22, folders 8, 11, Library of Congress

WNY—Western New York Historical Newspapers Database

INTRODUCTION

1. *Hearings before the Subcommittee to Investigate Juvenile Delinquency of the Committee on the Judiciary United States Senate, 83rd Congress, 2nd Session Pursuant to S. 190, April 21, 22, and June 4, 1954* (Washington DC: United States Government Printing Office, 1954), 103.

2. For a history of the progressive-era ideologies on children and criminality that resulted in the creation of the juvenile court system in the United States, see David S. Tanenhaus, *Juvenile Justice in the Making* (Oxford: Oxford University Press, 2004); Elizabeth J. Clapp, *Mothers of All Children: Women Reformers and the Rise of Juvenile Courts in Progressive Era America* (University Park, PA: The Pennsylvania State University Press, 1998); and Ellen Ryerson, *The Best Laid Plans: America's Juvenile Court Experiment* (New York: Hill and Wang, 1978).

3. "Tabs Horror Comics Thrill-Kill Blueprint," *Brooklyn Daily Eagle* (hereafter, *BE*), Aug. 23, 1954, Western New York Historical Newspapers (hereafter, *WNY*); Testimony of Dr. Fredric Wertham, in the New York State Legislative Committee to Study the Publication of Comic Books, *Transcript of the Proceedings* (New York: Municipal Stenographic Service, 1955), in *Senate Judiciary Committee: Subcommittee to Investigate Juvenile Delinquency, 1953–61*, the National Archives, box 211, "Comic Books" (hereafter, NYSLC, transcript); Edith C. Jackson, "2 Thrill Killers Steeped in Horror Books," *New York World-Telegram* (hereafter, *NYWT*), Dec. 15, 1954, Fredric Wertham papers, box 22, folder 11, Library of Congress (hereafter, Wertham papers).

4. Peter N. Stearns, *Anxious Parents: A History of Modern Childrearing in America* (New York: New York University Press, 2003).

5. Similarly, historian James A. Gilbert, in his groundbreaking work *A Cycle of Outrage*, posits that the midcentury obsession with juvenile delinquency was merely an overreaction to decreased parental control over emerging youth cultures. See David Hajdu, *The Ten-Cent Plague: The Great Comic-Book Scare and How It Changed America* (New York: Farrar, Straus and Giroux, 2008); Jim Trombetta, *The Horror! The Horror! Comic Books the Government Didn't Want You to Read* (New York: Abrams, 2010); Craig Yoe, *Secret Identity: The Fetish Art of Superman's Co-creator Joe Shuster* (New York: Abrams, 2009). In the historiography of comic books, the comic book industry is often portrayed as a group of embattled, beleaguered artists suffering under McCarthyist rule, rather than as the capitalist endeavor they ultimately were.

6. I am using the term "moral panic" here within its sociological definition, originally introduced by Jock Young (1971, 1973) and Stanley Cohen (1971, 1973), who explored how agents of social control often "amplified" deviance, as well as how the media was both complicit in the amplification as well as providing a type of handbook for new deviants. See Stanley Cohen, ed., *Images of Deviance* (Harmondsworth: Penguin, 1971); Stanley Cohen and Jock Young, eds., *The Manufacture of the News: Deviance, Social Problems and the Mass Media* (London: Constable, 1973); Jock Young, *The Drugtakers: The Social Meaning of Drug Use* (London: Palladin, 1971). For an essay on the history of the sociological theory of moral panics, see Angela McRobbie and Sarah L. Thornton, "Rethinking 'Moral Panic' for Multi-mediated Social Worlds," *The British Journal of Sociology* 46, no. 4 (1995): 559–574. There is debate within the field of "moral panic" studies as to whether the term has become so flexible that it now "lacks any precise theoretical grounding" (Munice, 1987). David

Miller and Jenny Kitzinger observed that the term has been overly applied to issues ranging from single mothers to guns to pornography to government censorship, and several sociologists (including Hier, Jewkes, and Thompson) have argued that it is often used indiscriminately by journalists to describe a large variety of social reactions. See John Munice, "Much Ado about Nothing? The Sociology of Moral Panics," *Social Studies Review* 3, no. 2 (1987): 42–46; David Miller and Jenny Kitzinger "AIDS, the Policy Process and Moral Panics," in *The Circuit of Mass Communication: Media Strategies, Representation and Audience Reception on the AIDS Crisis*, Miller, et al., eds. (London: Sage Publications, 1998) 213–222; Sean Hier, "Raves, Risks and the Ecstasy Panic: A Case Study in the Subversive Nature of Moral Regulation," *Canadian Journal of Sociology* 27, no. 1 (2002): 33–57; Yvonne Jewkes, *Media and Crime* (London: Sage Publications, 2004); and Kenneth Thompson, *Moral Panics* (New York: Routledge, 1998). As further noted by Cohen, "Cases where the moral outrage appears driven by conservative or reactionary forces . . . [where] the point [of research] was to expose social reaction not just as over-reaction . . . [but also as] *tendentious* (that is, slanted in a particular ideological direction) and . . . as *misplaced* or *displaced* (that is, aimed—whether deliberately or thoughtlessly—at a target which was not the 'real' problem)." See S. Cohen, *Folk Devils and Moral Panics: The Creation of the Mods and Rockers* (3rd ed.) (London: Routledge, 2002). Citation from A. Rohloff and S. Wright, "Moral Panic and Social Theory: Beyond the Heuristic," *Current Sociology* 58, no. 3 (2010): 403–419.

7. Sean P. Hier, "Tightening the Focus: Moral Panic, Moral Regulation and Liberal Government," *The British Journal of Sociology* 62, no. 3 (2011), 524; A. Rohloff and S. Wright, "Moral Panic and Social Theory: Beyond the Heuristic," 403–419; Sean P. Hier, "Conceptualizing Moral Panic through a Moral Economy of Harm," *Critical Sociology* 28, no. 3 (2002), 311–334; and Sean P. Hier, "Thinking beyond Moral Panic: Risk, Responsibility, and the Politics of Moralization," *Theoretical Criminology* 12, no. 2 (2008), 173–190.

8. Joel Best, *Random Violence: How We Talk about New Crimes and New Victims* (Berkeley: University of California Press, 1999).

CHAPTER 1

1. "Soggy Weather to Lift for Cooler Front Today," *New York Times* (New York) (hereafter, *NYT*), August 17, 1954; "Weather throughout the Nation," *NYT*, Aug. 17, 1954; and Edward De Blasio, "Boy Hitler of Flatbush Ave," *Inside Detective Magazine*, November 1954, 35.

2. Testimony of Robert Trachtenberg, *People of the State of New York v. Jack Koslow, Melvin Mittman* (N.Y. App. Div. 1958) (tr. at 685) (hereafter, *People v. Koslow*).

3. "Thrill-Killers' Victim Found in East River," *New York Journal American* (New York) (hereafter, *NYJA*), Aug. 19, 1954, reproduced in *People v. Koslow* (N.Y. App. Div. 1958) (Ex. G.) (hereafter, Ex. G); and "Teen-age Killers Pose a Mystery," *New York Herald Tribune* (New York) (hereafter, *NYHT*), Aug. 19, 1954, in Wertham papers.

4. The basket weaver's name was Joseph Kostyra, and the homeless man accosted on August 4 was Eddie Walsh. Harold Phelan and Sid Frigand, "Believe Body Found in River Teen Thrill Killers' Victim," *BE*, Aug. 19, 1954, final edition, *WNY*; "Vagrant Is Witness in Teen Thrill Case," *NYT*, Sept. 3, 1954; and Robert Jones and

Wilfred Alexander, "Mental Tests Ordered for Thrill Killers," *New York Daily Mirror* (hereafter, *NYDM*) Aug. 19, 1954, Ex. G.; and notes, Wertham papers. Photos of Joseph Kostyra's injuries ran in the *Daily News* (New York) (Aug. 19, 1954); the *New York Times* (Aug. 19, 1954); and the *New York Herald Tribune* (Aug. 19, 1954). The images were taken fourteen days after the assault had allegedly occurred.

5. Charlotte Herzog, "The Movie Palace and the Theatrical Sources of Its Architectural Style," *Cinema Journal* 20, no. 2 (April 1, 1981): 15–37. Images of The Republic were accessed on October 25, 2012, at http://cinematreasures.org/theaters/3971/photos/54946.

6. Bosley Crowther, "'Gorilla at Large' Is on View at Globe," *NYT*, June 12, 1954; grand jury testimony of Detective Casimir Czarnowski, *People of the State of New York v. Melvin Mittman and Jerome Lieberman* (N.Y. App. Div. 1958) (tr. at 51) (hereafter, *People v. Mittman*); and statement of Robert Trachtenberg, *People v. Koslow* (Ex. 23).

7. "Portraits of 4 Boys in Terrorist Orgy," *NYWT*, Aug. 18, 1954, Ex. G; grand jury testimony of Detective Casimir Czarnowski, *People v. Mittman* (tr. at 51); and statement of Robert Trachtenberg, *People v. Koslow* (Ex. 23).

8. St. Paul's Evangelical Lutheran Church, Sunday School and Parsonage, Landmarks Preservation Commission, April 12, 2011 (Designation List 441 LP-2418), accessed on October 25, 2012, www.nyc.gov/html/lpc/downloads/pdf/reports/2418.pdf.

9. "Rodney Park Center," City of New York Parks and Recreation, www.nycgovparks.org/parks/B223P01/history, accessed October 25, 2012; grand jury testimony of Detective Casimir Czarnowski, *People v. Mittman* (tr. at 51); and grand jury testimony of John Perrett, *People v. Mittman* (tr. at 38).

10. Affidavit of Raymond E. Duggan, Kings County District Attorney's Case Files, New York Municipal Archives, Indictment 1916/1954; "Portraits of 4 Boys in Terrorist Orgy"; grand jury testimony of Detective Casimir Czarnowski, *People v. Mittman* (tr. at 51); statement of Robert Trachtenberg, *People v. Koslow* (Ex. 23); grand jury testimony of John Perrett, *People v. Mittman* (tr. at 38); and Edwin Ross and Henry Lee, "Barge Skipper at Thrill Quiz; May Have Seen River Killing," Ex. G.

11. Grand jury testimony of Detective Casimir Czarnowski, *People v. Mittman* (tr. at 51); statement of Robert Trachtenberg, *People v. Koslow* (Ex. 23); grand jury testimony of John Perrett, *People v. Mittman* (tr. at 38); grand jury testimony of Dr. George W. Ruger, *People v. Mittman* (tr. at 70); and Edward De Blasio "Boy Hitler of Flatbush Ave."

12. Grand jury testimony of Detective Casimir Czarnowski, *People v. Mittman* (tr. at 51); statement of Robert Trachtenberg, *People v. Koslow* (Ex. 23); and grand jury testimony of John Perrett, *People v. Mittman* (tr. at 38).

13. Ibid.

14. Colloquy, *People v. Koslow* (tr. at 1406).

15. Statement of Jerome Lieberman, *People v. Koslow* (Ex. 28).

16. *People v. Koslow* (Ex. 4, 21).

17. Colloquy, *People v. Koslow* (tr. at 469).

18. "McCarren Park," City of New York Parks and Recreation, www.nycgovparks.org/parks/mccarrenpark/history, accessed November 6, 2012.

19. Notes, Wertham papers.

20. Edward De Blasio, "Boy Hitler of Flatbush Ave."; notes, Wertham papers; and statement of Jack Koslow, *People v. Koslow* (Ex. 26).

21. Fred Espenak, "Six Millennium Catalog of Phases of the Moon," NASA/ GSFC, http://eclipse.gsfc.nasa.gov/phase/phases1901.html, accessed November 18, 2012.

22. Testimony of Charles Menter and testimony of Robert Trachtenberg, *People v. Koslow* (tr. at 752, 2054); statement of Robert Trachtenberg, *People v. Koslow* (Ex. 23); statement of Jack Koslow, *People v. Koslow* (Ex. 26); and statement of Jerome Lieberman, *People v. Koslow* (Ex. 28). The boys later expressed uncertainty about whether the men at the first bench were playing checkers or chess.

23. Testimony of Robert Trachtenberg, *People v. Koslow* (tr. at 2171); and Owen Fitzgerald and Sid Frigand, "Teen Thrill Killers Seized," *BE*, Aug. 18, 1954, final edition, *WNY*.

24. Testimony of Robert Trachtenberg, *People v. Koslow* (tr. at 2171); and Marya Mannes, "The Night of Horror in Brooklyn," *The Reporter*, Jan. 1955. There is some confusion as to whether it was Jack Koslow who gave the command (according to Robert Trachtenberg's testimony) or Melvin Mittman (according to Jack Koslow's statement).

25. Testimony of Robert Trachtenberg, *People v. Koslow* (tr. at 2192).

26. Ibid. (tr. at 780).

27. Ibid.

28. "Portraits of 4 Boys in Terrorist Orgy"; Phelan and Frigand, "Believe Body Found in River"; and autopsy report, *People v. Koslow* (Ex. 3).

29. *People v. Koslow* (Ex. 8, 9, and 10); National Register of Historic Places— Inventory Nomination Form: Williamsburgh Savings Bank, United States Department of the Interior Heritage Conservation and Recreation Service, www.oprhp.state. ny.us/hpimaging/hp_view.asp?GroupView=3077, accessed November 13, 2012; statement of Jack Koslow, *People v. Koslow* (Ex. 29); and notes, Wertham papers.

30. See Isabel Wilkerson, *The Warmth of Other Suns: The Epic Story of America's Great Migration* (New York: Random House, 2010); Alferdteen Harrison, ed., *Black Exodus: The Great Migration from the American South* (Jackson, MS: University Press of Mississippi, 1991); and James N. Gregory, *The Southern Diaspora: How the Great Migrations of Black and White Southerners Transformed America* (Chapel Hill, NC: University of North Carolina Press, 2005).

31. Blowing machines were specialized equipment used by secondhand burlap bag dealers to clean and sanitize the bags so they could be reused or resold. Testimony of Raymond E. Duggan, *People v. Koslow* (tr. at 1742).

32. Virginia Parks, "Revisiting Shibboleths of Race and Urban Economy: Black Employment in Manufacturing and the Public Sector Compared, Chicago 1950– 2000," *International Journal of Urban & Regional Research* 35, no. 1 (2011): 110– 129; Michael B. Katz, Mark J. Stern, and Jamie J. Fader, "The New African American Inequality," *The Journal of American History* 92, no. 1 (June 2005): 75–108; "Insanity Plea Set for 'Brains' of Mob," *BE*, Aug. 20, 1954, final edition, *WNY*; "Thrill-Killer Victim's"; Edwin Ross and Neal Patterson, "Indict, Arraign the 4; There's No Thrill in It," *Daily News* (New York) (hereafter, *DN*), Aug. 27, 1954 (Ex. G.); Milton Bracker, "Teen-age Killers Identify Body of 2d Victim, Taken from River," *NYT*, Aug. 20, 1954; and testimony of Emma Menter and testimony of Charles Menter, *People v. Koslow*.

33. Testimony of Emma Menter, testimony of Charles Menter, and testimony of Joe Manson, *People v. Koslow*; Bracker, "Teen-age Killers Identify Body."

34. Although the employment rate had declined from a high of 4,500 workers in 1919, it was still one of the largest employers in the area with 1,500 workers in 1959. "Havemeyers & Elder Filter, Pan & Finishing House," Landmarks Preservation Commission Report, September 25, 2007, www.nyc.gov/html/lpc/downloads/pdf/reports/domino.pdf, accessed December 6, 2012; George Kranzler, *Williamsburg: A Jewish Community in Transition: A Study of the Factors and Patterns of Change in the Organization and Structure of a Community in Transition* (New York: Philipp Feldheim, Inc., 1961); and Elliot Willensky, *When Brooklyn Was the World, 1920–1957* (New York: Harmony Books, 1986).

35. Testimony of Robert Trachtenberg, *People v. Koslow* (tr. at 2206); and photographs of view looking down South Fifth Street across Kent Avenue, *People v. Koslow* (Ex. 2 and 2A). Today, the sanitation building located at 17 South Sixth Street is used by the New York City Department of Transportation.

36. The Yiddish has been rewritten here to conform to the YIVO standard of Yiddish transliteration. The original transliteration in the trial transcript was "Villst Kloppen?"

37. Statement of Jack Koslow, *People v. Koslow* (Ex. 26); and testimony of Robert Trachtenberg, *People v. Koslow* (tr. at 2214).

38. Testimony of Robert Trachtenberg, *People v. Koslow* (tr. at 2214); Trachtenberg statement, *People v. Koslow* (Ex. 22); Lieberman statement, *People v. Koslow* (Ex. 28); Koslow statement, *People v. Koslow* (Ex. 26); and Mittman statement, *People v. Koslow* (Ex. 27).

39. Testimony of Robert Trachtenberg, *People v. Koslow* (tr. at 2214); Trachtenberg statement, *People v. Koslow* (Ex. 22); Lieberman statement, *People v. Koslow* (Ex. 28); Koslow statement, *People v. Koslow* (Ex. 26); and Mittman statement, *People v. Koslow* (Ex. 27).

40. "Sobel Playground," City of New York Parks and Recreation, www.nyc-govparks.org/parks/sobelplayground, accessed November 15, 2012; testimony of Detective John Burke, *People v. Koslow*; Fitzgerald and Frigand, "Teen Thrill Killers Seized"; Norton Mockridge, "Teen Thrill Slayers Baffle Judges and Sicken Officials," *NYWT*, Aug. 18, 1954, Ex. G.; "National Affairs: Senseless," *Time Magazine*, August 30, 1954; and notes, Wertham papers.

CHAPTER 2

1. While the northernmost border was mostly Broadway, parts of Jewish Williamsburg extended as far north as South Second Street. George Kranzler, *Williamsburg: A Jewish Community in Transition: A Study of the Factors and Patterns of Change in the Organization and Structure of a Community in Transition.* (New York: Philipp Feldheim, Inc., 1961), 14.

2. Ibid., 16.

3. Sharon Reier, *The Bridges of New York* (New York: Quadrant Press, 1977); Donald C. Jackson, *Great American Bridges and Dams* (Washington DC: Preservation Press–John Wiley and Sons, 1988); Henry Petroski, *Engineers of Dreams: Great Bridge Builders and the Spanning of America* (New York: Vintage Books–Random

House, 1995); Kranzler, 17; Jenna Weissman Joselit, *New York's Jewish Jews: The Orthodox Community in the Interwar Years* (Bloomington: Indiana University Press, 1990); and Samuel Abelow, *History of Brooklyn Jewry* (Brooklyn: Scheba Publishing Co., 1937). According to Abelow, "The migration of Jews into Williamsburg and Greenpoint was not received gracefully by the old settlers. The bearded Jew who ventured far from his home, was not certain of returning without scars on his face made by rowdies. Nor was the unbearded Jew safe . . . the increasing number of Jews and their readiness to give blow for blow cowed the hooligans." (Quoted in Kranzler, 17).

4. Kranzler, 18.

5. Ibid.

6. Ibid., 19–20; Philip Fishman, *A Sukkah Is Burning: Remembering Williamsburg's Hasidic Transformation* (Minneapolis: Mill City Press, 2012).

7. Philip Fishman, *x*, 52; Menachem Daum and Oren Rudavsky, "Interview with Arthur Hertzberg," "Interview with Yaffa Eliach," and "Interview with Mayer Horowitz," *A Life Apart: Hasidism in America* (New York: First Run Features, 2001).

8. Menachem Daum and Oren Rudavsky, "Interview with Samuel Heilman," *A Life Apart: Hasidism in America* (New York: First Run Features, 2001); "Brooklyn-Queens Expressway," *South Williamsburg Project*, http://southwilliamsburgproject.weebly.com/brooklyn-queens-expressway.html, accessed January 12, 2013.

9. This is surmised from the fact that, in the 1930 census, he was listed as emigrating from Poland, while in the 1940 census he was listed as emigrating from Austria, making it likely he originated from southwestern Poland, which was controlled by Austria after the First Partition in the late eighteenth century.

10. *U.S. Census of Population and Housing, 1930*, accessed through Ancestry.com on December 27, 2012; *U.S. Census of Population and Housing, 1940*, accessed through http://1940census.archives.gov/ on December 27, 2012; deposition for bail for Harry Lieberman, Kings County district attorney's case files, New York Municipal Archives, indictment no. 1916/1954.

11. Norton Mockridge, "Teen Thrill Slayers Baffle Judges and Sicken Officials," *NYWT*, August 18, 1954, Ex. G.

12. Dovid Liberzon, "What the Parents of the Four Young Criminals Tell about Them," *Forverts*, Aug. 25, 1954.

13. Edwin Ross and Henry Lee, "More 'Fun': Boys Drenched Man with Gas, Set Him Afire," *DN*, August 19, 1954, Ex. G; "Portraits of 4 Boys in Terrorist Orgy," *NYWT*, Aug. 18, 1954, Ex. G; James O'Connor and Joseph Carter, "A Puny 'Super-Boy,' Killer-Pack's Chief," *DM*, Aug. 19, 1954, Ex. G; Murray Schumach, "Case Study Finds All Were Bookish," *NYT*, Aug. 19, 1954; and Liberzon, "What the Parents."

14. O'Connor and Carter, "A Puny 'Super-Boy.'"

15. Liberzon, "What the Parents."

16. Ibid. Other sources used for the biographical section on Jerome Lieberman include: Ross and Lee, "More 'Fun'"; Owen Fitzgerald and Sid Frigand, "Teen Thrill Killers Seized," *BE*, Aug. 18, 1954, final edition, *WNY*; "Police Ask Aid to Find Victims of Thrill Killers," *NYJA*, August 18, 1954, Ex. G; I. Kaufman, "Parents Are Stunned by Youths' Arrest in Torture Murders," *BE*, final edition, Aug. 18, 1954, *WNY*; Mockridge, "Teen Thrill Slayers Baffle"; and Harold Wolfson, "Koslow Showed Sadistic Streak, Neighbors Reveal," *NYJA*, Aug. 20, 1954, Ex. G.

17. *U.S. Census of Population and Housing, 1930,* accessed through Ancestry.com on December 27, 2012; and *U.S. Census of Population and Housing, 1940,* accessed through http://1940census.archives.gov on December 27, 2012. "Portraits of 4 Boys in Terrorist Orgy."

18. Fitzgerald and Frigand, "Teen Thrill Killers Seized."

19. Liberzon, "What the Parents."

20. "Portraits of 4 Boys in Terrorist Orgy"; Liberzon, "What the Parents"; Ross and Lee, "More 'Fun.'"

21. Liberzon, "What the Parents."

22. Ibid.

23. Schumach, "Case Study Finds."

24. Mockridge, "Teen Thrill Slayers Baffle."

25. "Portraits of 4 Boys in Terrorist Orgy."

26. Emanuel Perlmutter, "Court Debate," *NYT,* Aug. 19, 1954.

27. Liberzon, "What the Parents."

28. Other sources on the biography of Robert Trachtenberg include: "Police Ask Aid"; Kaufman, "Parents Are Stunned"; O'Connor and Carter, "A Puny 'Super-Boy'"; Perlmutter, "Court Debate"; and Wolfson, "Koslow Showed Sadistic Streak."

29. Wolfson, "Koslow Showed Sadistic Streak"; and Fitzgerald and Frigand, "Teen Thrill Killers Seized."

30. *U.S. Census of Population and Housing, 1930,* accessed through Ancestry.com on December 27, 2012; *U.S. Census of Population and Housing, 1940,* accessed through http://1940census.archives.gov/ on December 27, 2012; O'Connor and Carter, "A Puny 'Super-Boy'"; and "Teen-age Killers Pose a Mystery."

31. Ross and Lee, "More 'Fun'"; Liberzon, "What the Parents"; and "Portraits of 4 Boys in Terrorist Orgy."

32. Liberzon, "What the Parents"; and Harold Smith, "7 More Tell Jury of Thrill Killings," *BE,* Aug. 24, 1954, final edition, *WNY.*

33. Liberzon, "What the Parents."

34. "Portraits of 4 Boys in Terrorist Orgy."

35. Ibid.

36. Wolfson, "Koslow Showed Sadistic Streak."

37. O'Connor and Carter, "A Puny 'Super-Boy.'"

38. "Portraits of 4 Boys in Terrorist Orgy"; other sources for Melvin Mittman's biographical background include: "Police Ask Aid"; Kaufman, "Parents Are Stunned"; Perlmutter, "Court Debate"; Ross and Lee, "More 'Fun'"; Mockridge, "Teen Thrill Slayers Baffle"; and Schumach, "Case Study Finds."

39. Sig Arno was a well-known German Jewish film and theater actor who appeared in over 140 films between 1915 and 1961. His most famous role was as Toto in *The Palm Beach Story* (1942), and he was nominated for a Tony Award in 1958 for his starring role in the Jean Anoulih play *Time Remembered.*

40. O'Connor and Carter, "A Puny 'Super-Boy.'"

41. *Census of Population and Housing, 1940,* accessed through http://1940census.archives.gov on December 27, 2012; Elizabeth Toomey, "What Did I Do Wrong? Mother Sobs," *NYWT,* Aug. 20, 1954, Ex. G., also run in the *Brooklyn Daily Eagle* under the same title (*BE,* Aug. 20, 1954, final edition, *WNY*). Excerpts from the Toomey interview were reprinted by the *Daily Mirror* in an article by Fred Zepp, "Where Did We Fail, Cry Parents of 4" *DM,* Aug. 21, 1954, Ex. G.

42. All quotes attributed to Jack Koslow in this section are transcribed from the notes written by Dr. Fredric Wertham in his psychiatric interviews with Koslow at the Raymond Street Jail on December 3 and 4, 1954 (hereafter, interview notes). Wertham papers.

43. Toomey, "What Did I Do Wrong?"

44. Wertham, interview notes.

45. Ibid.

46. Wolfson, "Koslow Showed Sadistic Streak."

47. Edwin Ross and Henry Lee, "Barge Skipper at Thrill Quiz; May Have Seen River Killing," Aug. 25, 1954, Ex. G.

48. Wolfson, "Koslow Showed Sadistic Streak."

49. Milton Bracker, "Boy Killer Insane His Counsel Says," *NYT*, Aug. 21, 1954, Wertham papers; and John Feeney and Joseph Carter, "Thrill Slayer Told All After 'Deal' over Girl," *DM*, Aug. 22, 1954, Ex. G.; Wertham, interview notes.

50. Nathan Kanter and Harry Schlegel, "Thrill Boss Psycho as Child," *DN*, Aug. 23, 1954, reproduced in *People v. Koslow*, Ex. G.; and "Koslow, at 7, Was Psychiatric Case," *NYT*, Aug. 23, 1954, Wertham papers.

51. Wertham, interview notes.

52. Toomey, "What Did I Do Wrong?"

53. Wertham, interview notes.

54. Toomey, "What Did I Do Wrong?"

55. Wertham, interview notes.

56. William Longgood, "Thrill-Killer Once Described as Normal by Psychiatrist," *NYWT*, Aug. 20, 1954, Ex. G; "Crime Boys Love Books and Music," *NYT*, Aug. 19, 1954, Wertham papers; Bracker, "Boy Killer Insane His Counsel Says"; and Wertham, interview notes.

57. Wertham, interview notes.

58. Longgood, "Thrill-Killer Once Described as Normal"; and Wertham, interview notes.

59. Wertham, interview notes.

60. Notes from telephone call with Morris Einstein, November 29, 1954, Wertham papers.

61. Wertham, interview notes; and Longgood, "Thrill-Killer Once Described as Normal." Although this will be dealt with more fully in a subsequent chapter, it is important to note that schizophrenia in the 1950s was the product of "widespread conceptual instability" and that there were a variety of competing professional definitions of what exactly constituted dementia praecox and schizophrenia (see Kieran McNally, "Definitions of Schizophrenia, 1908–1987: The Failed Essentialism," *Theory & Psychology* 22, no. 1(2012): 91–113). Further complicating the diagnosis, schizoaffecive psychosis, introduced in 1933 by Jacob Kasanin, was used to describe an illness that was "between schizophrenia and manic-depressive psychosis." Gregory Zilboorg identified "ambulatory schizophrenia" to describe "odd thoughts, unstable interpersonal relationships, and variable life pursuits among schizophrenics," while the team of Hoch and Polatin coined the term "pseudoneurotic schizophrenia" to describe "free-floating anxiety, multiple neurotic symptoms, and diverse and perverse sexual practices." (See Adityanjee et al., "Dementia Praecox to Schizophrenia: The First 100 Years," *Psychiatry and Clinical Neurosciences* 53 (1999): 437–448.) For a discussion of the shift from dementia praecox to schizophrenia, see Richard Noll,

American Madness: The Rise and Fall of Dementia Praecox (Cambridge, MA: Harvard University Press, 2011). For a feminist interpretation concerning how the diagnosis of schizophrenia in the 1950s was often made along gendered lines, typically when a patient was seen as not being able to adequately fulfill her gender role, see Carol A. B. Warren, *Madwives: Schizophrenic Women in the 1950s* (New Brunswick, NJ: Rutgers University Press, 1987).

62. Wertham, interview notes.

63. Ibid.

64. Ibid.; and "Portraits of 4 Boys in Terrorist Orgy."

65. Wertham, interview notes.

66. Wolfson, "Koslow Showed Sadistic Streak."

67. Bracker, "Boy Killer Insane His Counsel Says"; and David Lieberzohn, "A Telephone Could Have Perhaps Prevented the Entire Criminal Career of the Four Youths," *Forverts*, Aug. 22, 1954.

68. Wertham, interview notes; and Feeney and Carter, "Thrill Slayer Told All."

69. Feeney and Carter, "Thrill Slayer Told All."

70. Wertham, interview notes.

71. Further biographical information on Jack Koslow was obtained from the following sources: "Police Ask Aid"; Ross and Lee, "More 'Fun'"; Fitzgerald and Frigand, "Teen Thrill Killers Seized"; Kaufman, "Parents Are Stunned"; Joseph Carter, "Thrill Murder Chief Insane Two Years," *DM*, Aug. 21, 1954, Ex. G; "Thrill Killers Face Murder Indictments," *BE*, Aug. 18, 1954, final edition, *WNY*; Perlmutter, "Court Debate"; Mockridge, "Teen Thrill Slayers Baffle"; Schumach, "Case Study Finds"; Liberzon, "What the Parents"; "Teen-age Killers Pose a Mystery"; and Smith, "7 More Tell Jury of Thrill Killings."

CHAPTER 3

1. Sid Frigand, "Teen Gangs Battle, Two Passerbys Shot," *BE*, Mar. 21, 1954, final edition, *WNY*; "Adams Wars on Hoods Here," *BE*, Aug. 3, 1954, final edition, *WNY*; "Girl, 15, and Marine Both Face Murder Trial in Tub-slaying," *BE*, Mar. 31, 1954, final edition, *WNY*; "Youth Guilty in Attempt to Kidnap Boy, 7," *BE*, Aug. 4, 1954, final edition, *WNY*; Richard J. Roth, "A Shocked Brooklyn Asks Why," *BE*, July 18, 1954, final edition, *WNY*.

2. James Gilbert, *A Cycle of Outrage: America's Reaction to the Juvenile Delinquent in the 1950s* (New York: Oxford University Press, 1986), 64–66.

3. Acting on motion S. Res. 89, 83d Cong., put forth by Senator Robert C. Hendrickson, R-New Jersey.

4. *Juvenile Delinquency (National, Federal, and Youth-serving Agencies): Hearings Before the Subcommittee to Investigate Juvenile Delinquency of the Committee on the Judiciary United States Senate, Eighty-third Congress, First Session, Pursuant to S. Res. 89 Investigation of Juvenile Delinquency in the United States* (hereafter, *Juvenile Delinquency Hearings*) (New York: Greenwood Press, 1969 [Reprint]), 9, 14, 52. According to Dr. Eliot, "Less densely populated areas of the country seem to be experiencing even sharper increases than 29 percent. . . . It is clear from this that juvenile delinquency is not just a 'big city problem'" (12).

5. Shaw and McKay built on the work of famed sociologists Robert Park and Ernest Burgess, particularly the 1925 work *The City: Suggestions for the Study of Human Nature in the Urban Environment*. Park and Burgess suggested that the city could be studied similarly to an environment found in nature and that many of the same processes of Darwinian evolution were at play in cities as in other ecosystems. In particular, competition for urban resources (such as land) created zones of desirability and created ecological niches where residents shared similar social characteristics.

6. Gilbert, *Cycles of Outrage*, 128–129. An example of the "Chicago School" theories that persisted in the 1950s is found in Solomon Kobrin, "The Conflict of Values in Delinquency Areas," *American Sociological Review* 16, no. 5 (1951): 653–661. Kobrin argues that

> urban areas of high rates of delinquents are characterized by a duality of conduct norms rather than by the dominance of either a conventional or a criminal culture. This hypothesis appears to be useful in explaining the variability of behavior status on the part of boys in delinquency areas; in constructing a typology of delinquency areas based on degrees of integration of opposing value schemes; and in accounting for certain psychological mechanisms involved in the origin and persistence of the subculture of the delinquent boys' gang.

7. Sheldon and Eleanor T. Glueck, *One Thousand Juvenile Delinquents* (Cambridge: Harvard University Press, 1934) chapters 5, 9.

8. Sheldon and Eleanor Glueck, *Delinquents in the Making: Paths to Prevention* (New York: Harper and Row, 1952) chapters 4, 5.

9. While the Gluecks advocated that the affectional relationship and its correlation to delinquency existed irrespective of socioeconomic issues, other authors suggested a parallel between socioeconomic status and the adjustment of adolescents to parents. See Ivan Nye, "Adolescent-Parent Adjustment–Socio-Economic Level as a Variable," *American Sociological Review* 16, no. 3 (1951): 341–349.

10. Glueck, *Delinquents in the Making*, chapter 6; and *Juvenile Delinquency Hearings*, 91.

11. For an exploration of David Riesman's *The Lonely Crowd* and his conception of the crisis of masculinity, see James Gilbert, *Men in the Middle: Searching for Masculinity in the 1950s* (Chicago: University of Chicago Press, 2005), chapter 3, "Lonely Men: David Riesman and Character."

12. William W. Wattenberg and James Balistrieri, "Gang Membership and Juvenile Misconduct," *American Sociological Review* 15, no. 6 (1950): 744–752.

13. *Juvenile Delinquency Hearings*, 94.

14. The phrase "white-collar" delinquency appears to have been used to indicate a class of delinquency that was nonviolent and perpetuated by middle- and upper-class youths.

15. Robert J. Havighurst and Hilda Taba, *Adolescent Character and Personality* (New York: John Wiley & Sons, 1949).

16. William W. Wattenberg and James Balistrieri, "Automobile Theft: A 'Favored-Group' Delinquency," *American Journal of Sociology* 57, no. 6 (1952): 575–579.

17. "Conditions Conducive to Youth Crime," *Congressional Digest* 33, no. 4 (1954): 291, 301.

18. Clara S. Logan, "TV—Are the Industry's Standards Effective?—Con," Harold E. Fellows, "TV—Are the Industry's Standards Effective?—Pro," Dr. Fredric M. Thrasher, "Do the Crime Comic Books Promote Juvenile Delinquency?—Con," Dr. Fredric Wertham, "Do the Crime Comic Books Promote Juvenile Delinquency?—Pro," *Congressional Digest* 33, no. 4 (1954).

19. William Dienstein, "Facts and Fancies about Delinquency," *The Phi Delta Kappan* 35, no. 6 (1954): 227–230. Emphasis is Dienstein's.

20. Ralph B. Spence, "Impact of Education on Juvenile Delinquency," *Journal of Educational Sociology* 24, no. 1 (1950): 3–9.

21. Rachel Devlin, in an article on female delinquency in the postwar period, has argued that community responses to deviancy were fraught with gendered ideology. While sociologists and criminologists concentrated on the delinquency of boys, rebellious girls became the domain of psychoanalysts who argued the young women posed a threat to the Cold War family and, by extension, the social order. Devlin finds that the behavior of delinquent girls was understood as plagued by class-specific problems underlying the father-daughter relationship and was therefore safely "contained" within the matrix of the family. See Rachel Devlin, "Female Juvenile Delinquency and the Problem of Sexual Authority in America, 1945–1965," in *Delinquents and Debutantes: Twentieth-century American Girls' Cultures*, ed. Sherrie A. Inness (New York and London: New York University Press, 1998).

22. "Parental Responsibility Rates More Attention in Crime Wave," *BE*, Feb. 8, 1954, final edition, *WNY*; Richard J. Roth, "McMullen Asks Legislature Probe Youth Crime Wave," *BE*, Feb. 12, 1954, Final edition, *WNY*; and New York (State), *Youth and Delinquency: A Statewide Inquiry by Citizens and Officials of the State of New York. Source Book Report of the Regional Hearings and Statewide Conference of the New York Temporary Commission on Youth and Delinquency* (New York: 1956) accessed through HathiTrust Digital Library, February 28, 2013, permalink http://catalog. hathitrust.org/Record/001135844.

23. "Test Plan to Spot and Treat Potential Child Delinquents," *BE*, Feb. 8, 1954, final edition, *WNY*.

24. "Deluge Dewey with Demands to Ban Switchblades, Cone Urges," *BE*, Feb. 25, 1954, final edition, *WNY*; and "Brooklyn Trial Lawyers Ask All-out Ban on Switchblades," *BE*, Feb. 25, 1954, final edition, *WNY*. The "crisis" of switchblades began with the 1950's *Woman's Home Companion* article "The Toy That Kills" (Jack H. Pollack, "The Toy That Kills," *Women's Home Companion Magazine*, November 1950, 77), which instigated a national campaign to ban the sale and possession of switchblade knives. In New York, the legislation to criminalize switchblades began in 1952 with the legislature barring the sale of the weapon to minors under the age of sixteen.

25. "Mayor Wagner Takes Sound Steps to Curb Teen-age Hoodlumism," *BE*, Mar. 5, 1954, final edition, *WNY*; Al Salerno, "Foes Lash Out at Progressive Education (Third in a Series)," *BE*, Mar. 9, 1954, final edition, *WNY*; and "Says Schools Get Too Much Blame for Youth Crime," *BE*, Mar. 12, 1954, final edition, *WNY*.

26. "Special Schools Urged for Juvenile Delinquents," *BE*, Mar. 10, 1954, final edition, *WNY*.

27. Letter from the New York Teacher's Guild to Mayor Robert Wagner, March 10, 1954, Municipal Archives, box 152, folder 2138.

28. "Parents, Not School or Church, Blamed for Soaring Youth Crimes," *BE*, Mar. 18, 1954, final edition, *WNY*.

29. "Urges City Consulting Service for Parents with Unruly Children," *BE*, Mar. 18, 1954, final edition, *WNY*.

30. "Urges Strong-arm Tactics for Youth," *BE*, Mar. 19, 1954, final edition, *WNY*.

31. "Boro Solons Pledge '55 Zip Gun Drive," *BE*, Mar. 21, 1954, final edition, *WNY*.

32. "Press for Formation of Boro Committee to Battle Delinquency," *BE*, Mar. 23, 1954, final edition, *WNY*; and "Delinquency Study Launched by Women of Youth United," *BE*, Mar. 30, 1954, final edition, *WNY*.

33. Dorothy O'Keefe, "Shelter Takes New Approach to Delinquency" *BE*, Apr. 4, 1954, final edition, *WNY*; "$41,000,000 Drive On Juvenile Crime Studied by Wagner," *BE*, Apr. 5, 1954, final edition, *WNY*.

34. "Civic-minded Citizenry Seen Best Antidote for Delinquency," *BE*, Apr. 8, 1954, final edition, *WNY*.

35. "Urges Stiffer Penalties for Filth Merchants," *BE*, Apr. 12, 1954, final edition, *WNY*; and "Cone Urges Sales KO of Crime Comic Books," *BE*, May 3, 1954, final edition, *WNY*.

36. "Sport, Home Show to Bolster Fight on Delinquency," *BE*, March 21, 1954, final edition, *WNY*.

37. "67 Pct. Council Committee Details Delinquency Plans," *BE*, May 13, 1954, final edition, *WNY*.

38. "Flatbush Panelists Agree: Curbs on Delinquency Must Be Set at Home," *BE*, May 21, 1954, final edition, *WNY*.

39. Irene Corbally Kuhn, "Parents' Failure to Discipline Blamed for Child Delinquency," *BE*, June 21, 1954, final edition, *WNY*.

40. "Teen-age Pair Admits Slaying Boro Executive: His Humming Self Was Provocation," *BE*, July 11, 1954, final edition, *WNY*; Richard J. Roth, "A Shocked Brooklyn Asks Why," *BE*, July 18, 1954, final edition, *WNY*; and "Stomp Murder Trial Resumes Wednesday," *BE*, September 11, 1954, final edition, *WNY*.

41. "Jury Weighs Stomp Verdict," *BE*, Sept. 20, 1954, final edition, *WNY*.

42. "Wants Cops Back on Beat, Using Their Nightsticks," *BE*, July 21, 1954, final edition, *WNY*.

43. "Boro Leaders Vow Parents Must Answer for Hoodlums," *BE*, July 25, 1954, final edition, *WNY*.

44. Ibid.

45. "Tougher Cops, Judges Urged as Key Cures for Young Hoodlums," *BE*, July 30, 1954, final edition, *WNY*.

46. Ibid.

47. "Text of Commissioner Adams' Talk on the City Crime Crisis," *New York Times*, Aug. 2, 1954.

48. Ibid.

49. "Adams Wars on Hoods Here: Coney Island, Downtown Are Targets," *BE*, Aug. 3, 1954, final edition, *WNY*.

50. "Crime Orgy Runs Riot in Boro; Civic Groups Ask Cop Raise," *BE*, Aug. 9, 1954, final edition, *WNY*; Joseph Ingraham, "Adams Asks Paid Overtime to Strengthen Police Force," *New York Times*, Aug. 4, 1954.

51. Remarks by Mayor Robert F. Wagner, "Mayor's Conference," broadcast on WOR-TV, Friday, August 13, 1954, 7:00–7:30 p.m., Wagner Collection, Municipal Archives.

52. Robert Jones and Wilfred Alexander, "Mental Tests Ordered for Thrill Killers," *DM*, Aug. 19, 1954, reproduced in *People v. Koslow* (N.Y. App. Div. 1958) (Ex. G).

CHAPTER 4

1. Trial testimony of Detective Casimir Czarnowski, *People v. Koslow* (tr. at 1317).

2. Ibid.

3. Ibid.

4. Ibid.

5. Ibid.

6. Trial testimony of Detective Raymond E. Duggan, *People v. Koslow* (tr. at 1433).

7. These allegations can be surmised from the cross-examination of Det. Raymond Duggan by Koslow's defense attorney.

8. Trial testimony of Detective Raymond E. Duggan, *People v. Koslow* (tr. at 1433).

9. Ibid.

10. Statement of Jack Koslow, *People v. Koslow*, People's Exhibit 24 (tr. at 2848); "Study in Savagery," photo, *BE*, Aug. 19, 1954, Brooklyn Public Library, Brooklyn Collection; "Remembers It Well," photo, *BE*, Aug. 19, 1954, Brooklyn Public Library, Brooklyn Collection; "Three Adolescent Boys with Assistant District Attorney and Stenographer," photo, *BE*, Aug. 19, 1954, Brooklyn Public Library, Brooklyn Collection; and trial testimony of Arthur Monford, *People v. Koslow*.

11. Ibid.

12. I use the term "girls" here to describe the gang's female victims because it was the term used in the trial transcripts, the press coverage, and Jack's psychiatric interview with Dr. Fredric Wertham, as well as the fact that all of the female victims were under eighteen years of age.

13. Ibid.

14. Ibid.

15. Ibid.

16. Statement of Melvin Mittman, *People v. Koslow*, People's Exhibit 24 (tr. at 2904).

17. Ibid.

18. Ibid.

19. Fifty-three years later, the Brooklyn Psychiatric Center's Williamsburg-Greenpoint Clinic would be renamed the Edward S. Lentol Clinic at a ceremony presided over by his equally civic-minded son, Assemblyman Joseph R. Lentol. Brooklyn Care Works, press release: "Brooklyn Psychiatric Centers Renames Williamsburg-Greenpoint Clinic in Honor of the Late Honorable Edward S. Lentol," www.creativesource.com/BrooklynCareworks/pressreleases/may_24_04.html, accessed March 21, 2013.

20. E. J. Dimock, "Review: Listen to Leaders in Law," *American Bar Association Journal* 49, no. 7 (1963): 679; and Julian Fox, "Brooklyn's Man of the Week: Urges Prevention, Not Punishment," *BE*, Dec. 19, 1954, final edition, *WNY*.

21. Norton Mockridge, "Teen Thrill Slayers Baffle Judges and Sicken Officials," *NYWT*, Aug. 18, 1954, Ex. G; and Julian Fox, "Brooklyn's Man of the Week."

22. Dovid Liberzon, "District Attorney Silver Tells Why They Moved from a House Fifty Years Ago," *Forverts*, Sept. 1, 1954.

23. Fox, "Brooklyn's Man of the Week."

24. Ibid.

25. Mockridge, "Teen Thrill Slayers Baffle."

26. Robert Jones and Wilfred Alexander, "Mental Tests Ordered for Thrill Killers," *DM*, Aug. 19, 1954, Ex. G.

27. Emanuel Perlmutter, "Court Debate," *NYT*, Aug. 19, 1954, Wertham papers; and Mockridge, "Teen Thrill Slayers Baffle."

28. Perlmutter, "Court Debate"; and Mockridge, "Teen Thrill Slayers Baffle."

29. Locally, the case headlined the *New York Journal-American*, the *Brooklyn Daily Eagle*, the *Daily News*, and the *New York World-Telegram*, and it made the front page of the *New York Times*. It was front-page news throughout the state, including newspapers in Amsterdam, Binghamton, Gloversville, Kingston, Auburn, Schenectady, and Utica. And across the country, the case made the front-page as far away as Los Angeles, Boston, and Washington DC.

30. "Storms Cool Off City; Humidity Remains High," *NYT*, Aug. 20, 1954.

31. Trial testimony of Arthur Drucker, *People v. Koslow* (tr. at 2970, 3039).

32. This fact was noted by the trial judge, Hyman Barshay, on application by State Senator Fred G. Moritt for the dismissal of charges against Jack Koslow:

> The Court: . . . I must also tell you now that the law is, and I will charge it to the jury, that under the law of the State of New York, there is no obligation on the part of the District Attorney to advise a defendant that his failure, his refusal or failure to answer questions may not be held against him. . . . The law of the State is that the District Attorney is not required to advise a defendant when he questions him "whatever you say may be used against you." *People v. Koslow* (tr. at 3689–91)

33. Milton Bracker, "Teen-age Killers Identify Body of 2d Victim, Taken from River," *NYT*, Aug. 20, 1954.

34. "Eyes flickered," from Milton Bracker, "Teen-age Killers," and John Ferris, "2d Victim Found in River," *NYWT*, Aug. 19, 1954, Ex. G; "shaking voice," from Bracker, "Teen-age Killers"; "Thrill-Killer's Victim Found in East River," *NYJA*, Aug. 19, 1954, Ex. G; and "he gulped," from John Ferris, "Thrill Victim Found in River," *NYWT*, Aug. 19, 1954, Ex. G.

35. Although this quote was taken by several reporters and published by various newspapers, it mysteriously did not make it into any "official" statements taken by the district attorney's office, a fact that would subsequently be expounded upon at the trial. Bracker, "Teen-age Killers"; John Ferris, "Thrill Victim Found in River"; and "Thrill-Killer's Victim Found in East River."

36. Ferris, "Thrill Victim Found in River"; and Harold Phelan and Sid Frigand, "Believe Body Found in River Teen Thrill-Killers' Victim," *BE*, Aug. 19, 1954, final edition, *WNY*.

37. Bracker, "Teen-age Killers Identify"; Ferris, "Thrill Victim Found in River"; and "Thrill-Killer's Victim Found in East River."

38. Ibid.

39. Ibid.

40. Paul Rice, "A Deed to Haunt Them," photo, *NYJA*, Aug. 19, 1954, Ex. G; "That's Him!," photo, *DM*, Aug. 20, 1954, reproduced in *People v. Koslow* (N.Y. App. Div. 1958) (Ex. J); Stanziola, "Dramatic Scene," photo, *NYWT*, Aug. 19, 1954, reproduced in *People v. Koslow* (N.Y. App. Div. 1958) (Ex. J); and Fox, "Thrill Victim?" photo, *BE*, Aug. 19, 1954, *WNY*.

41. "Kill for Thrill Gang," photo, *BE*, Aug. 18, 1954, *WNY*.

42. "Human Torch," photo, *BE*, Aug. 19, 1954, *WNY*.

43. Mel Finkelstein, "The Finger Points," photo, *NYJA*, Aug. 19, 1954, Ex. G.

44. "Mrs. Voigt Hopes Codarre Pays in the Chair, Says She Will Avoid Trial unless D.A. Calls Her," *Poughkeepsie Journal*, Sept. 10, 1943.

45. "Prosecutor Favors Death for Camp Slayer," *Poughkeepsie Journal*, Aug. 8 1943.

46. "Case Is Completed in Turk Boy's Trial: Prosecution Fails to Ask for Death Penalty—Jury to Be Charged Today," *NYT*, May 7, 1946.

47. "State Liberalizes Child Trial Status: Capital Crimes Action," *NYT*, Mar. 31, 1948. The various groups included the Society for the Prevention of Crime, the State Charities Aid Association, the Prison Association of New York, the District Attorneys Association, the Jewish Board of Guardians, the State Department of Correction, and the State Board of Parole.

48. By an overwhelming majority of 400,000 votes, the amendment was accepted by New York State voters in 1921. New York State Constitutional Convention, Document No. 42 (Albany 1915), 16.

49. Joseph R. Clevenger, *Penal Law and the Code of Criminal Procedure of the State of New York with Amendments Passed by the Legislature to the end of the Regular Session of 1942.* 24th ed. (Albany: Matthew Bender & Company, Inc., 1942), 100.

50. "Governor's Memoranda," *New York State Legislative Annual 1948* (New York: New York Legislative Service, Inc., 1948), 210–11.

51. Ibid.

52. A. P. Dick and A. G. Beckett, "Some Observations on the Treatment of Ulcerative Colitis with A.C.T.H.," *The British Medical Journal* 2, no. 4884 (1954): 378–383; Franz Alexander, *Psychosomatic Medicine* (New York: Norton, 1950). Alexander argued that a duodenal ulcer was an expression of the conflict between dependent and independent needs and that ulcer patients typically had dependent needs that were repressed, thereby causing a compensatory need for striving and achievement; see also Jurgen Ruesch et al., *Duodenal Ulcer: A Sociopsychological Study of Naval Enlisted Personnel and Civilians* (London: Cambridge University Press, 1950).

53. "Insanity Plea Set for 'Brains' of Mob," *BE*, Aug. 20, 1954, *WNY*; Joseph Carter, "Thrill Murder Chief 'Insane' 2 Years," *DM*, Aug. 21, 1954, Ex. G; Edwin Ross and James Davis, "Thrill-Kill Leader Loses Round in Fight to Escape Chair," *DN*, Aug. 21, 1954, Ex. G; and Harold Smith and I. Kaufman, "'Thrill' Killers Face Murder Indictments," *BE*, Aug. 21, 1954, *WNY*.

54. John Feeney and Joseph Carter, "Thrill Slayer Told All after 'Deal' over Girl," *Sunday Mirror*, Aug. 22, 1954, Ex. G; Sid Frigand, "Koslow Confessed in Deal on 'Fiancée'," *BE*, August 22, 1954, *WNY*; and "Murder Charges Face Teen Killers," *NYT*, Aug. 22, 1954.

55. "Central Courts Brooklyn," New York Citywide Administrative Services webpage, www.nyc.gov/html/dcas/html/about/brook_centralcourt.shtml, accessed April 9, 2013; and personal observation.

56. "Jerry Lieberman Refuses to Speak before the Jury," *Forverts*, Aug. 26, 1954.

57. Ibid.

58. Morris Kaplan, "Top Counsel Hired for Teen Killers," *NYT*, Aug. 26, 1954.

59. Turk was ultimately prosecuted as a juvenile delinquent in the Children's Court because of Murray's skillful legal maneuverings.

60. "Killer of 4 Cited as Neurotic in '46," *NYT*, June 8, 1954; and "Roche Is Indicted in Four Slayings," *NYT*, June 17, 1954.

61. Morris Kaplan, "Top Counsel Hired for Teen Killers," *NYT*, Aug. 26, 1954.

62. "Thrill Killer Balks at Telling on Pals before Grand Jury," *BE*, Aug. 25, 1954, *WNY*; Edwin Ross and Henry Lee, "Report Murder Indictment Voted against Thrill Killers," *DN*, Aug. 26, 1954, Ex. G; and "Reject 'Deal' to Save Thrill-Kid from Chair," *DM*, Aug. 26, 1954, Ex. G.

63. "5-day Heat Wave Here Slated to Boil Up Today," *NYT*, Aug. 25, 1954.

64. Kaplan, "Top Counsel."

65. Edmund Elmaleh, *The Canary Sang but Couldn't Fly : The Fatal Fall of Abe Reles, the Mobster Who Shattered Murder, Inc.'s Code of Silence* (New York: Lewes, 2009).

66. Kaplan, "Top Counsel"; and Ross and Lee, "Report Murder Indictment."

67. Kaplan, "Top Counsel"; "Jury Set to Indict All 4 Thrill-Killers," *BE*, August 26, 1954, *WNY*.

68. Harold Smith and Sid Frigand, "Quartet Charged with First Degree Torture Slaying," *BE*, Aug. 27, 1954, *WNY*; Edwin Ross and Neal Patterson, "Indict, Arraign the 4; There's No Thrill in It," *DN*, Aug. 27, 1954, Ex. G; Stanley Hall, "Not Getting a 'Kick' out of Plight," photo, *DM*, Aug. 27, 1954, Ex. G; Fred Zepp, "4 Killers Indicted, Fight to Beat Chair," *DM*, Aug. 27, 1954, Ex. G; and Milton Hong, "4 Teen-age Killers Are Indicted in First Degree in River Murder," *NYT*, Aug. 27, 1954.

69. Smith and Frigand, "Quartet Charged"; Ross and Patterson, "Indict, Arraign the 4"; Hall, "Not Getting a 'Kick' out of Plight"; Zepp, "4 Killers Indicted"; and Hong, "4 Teen-age Killers."

70. Indictment (tr. at 31–33), *People v. Koslow*.

71. Statement of Melvin Mittman, People's Exhibit 27, *People v. Koslow*.

CHAPTER 5

1. According to the *Forverts*, "Police pursuit of suspicious people in the streets and in the parks of New York began ten days ago, but due to the tragic event with the four boys in Williamsburg . . . police increased the force behind the campaign." "160 Arrested in New York Police Raids," *Forverts*, Aug. 22, 1954.

2. Ralph W. Whelan, "New York City Youth Board Memorandum–Emergency Appropriation," Aug. 23, 1954, Wagner Collection, Municipal Archives.

3. "Boys Clubs," memo, Wagner Collection, Municipal Archives.

4. Remarks by Mayor Robert F. Wagner at Brownsville Boys' Club Annual Dinner, Waldorf Astoria Hotel, Sunday evening, September 19, 1954, Wagner Collection, Municipal Archives.

5. For this chapter, what I refer to as the opinion of the "Jewish Community" is largely gleaned from the Yiddish newspaper the *Forverts*, in particular, the editorial columns and letters from readers to the editor. My decision to rely on this newspaper as a representative of the opinions of the larger Brooklyn Jewish community was because of several factors: first, that the newspaper was published in Yiddish necessarily limited its readership to members of the Jewish community; second, while the newspaper had declined from its heyday when circulation boasted 225,000 subscriptions, it still had a substantial subscription base in the 1950s (circulation in 1962 was 56,126 daily and 59,636 Sunday, according to an article in *Time Magazine* ["The Victim of Success." *Time*, Dec. 28, 1962]); and, third, the paper traditionally held a moderate, democratic-socialist view, appealing to a more modern, assimilationist Jewish audience. See Ehud Manor, *Forward: The Jewish Daily Forward (Forverts) Newspaper: Immigrants, Socialism and Jewish Politics in New York, 1890–1917* (Eastbourne, England: Sussex Academic Press, 2009). A fourth reason was because, as evidenced by the editorials and letters from readers, the newspaper had become a public forum where members of the Jewish community could express their opinions on this particular case. That the *Forverts* sought to provide this type of space for communal interaction can be seen in its incorporation of the regular column "From Folk to Folk," in which readers could both write in on current issues as well as comment on previous letters. All quotes in this chapter and throughout this book that originated in the *Forverts* were translated by Yiddish scholar Ri J. Turner, for whose assistance I am extremely grateful.

6. B. Shepner, "Bad Children and Foolish Parents," *Forverts*, Aug. 24, 1954.

7. Ibid.

8. Ibid.

9. Comments made at the Family Service Association of America convention in Los Angeles. H. Lang, "From Atlantic to Pacific: Happenings and Occurrences," *Forverts*, Sept. 14, 1954.

10. The rate of juvenile delinquency among Jews in this period is very low, only 3 percent of juvenile delinquency petitions while Jews made up 27 percent of the white population under the age of fifteen. There was a significant drop between 1930 and 1952 in the number of juvenile delinquency cases among Jews, with the majority being "wrongful appropriation of property" (43 percent). Jewish children ranked slightly higher in the following categories: (1) auto theft (11 percent compared to 7 percent); (2) ungovernable behavior (20 percent compared to 9 percent); and (3) injury to persons (10 percent in comparison to 6 percent). But theft offenses were only 43 percent compared to 54 percent for the overall population. See Sophia Robinson, "A Study of Delinquency among Jewish Children in NYC," in *The Jews: Social Patterns of an American Group*, Marshall Sklare, ed. (Glencoe, IL: Free Press, 1958). L. Davidzon, "A Conversation with Dr. Harris Peck, the Chief Psychiatrist from the New York Children's Court," *Forverts*, Sept. 3, 1954.

11. In 1930, the percentage of Jewish children who were charged with delinquency was 14 percent, and the number of Jewish adults accused of serious crimes in 1930 represented 20 percent of the criminal population. See Dovid Liberzon, "Crimes among Jewish Children Decrease," *Forverts*, Aug. 26, 1954.

12. Ibid.

13. *Yiddishkeit* is a word packed with a great deal of meaning: *Yiddishkeit* is defined as "the group of qualities that define Jewishness; a feeling or flavor of Jewish

traditions, culture, ethnicity or manners." Joyce Eisenberg and Ellen Scolnic, *Dictionary of Jewish Words: A JPS Guide* (Philadelphia: The Jewish Publication Society, 2006), 189. The *New Oxford American Dictionary* (3rd ed., Angus Stevenson and Christine A. Lindberg, eds. (Oxford: Oxford University Press, 2010)) defines *Yiddishkeit* as "the quality of being Jewish; the Jewish way of life or its customs and practices." But the best definition I have found is on the website of the Orange County Yiddish Organization, which defines *Yiddishkeit* as follows: "'Yiddishkeit' means 'Jewishness,' i.e., a 'Jewish way of life.' It encapsulates the expressed culture or folk practices of Yiddish speaking Jews through humor, klezmer music, ideologies, practices, tradition, and food. In other words, it is the Jewish heritage of Eastern and Central Europe and Russia." ("What Is Yiddishkeit?" Orange County Yiddish, www.ocyiddish.org/index. php?option=com_content&view=article&id=9&Itemid=11, accessed June 4, 2013.)

14. Quentin Reynolds, *Courtroom: The Story of Samuel S. Leibowitz* (New York: Popular Library, 1950; reprint New York: Farrar, Straus and Giroux, 1999).

15. Dovid Liberzon, "A Conversation with Judge Leibowitz about Juvenile Crime," *Forverts*, Aug. 27, 1954.

16. I. Kaufman, "Charges Adolescent Court Looses Criminals on Public," *BE*, Aug. 20, 1954, final edition, *WNY*.

17. Ibid.

18. Leibowitz was so fervently pro-Zionist that he actually loaned the chief of the Kings County probation department to Israel to assist in the creation of Israel's probation system.

19. "Panken Raps Leibowitz on Leniency Charge," *BE*, Aug. 19, 1954, final edition, *WNY*.

20. "On to the Chair," editorial, *NYWT*, Aug. 20, 1954, Municipal Archives, Indictment 1917/1954; L. Fogelman, "The Riddle of the 4 Young Criminals," *Forverts*, Aug. 20, 1954; Dovid Liberzon, "A Conversation with Judge Leibowitz"; and "Judge Leibowitz Merits Victory in Three-cornered Primary Fight," *BE*, Sept. 10, 1954, final edition, *WNY*.

21. For the purposes of this chapter, the "mainstream" press consists of the following newspapers: the *New York Times, New York Journal-American, New York Daily News, New York Post, New York World Telegram and Sun, New York Daily Mirror*, and the *Brooklyn Eagle*. Newspapers consulted from outside of New York City include the following: the *Amsterdam Daily Democrat and Evening Recorder*, the *Binghamton Press, Geneva Daily Times*, the *Leader-Republican* (Geneva, NY), the *Kingston Daily Freeman*, the *Millbrook Round Table, Oswego-Palladium Times*, the *Citizen-Advertiser* (Auburn, NY), *Niagara Gazette, Tonawanda Evening News*, the *Daily Gazette* (Schenectady, NY), *Utica Daily Press*, the *Herald Statesman* (Yonkers, NY), and the *Los Angeles Times*. However, as the articles in all of these non–New York City newspapers were reprinted from the United Press, and therefore derivative of the original content published in the New York City newspapers, the New York City Press has been privileged for the purposes of this chapter.

22. Fogelman, "The Riddle"; Liberzon, "A Conversation with Judge Leibowitz"; "More Police, Fewer Criminals," *Forverts*, Sept. 14, 1954; and "Crime Past Understanding," *NYT*, Aug. 19, 1954, Wertham papers. See chapter 3 for a discussion on the call for more police by the mainstream press.

23. "Crime Past Understanding"; "Youthful Crimes Laid to Society," *NYT*, Aug. 19, 1954, Wertham papers; and Meyer Berger, "About New York: Teen-age Brooklyn

Killers Not Explained by Crowded, Run-down Neighborhood," *NYT*, Aug. 20, 1954, Wertham papers.

24. Sid Frigand, "Psychiatrists Split on Views about Killers," Aug. 20, 1954, *BE*, final edition, *WNY*.

25. William Longgood, "Psychiatrist Lays Teen Killers' Acts to Sex Fears and Aggressive Hate," *NYWT*, Aug. 19, 1954, Ex. G.

26. "Insanity Plea Set for 'Brains' of Mob," *BE*, final edition, Aug. 20, 1954, *WNY*; William Longgood, "Thrill-Killer Once Described"; Harold Wolfson, "Koslow Showed Sadistic Streak, Neighbors Reveal," *NYJA*, Aug. 20, 1954, Ex. G; Joseph Carter, "Thrill Murder Chief 'Insane' 2 Years," *DM*, Aug. 21, 1954, Ex. G.

27. L. Fogelman, "The Riddle of the 4 Young Criminals," *Forverts*, Aug. 20, 1954.

28. Tsivyon, "Jewish Interests," *Forverts*, Sept. 4, 1954.

29. Letter from Gedalia Kaplan, "From Folk to Folk: *Forverts*-readers Discuss the Question about Child-criminals," *Forverts*, Sept. 15, 1954.

30. Dovid Eynhorn, "Tragic Offender from a Confused Generation," *Forverts*, Aug. 29, 1954.

31. Dovid Liberzon, "What Can We Learn from the History with the 4 Jewish Boys?," *Forverts*, Sept. 7, 1954.

32. Letter from Gedalia Kaplan.

33. Dovid Liberzon, "The 4 Boys Didn't Have Any Jewish Education, Says Rabbi Honig," *Forverts*, Aug. 31, 1954.

34. Letter from Gedalia Kaplan.

35. The actual biblical quote is "יִשְׁמְרֵאֵנִי כְּאִישׁוֹן בַּת עָיִן בְּצֵל כְּנָפֶיךָ תַּסְתִּירֵנִי." literally "Guard me as the pupil of your eye," which the writer then paraphrased. Tehillim, 17:8.

36. Letter from Mrs. P. Meyers, "From Folk to Folk: *Forverts*-readers Discuss the Question about Child-criminals," *Forverts*, Sept. 15, 1954.

37. Golda Miller, "The Woman and the Home: The Four Young Murderers Have Disturbed the Complacency of Many Parents," *Forverts*, Sept. 12, 1954.

38. Mary Royz, "The Woman and the Home: The Four Young Criminals and the School-child," *Forverts*, Sept. 17, 1954.

39. Hillel Rogoff, "Editorial: Tell Me Who Your Friends Are," *Forverts*, Dec. 11, 1954.

40. Letter from Binyumen Greenberg, "From Folk to Folk: *Forverts*-readers Discuss the Question about Child-criminals," *Forverts*, Sept. 10, 1954; letter from Simon Braginsky, "From Folk to Folk: *Forverts*-readers Discuss the Question about Child-criminals," *Forverts*, Sept. 15, 1954.

41. Miller, "The Woman and the Home."

42. Eli Stolpner, "What Does Your Child Do with His Free Time?" *Forverts*, Sept. 8, 1954.

43. Dovid Eynhorn, "Tragic Offender."

44. Davidzon, "A Conversation with Dr. Harris Peck."

45. Shepner, "Bad Children and Foolish Parents."

46. Liberzon, "A Conversation with Judge Leibowitz."

47. Eynhorn, "Tragic Offender."

48. Davidzon, "A Conversation with Dr. Harris Peck."

49. See endnote 13 for a discussion of *Yiddishkeit*.

50. Liberzon, "The 4 Boys Didn't Have Any Jewish Education."

51. Ibid.

52. Dovid Liberzon, "District Attorney Silver Tells Why They Moved from a House Fifty Years Ago," *Forverts*, Sept. 1, 1954.

53. D. Zlotovsky, "Why Are More Crimes Committed Here than Previously among Jews in the Old Country?" *Forverts*, Dec. 25, 1954.

54. A. Menes, "The Education of Jewish Youth," *Forverts*, Sept. 5, 1954.

55. Letter from Yisroel Friedman, "From Folk to Folk: *Forverts*-readers Discuss the Question about Child-criminals," *Forverts*, Sept. 10, 1954.

56. Letter from Gedalia Kaplan, letter from Simon Braginsky, "From Folk to Folk."

57. Tsivyon, "Jewish Interests," *Forverts*, Sept. 4, 1954. Ben-Tsiyon Hoffman was an ordained rabbi from Vilna, a foreign correspondent for the *Forverts*, and a Bundist activist. See entry for "Tsivyon" in *Guide to the YIVO Archives*, www.yivoarchives.org/index.php?p=collections/controlcard&id=34177, accessed June 5, 2013.

58. Shepner, "Bad Children and Foolish Parents"; and Dovid Eynhorn, "What Our Youth Lack," *Forverts*, Sept. 4, 1954.

59. Hasia R. Diner, *We Remember with Reverence and Love: American Jews and the Myth of Silence after the Holocaust, 1945–1962* (New York: New York University Press, 2009), chapter 6; Arthur Green, "New Directions in Jewish Theology in America," in Deborah Dash Moore, ed., *American Jewish Identity Politics* (Ann Arbor, MI: University of Michigan Press, 2008), 207.

60. Diner, *We Remember*.

61. For a discussion of the religious revival of the 1950s, see Robert S. Ellwood, *The Fifties Spiritual Marketplace: American Religion in a Decade of Conflict* (New Brunswick, NJ: Rutgers University Press, 1997); James Hudnut-Beumler, *Looking for God in the Suburbs: The Religion of the American Dream and Its Critics, 1945–1965* (New Brunswick: Rutgers University Press, 1994); Peggy Bendroth, *Growing Up Protestant: Parents, Children and Mainline Churches* (New Brunswick, NJ: Rutgers University Press, 2002); and Penny Edgell, *Religion and Family in a Changing Society* (Princeton, NJ: Princeton University Press, 2005). That the trend was mirrored in the Jewish community, see Will Herberg, *Protestant, Catholic, Jew: An Essay in American Religious Sociology* (Chicago: University of Chicago Press, 1960).

62. Arthur A. Goren, "A 'Golden Decade' for American Jews: 1945–1955," in *A New Jewry: America since the Second World War*, Peter Y. Medding, ed. (New York: Oxford University Press, 1992), 3–20.

63. "Between the early 1940s and the early 1960s, the number of children attending Jewish schools tripled, from approximately 190,000 to 590,000 pupils, accounting for roughly 80 to 85 percent of all Jewish children between the ages of five and fourteen." See Rona Sheramy, "'Resistance and War': The Holocaust in American Jewish Education, 1945–1960," in *American Jewish History* 91, no. 2 (2003): 287–313. Statistics from Jack Wertheimer, "Jewish Education in the United States: Recent Trends and Issues," *American Jewish Year Book* 99 (1999): 38. Diner, *We Remember*; Hasia R. Diner, *The Jews of the United States, 1624–2000* (Berkeley: University of California Press, 2004), 259–304; Arthur A. Goren, "A 'Golden Decade' for American Jews: 1945–1955," in *A New Jewry: America since the Second World War*, Peter Y. Medding, ed. (New York: Oxford University Press, 1992), 3–20; Jonathan D. Sarna, *American Judaism: A History* (New Haven, CT: Yale University Press, 2004), 272–315.

64. Diner, *We Remember*, 330.

65. Davidzon, "A Conversation with Dr. Harris Peck"; Eynhorn, "Tragic Offender."

66. Ibid.

67. A. Menes, "The Education of Jewish Youth," *Forverts*, Sept. 5, 1954.

68. *Inside Detective Magazine*, Nov., 1954, 35; Gedalia Kaplan, letter to the editor.

69. Editorials that compared the "Thrill Killers" to Leopold and Loeb were Hillel Rogoff, "Modern Times," *Forverts*, Sept. 2, 1954 and Tsivyon, "Jewish Interests," Sept. 4, 1954.

70. As Seymour Lipset and Earl Rabb wrote in *Jews and the New American Scene* (Cambridge: Harvard University Press, 1995), "American Jews . . . were fully engaged in 'making it' in a benign postwar America" (117). The "consensus school" in which American Jewry was seen as remaining largely silent on the Holocaust in the 1950s started with Stephen Whitfield's article "The Holocaust and the American Jewish Intellectual" (*Judaism* 28, no. 4 (1979): 391–92, 398–99) and Leon Jick's article "The Holocaust: Its Uses and Abuses in the American Public" (*Yad Vashem Studies* 14 (1981): 303–18). Then, in his book *A Time for Healing: American Jewry since World War II*, published in 1992 (the first full-length study of postwar American Jewry), Edward Shapiro continued this argument, positing that there was little discussion of the Holocaust in America until the 1960s (Baltimore: Johns Hopkins University Press, 1992). The thesis was then reiterated by Edward T. Linenthal (*Preserving Memory: The Struggle to Create America's Holocaust Museum* (New York: Columbia University Press, 1995)), Deborah Lipstadt ("America and the Memory of the Holocaust, 1950–1965," *Modern Judaism* 16, no. 3 (1996): 195–214), Gerald Sorin (*Tradition Transformed: The Jewish Experience in America* (Baltimore: Johns Hopkins University Press, 1997)), Peter Novick (*The Holocaust in American Life* (Boston: Mariner Press, 1999), 63–123), Norman G. Finkelstein (*The Holocaust Industry: Reflections on the Exploitation of Jewish Suffering* (London: Verso, 2000)), Alan Mintz (*Popular Culture and the Shaping of Holocaust Memory in America* (Seattle: University of Washington Press, 2001)); Sherry Ortner (*New Jersey Dreaming: Capital, Culture, and the Class of 1958* (Durham, NC: Duke University Press, 2003), 300, 309), and Jonathan D. Sarna (*American Judaism: A History* (New Haven, CT: Yale University Press, 2004)).

71. See Whitfield, 1979; Jick, 1981; Novick 1999; and Lipstadt, 1996.

72. See Diner, *We Remember*, for an argument that within the Jewish community, there was intense commemoration of, education about, and discussion of the Holocaust in the mid-twentieth century.

73. Rona Sheramy, "'Resistance and War': The Holocaust in American Jewish Education, 1945–1960," *American Jewish History* 91, no. 2 (2003): 287–313.

74. See Jonathan D. Sarna, "American Jewish Education in Historical Perspective," *Journal of Jewish Education* 64, nos. 1–2 (1998): 12–13, and Jonathan D. Sarna, *American Judaism: A History* (New Haven, CT: Yale University Press, 2004), 80.

75. See Deborah Lipstadt, "America and the Memory of the Holocaust, 1950–1965," *Modern Judaism* 16, no. 3 (1996): 195–214; Deborah Dash Moore, "Reconsidering the Rosenbergs: Symbol and Substance in Second Generation American Jewish Consciousness," *Journal of American Ethnic History* 8, no. 1 (1988): 20–37;

and Arthur A. Goren, "A 'Golden Decade' for American Jews: 1945–1955," in *A New Jewry? America since the Second World War*, Peter Y. Medding, ed. (New York: Oxford University Press, 1992), 14–15.

76. Sheramy, "Resistance and War," 304; and Deborah Dash Moore, *GI Jews: How World War II Changed a Generation* (Boston: Belknap Press, 2006).

77. Wolfson, "Koslow Showed Sadistic Streak."

78. Only a couple of reported articles made mention of Jack's affinity for Nazism. One, by Dovid Lieberzohn, "Jake Kozlov, the Leader of the Group of Young Criminals," relayed that Jack had a mustache, "supposedly in imitation of Hitler" and that Jack had said "Heil Hitler" in school and was obsessed with Germany. Another article, "Judge Does Not Want to Declare Leader of Boys as Insane" (*Forverts*, Aug. 20, 1954), reported that "Kozlov had Nazi swastikas and Nazi books in his room."

Chapter 6

1. New York Corrections History Society, "Return to Raymond Street Jail," accessed April 17, 2013, www.correctionhistory.org/html/museum/gallery/raymondst/return2raymondst.html; excerpt, "Senators Begin Comic Book Probe," *Testimony before the Senate Subcommittee on Juvenile Delinquency*, Hearst Telenews 7, no. 80 (UCLA Film and Television Archive, Inventory #VA4775 T); "Psychiatrist Wertham—More Delinquents" photo, *Time Magazine*, Mar. 29, 1948; "Mercury Drops to 26.5, Autumn's Low to Date," *NYT*, Dec. 4, 1954; and "The Weather throughout the Nation," *NYT*, Dec. 4, 1954.

2. Letter from Wertham to Fink, December 12, 1954, Wertham papers.

3. Order, November 30, 1954, Kings County District Attorney's Case Files, New York Municipal Archives, Indictment 1917/1954.

4. Interview notes; and Marya Mannes, "The 'Night of Horror' in Brooklyn," *The Reporter*, Jan. 27, 1955.

5. Bart Beaty, *Fredric Wertham and the Critique of Mass Culture* (Jackson, MS: University Press of Mississippi, 2005), 16–17; Eric J. Engstrom, "'On the Question of Degeneration' by Emil Kraepelin (1908)," *History of Psychiatry* 18 (2007): 389–404; and Richard Kluger, *Simple Justice: The History of Brown v. Board of Education and Black America's Struggle for Equality* (New York: Vintage, 2004), 440–7.

6. Dennis Doyle, "'A Fine New Child': The Lafargue Mental Hygiene Clinic and Harlem's African American Communities, 1946–1958," *Journal of the History of Medicine and Allied Sciences* 65, no. 2 (2009): 173–212.

7. Kluger, *Simple Justice*, 441.

8. Fredric Wertham, *Dark Legend: A Study in Murder* (London: Victor Gollancz, Ltd., 1947), 116; For the significance of this statement, see David Mariott, "How Did Nietzsche Get into the Nursery?" in *Where Id Was: Challenging Normalization in Psychoanalysis*, Anthony Molino and Christine Ware, eds. (New York: Continuum, 2001); and Bruno Solby, review of *Dark Legend, a Study in Murder*, by Fredric Wertham, *Sociometry* 4, no. 4 (1941): 423–426.

9. Beaty, *Fredric Wertham*, 16–17.

10. "As a champion of the down-trodden," in Wendell Muncie, review of *The Show of Violence*, by Fredric Wertham, *The Quarterly Review of Biology* 24, no. 3 (1949): 268–269.

11. Doyle, "'A Fine New Child,'" 179. Doyle argues that the support of Rev. Shelton Hale Bishop, including the loaning of space at St. Philip's, was crucial to the success of the clinic as it gave the clinic legitimacy among the local population and helped in fostering an image of the clinic as a "home-grown" institution.

12. Doyle, "'A Fine New Child,'" 173–212; and Kluger, *Simple Justice*, 440–447.

13. Transcript, "Delaware Group," Fredric Wertham papers, box 18, folder 11, Library of Congress; and trial testimony of Fredric Wertham, *Belton, et al. vs. Gebhart, et al. and Bulah, et al. vs. Gebhart, et. al.*, Fredric Wertham papers, box 18, folder 16, Library of Congress, 2–5.

14. Trial testimony of Fredric Wertham, *Belton v. Gebhart*, 8.

15. Jeet Heer, "The Caped Crusader: Fredric Wertham and the Campaign against Comic Books," *Slate*, Apr. 4, 2008, www.slate.com/articles/arts/culture-box/2008/04/the_caped_crusader.html, accessed April 24, 2013.

16. Letter, Fredric Wertham to Harold Leventhal, November 19, 1947, Fredric Wertham papers, box 23, folder 1, Library of Congress.

17. For a complete discussion of the critique of comic books from the early 1940s forward, see Bart Beaty, *Fredric Wertham and the Critique of Mass Culture*, chapter 4, "Wertham and the Critique of Comic Books" (Jackson, MS: University Press of Mississippi, 2005).

18. Bart Beaty, *Fredric Wertham*, 134–135.

19. Bart Beaty, *Fredric Wertham*, 125.

20. Fredric Wertham, *Seduction of the Innocent* (Laurel, NY: Main Road Books, reprint 2004), 31–32.

21. Ibid.

22. Wertham, *Seduction*, 101.

23. Wertham, *Seduction*, 104–105.

24. As historian Mary L. Dudziak demonstrates, the problem of American race relations was crucial to international perceptions of the United States. While the USSR spotlighted America's race issues to curry favor in nonwhite regions, the United States Information Agency tried to present a progressive story of American race relations using a variety of propaganda methods that emphasized America's democratic process. See Mary L. Dudziak, *Cold War Civil Rights: Race and the Image of American Democracy* (Princeton, NJ: Princeton University Press, 2000). For an examination of the difficulty presented in trying to "sell" American democracy to the world in spite of intense opposition to America's segregation, see Laura A. Belmonte, *Selling the American Way: U.S. Propaganda and the Cold War* (Philadelphia: University of Pennsylvania Press, 2008), particularly chapter 6.

25. Wertham, *Seduction*, 100.

26. Wertham, *Seduction*, 290. For the chapter on international reception of American comics, see chapter 11, "Murder in Dawson Creek: The Comics Abroad."

27. Lee Elias, *First Love Illustrated*, no. 35, December 1935, Harvey Comics, panel inset in *Seduction of the Innocent* (Laurel, NY: Main Road Books, reprint 2004).

28. Direct examination of Dr. Fredric Wertham, post office obscenity hearing, Fredric Wertham papers, box 23, folder 2, Library of Congress, 33.

29. Wertham, *Seduction*, 184.

30. All quotes attributed to Jack Koslow in this section are transcribed from the notes written by Dr. Fredric Wertham in his psychiatric interviews with Koslow at the

Raymond Street Jail on December 3 and 4, 1954 (hereafter, interview notes). Fredric Wertham papers, box 22, folder 11, Library of Congress.

31. This is based on Jack's memory of the radio broadcast and is likely not a verbatim rendering.

32. Wertham, interview notes; Milton Bracker, "Sanity Plea Made for Youth Slayer," *NYT*, Aug. 21, 1954; and Harold Smith and I. Kaufman, "'Thrill' Killers Face Murder Indictments," *BE*, Aug. 21, 1954, *WNY*.

33. Wertham, interview notes.

34. Eric L. Goldstein, *The Price of Whiteness: Jews, Race and American Identity* (Princeton, NJ: Princeton University Press, 2007), 2.

35. According to Karen Brodkin, "Some resist white privilege, others do not see Jews as white," *How Jews Became White Folks and What That Says about Race in America* (Piscataway, NJ: Rutgers University Press, 1999), 138.

36. Ibid. There is substantial controversy concerning the role of Jews in the Civil Rights Movement. Murray Friedman (*What Went Wrong: The Creation and Collapse of the Black-Jewish Alliance* (New York: Free Press, 1995)) argues for a golden age, which was felled when militant black nationalist separatists expelled all whites from the movement, began to spout anti-Semitic rhetoric, and allied themselves with global anti-Zionist movements. Conversely, Harold Cruse (*The Crisis of the Negro Intellectual* (New York: Morrow, 1967)) argued that Jews essentially infiltrated the Civil Rights movement to promote Jewish equality and were rightfully purged from what was becoming an increasingly nationalist struggle for self-determination. For Jonathan Kaufman (*Broken Alliance: The Turbulent Times between Blacks and Jews in America* (New York: Charles Scribner's Sons, 1988)), the cooperation was only because of overlapping agendas, and the alliance was only a means to an end and meant to be dissolved once the end was reached. Other scholars, such as David Levering Lewis ("Parallels and Divergences: Assimilationist Strategies of Afro-American and Jewish Elites from 1910 to the Early 1930s," in J. Salzman, ed., *Bridges and Boundaries: African Americans and American Jews* (Braziller/Jewish Museum, 1992), 17–35) and Herbert Hill ("Black-Jewish Conflict in the Labor Context," in Vincent P. Franklin, ed., *African Americans and Jews in the Twentieth Century: Studies in Convergence and Conflict* (1998), 294–286) have argued that it was only Jewish and African American elites who collaborated, with nonelite Jews, fearing the encroachment on their hard-won advances in claiming whiteness, and only African American elites viewed Jews as being in any way different from other whites. But Hasia Diner (*In the Almost Promised Land: American Jews and Blacks 1915–1935* (Westport, CT: Greenwood Press, 1977)) argues that the coalitions between blacks and Jews extended throughout the various class levels and was not limited to elites. Most recently, Cheryl Lynn Greenberg (*Troubling the Waters: Black-Jewish Relations in the American Century* (Princeton, NJ: Princeton University Press, 2006)) argues that the peak and decline of Black-Jewish relations mirrors the peak and decline of American liberalism, as both groups advocated cultural pluralism, individual equality, and state protection of these ideals. And Seth Forman (*Blacks in the Jewish Mind: A Crisis of Liberalism* (New York: New York University Press, 1998)) claims that Jews sought to express their Jewishness through political liberalism and that this expression of social idealism found a ready and fertile ground in the Civil Rights movement.

37. See also Brodkin, *How Jews Became White Folks*; Samuel C. Heilman, *Portrait of American Jews: The Last Half of the 20th Century* (Seattle, WA: University of

Washington Press, 1993). To illustrate the extreme amount of identification some young Jews born in this era had with whiteness, there is the story of Daniel Burros, one year younger than Jack Koslow, who was identified in 1965 as the grand dragon of the Ku Klux Klan in New York State after being the national secretary for the American Nazi Party. Burros grew up in a Jewish family in Queens, and was reportedly a "star pupil" in Hebrew school. See McCandlish Phillips, "State Klan Leader Hides Secret of Jewish Origin," *NYT*, Oct. 31, 1965.

38. Brodkin, *How Jews Became White Folks*, 141. While this new, integrated Jewishness centered on male privilege, Jewish women were vilified as overbearing mothers whose prolific appetites—be it for love, loyalty, or material possessions—mirrored classic anti-Semitic stereotypes and therefore were blamed for the inability for Jews to completely "blend in" with America's white mainstream. See Riv-Ellen Prell, *Fighting to Become Americans: Jews, Gender, and the Anxiety of Assimilation* (Boston: Beacon Press, 1999).

39. Brodkin, *How Jews Became White Folks*, chapter 5.

40. Wertham, interview notes.

41. According to the *New York World Telegram*, "Local kids recalled he 'imitated the Fuehrer "just for fun." And on one occasion they said he insulted [a] Negro woman sitting on a park bench.'" "Portraits of 4 Boys in Terrorist Orgy," *NYWT*, August 18, 1954, Ex. G; Wolfson, "Koslow Showed Sadistic Streak."

42. Jack mentions the film is one of seven, making it likely one of the films in the Universal Pictures series that started in 1931 and concluded in 1945 and included the following films: *Frankenstein* (1931), *Bride of Frankenstein* (1935), *Son of Frankenstein* (1939), *The Ghost of Frankenstein* (1942), *Frankenstein Meets the Wolfman* (1943), *House of Frankenstein* (1944), and *House of Dracula* (1945).

43. Wertham, interview notes.

44. Ibid.

45. Ibid.

46. Wilfred Alexander, "Psychiatrists Call Killers Sex Deviates," *DM*, Aug. 20, 1954, Ex. G.

47. Ibid.

48. Nathan Kanter and Harry Schlegel, "Thrill Boss Psycho as Child," *DN*, Aug. 23, 1954, Ex. G.

49. "Koslow was suffering from dementia praecox and schizophrenic tendencies. Both are characterized by a loss of contact with reality, so it would have been entirely possible for Koslow to have a romance with a girl while still not being interested in a normal sex life." John Feeney and Joseph Carter, "Thrill Slayer Told All after 'Deal' over Girl," *Sunday Mirror*, Aug. 22, 1954, Ex. G.

50. Edward Zeltner, "Over the River," *DM*, Sept. 7, 1954, Ex. G.

51. David K. Johnson, *The Lavender Scare: The Cold War Persecution of Gays and Lesbians in the Federal Government* (Chicago: University of Chicago Press, 2004), 8.

52. Collin E. Cooper, "Letter to the Editor," *Journal of the American Medical Association* 209 (August 1969): 941, cited in Carolyn Herbert Lewis, *Prescription for Homosexuality: Sexual Citizenship in the Cold War Era* (Chapel Hill, NC: University of North Carolina Press, 2010), 3.

53. Lewis, *Prescription for Homosexuality*, 5.

54. Several newspapers commented on Jack's "effeminacy," including the *New York World Telegram*: "tall, thin-faced youth whose gestures are effeminate"; "People . . . said that young Koslow . . . never had anything to do with girls. Several of the

people . . . said they always had considered Koslow effeminate." (Norton Mockridge, "Teen Thrill Slayers Baffle Judges and Sicken Officials," *NYWT*, Aug. 18, 1954, Ex. G); "speaks in a frail, high voice . . . the teenagers think of him as delicate" ("Portraits of 4 Boys in Terrorist Orgy"); the *Daily Mirror* also described his voice as "thin and reedy" and Jack as "puny," "frail," and "giggly" (James O'Connor and Joseph Carter, "A Puny 'Super-Boy,' Killer-Pack's Chief," *DM*, Aug. 19, 1954, Ex. G.); and the Yiddish daily *Forverts* claimed Jack had a "high soprano voice" and was "more often thought 'feminine' than 'masculine.'" ("Father of One of the Boys Says 'It's All My Fault,'" *Forverts*, Aug. 19, 1954).

55. James Gilbert, *Men in the Middle: Searching for Masculinity in the 1950s* (Chicago: University of Chicago Press, 2005), 39–43.

56. Ibid., 80. This point was also addressed by Lizabeth Cohen in *Consumer's Republic: The Politics of Mass Consumption in Postwar America* (New York: Alfred A. Knopf, 2003). She essentially argues that men's domination of consumerism was at the expense of women, for whom lack of access to credit as well as increased advertising emphasizing women's untrustworthiness concerning major purchasing decisions created a more hostile consuming environment.

57. Alfred Kinsey et al., *Sexual Behavior in the Human Male* (Philadelphia: Saunders, 1948), 627.

58. Robert J. Corber, *Homosexuality in Cold War America: Resistance and the Crisis of Masculinity* (Durham, NC: Duke University Press, 1997), 10–11.

59. Ibid., 11–12.

60. Ibid., 8–9. See also Eric Schneider, *Vampires, Dragons and Egyptian Kings: Youth Gangs in Post-war New York* (Princeton, NJ: Princeton University Press, 2001).

61. Barbara Ehrenreich, *The Hearts of Men: American Dreams and the Flight from Commitment* (Garden City, NY: Anchor Press/Doubleday, 1983), 42–51.

62. Schneider, *Vampires, Dragons and Egyptian Kings*, 136.

63. "Father of One of the Boys Says 'It's All My Fault,'" *Forverts*, Aug. 19, 1954; and Dovid Liberzon, "What the Parents of the Four Young Criminals Tell about Them," *Forverts*, Aug. 25, 1954.

64. Lisa Lindquist Dorr, "The Perils of the Back Seat: Date Rape, Race and Gender in 1950s America," *Gender and History* 20, no. 1 (2008): 31.

65. Wertham, interview notes.

66. Ibid.

67. Ibid.

68. Ibid.

69. Letter from Wertham to Eisenstein, January 20, 1955, Wertham papers,

70. Letter from Wertham to Slochower, November 1, 1956, Wertham papers. According to the DSM I published in 1952, the schizoid personality was defined as

(1) avoidance of close relations with others, (2) inability to express directly hostility or even ordinary aggressive feelings, and (3) autistic thinking. These qualities result early in coldness, aloofness, emotional detachment, fearfulness, avoidance of competition, and day dreams revolving around the need for omnipotence. As children, they are usually quiet, shy, obedient, sensitive and rearing. At puberty, they frequently become more withdrawn, then manifesting the aggregate of personality traits known as introversion, namely, quietness, seclusiveness, "shut-in-ness," and unsociability, often with eccentricity.

American Psychiatric Association, *Diagnostic and Statistical Manual of Mental Disorders* (Washington DC: American Psychiatric Association Mental Hospital Service, 1952), 35.

71. Although an appellate court in the District of Columbia ruled in *Durham v. United States* in 1954 for a broader definition of mental illness, New York continued to use a modified version of the M'Naghten rule, in which the burden was on the defense to prove that the defendant (a) at the time of the commission of the crime was so deranged so as not to understand the nature or quality of his or her actions or (b) that if the defendant did know the nature or quality of his or her actions, he or she was too deranged to understand that the actions were legally and morally wrong.

72. Robert Jones and Wilfred Alexander, "Mental Tests Ordered for Thrill Killers," *DM*, Aug. 19, 1954; William Longgood, "Thrill-Killer Once Described as Normal by Psychiatrist," *NYWT*, Aug. 20, 1954; and Harold Smith and I. Kaufman, "Thrill Killers Face Murder Indictments," *BE* Aug. 21, 1954, all Ex. G.

73. Wertham, interview notes.

74. Wertham was never paid for his time, even though he had reduced his fee from the usual $500 to $400 in light of not testifying. Ultimately, Wertham referred the matter to a collection agency, which also had no luck in collecting the money, being told after repeated letters and phone calls that Mr. Eisenstein was no longer associated with the firm and that they had no idea where he was currently practicing. See letter from Greene to Wertham, December 29, 1955, Wertham papers.

CHAPTER 7

1. Al Salerno and I. Kaufman, "Trial of Thrill Killers Put Off for a Week," *BE*, Nov. 15, 1954, final edition, *WNY*; and Francis Sugrue, "Torture-slaying Trial of 4 Boys Put Off Week," *NYHT*, Nov. 16, 1954, Ex. G.

2. See chapter 4 for a brief description of the careers of these two attorneys.

3. In 1930, he was cleared of charges of "job buying," but the remaining stigma likely contributed to his resignation.

4. Jeanne Toomey, *Assignment Homicide: Behind the Headlines* (Santa Fe, NM: Sunstone Press, 1998), 59–60.

5. Al Salerno, "Brooklyn and Broadway Night Life," *BE*, Mar., 27, 1951, final edition, *WNY*. *Robert and Elizabeth* was reworked from Moritt's original script by Ron Grainer and Ronald Millar. It is an operetta-style musical that tells the story of the romance and elopement of poets Robert Browning and Elizabeth Barrett. The original 1964 London production was a success, starring Sir John Clements as Barrett, June Bronhill as Elizabeth, and Keith Michell as Robert. Several revivals have followed.

6. M. Tseder, "Last Act of the Tragedy with the Brooklyn Jewish Boys," *Forverts*, Dec. 13, 1954.

7. Harold H. Harris, "Politics and People," *BE*, Oct. 7, 1952, final edition, Western New York Historical Newspapers. Moritt was currently a favorite among the Kings County court clerks and staff, having championed a wage increase on their behalf in the state senate. See M. Tseder, "Last Act of the Tragedy with the Brooklyn Jewish Boys," *Forverts*, Dec. 13, 1954.

8. Interview notes, Wertham papers.

9. Max Lerner, "Portrait of a Tragedy," *NYP*, Dec. 3, 1954, Wertham papers; and "Thrill Killer Turns on Pals," *BE*, final edition, Nov. 15, 1954, *WNY*.

10. These included several telephone calls to an annoyed federal judge to release Healy from a trial in federal court and phone calls to the chief assistant district attorney in Manhattan to ensure that Mr. Murray was relieved after the grueling Roche case.

11. Emphasis mine. Colloquy (tr. at 313–314), *People v. Koslow et al.* (N.Y. App. Div. 1958). The *New York Herald-Tribune* called the request "A poor choice of words," and several newspapers made note of the statement. See Salerno and Kaufman, "Trial of Thrill Killers"; Sugrue, "Torture-slaying Trial"; "Open Trial of 4 In Thrill Killing," *NYJA*, Nov. 15, 1954, Ex. G.

12. Colloquy, *People v. Koslow* (tr. at 315–18).

13. *Sheppard v. Maxwell*, 384 U.S. 333 (1966).

14. In the Sheppard case, "the jury viewed the scene of the murder on the first day of the trial. Hundreds of reporters, cameramen and onlookers were there, and one representative of the news media was permitted to accompany the jury while it inspected the Sheppard home. The time of the jury's visit was revealed so far in advance that one of the newspapers was able to rent a helicopter and fly over the house taking pictures of the jurors on their tour." *Sheppard v. Maxwell*, 384 U.S. 333 (1966); and testimony of Arthur Drucker, *People v. Koslow* (tr. at 3131–3137).

15. Samuel P. Abelow, *History of Brooklyn Jewry* (Brooklyn, NY: Scheba, 1937), 275, 325; Burton B. Turkus and Sid Feder, *Murder, Inc.: The Story of "The Syndicate"* (New York: Farrar, Straus and Young, 1951), 371. On Lepke Buchalter trial, see Richard Norton Smith, *Thomas E. Dewey and His Times* (New York: Simon & Schuster, 1982) and Mary M. Stolberg, *Fighting Organized Crime: Politics, Justice and the Legacy of Thomas E. Dewey* (Boston: Northeastern University Press, 1995). Barshay was the defense counsel for Feldman's third and final trial, the only one in which he was found innocent. Interestingly, James D. C. Murray was the defense attorney at Feldman's second trial, at which he was found guilty.

16. "Spinning Drum Will Decide Judge to Try Thrill-Killers," *BE*, Aug. 28, 1954, final edition, *WNY*; and "To Hear Murder Case: Barshay Will Preside at Trial of Brooklyn Teen-agers," *NYT*, Sept. 4, 1954.

17. Colloquy, *People v. Koslow* (tr. at 350–363).

18. Colloquy, *People v. Koslow* (tr. at 362–365).

19. James Oldham, "The History of the Special (Struck) Jury in the United States and Its Relation to Voir Dire Practices, the Reasonable Cross-section Requirement, and Peremptory Challenges," *Wm. & Mary Bill Rts. J.* 6 (1998): 623, http://scholarship.law.wm.edu/wmborj/vol6/iss3/2.

20. A "Struck Jury" or "Donahue Model" is one in which, instead of performing voir dire in a strike-and-replace manner of challenges, the jurors are first questioned by the judge for dismissal for cause. Next, they are questioned as a group by the defense and prosecution, where discussion among the potential jurors is encouraged. Afterward, the defense and prosecution are given a list of the potential juror's names, and each side strikes off the names of those jurors they wish to disqualify, until a sufficient number has been reached. This model is still used in many states, although typically for civil rather than criminal cases.

21. The only caveat was that the county population needed to have exceeded 500,000. See Act of Apr. 23, 1896, ch. 378, 1896 N.Y. Laws 354.

22. Editorial, "Blue Ribbon Juries," *Pittsburgh Press*, Sept. 6, 1938.

23. Ibid.

24. "The 'Blue-Ribbon' Jury," *Harvard Law Review* 60, no. 4 (1947): 613–620. These juries were almost always exclusively white males, as both women and minorities typically did not meet the requirements. See *Fay v. People of State of New York*, 332 U.S. 261 (1947).

25. Motion by defendant Koslow, *People v. Koslow* (tr. at 336–337).

26. *Fay v. People of State of New York*, 332 U.S. 261 (1947).

27. M. Tseder, "Youngest of the Accused Boys Will Have Separate Trial," *Forverts*, Nov. 23, 1954.

28. For the newspaper reportage on rumors that Trachtenberg would turn, see Salerno and Kaufman, "Trial of Thrill-Killers"; "Thrill Killer Turns on Pals," *BE*, Nov. 15, 1954, final edition, *WNY*; and Nat Kanter, "1 of 4 Thrill Killers to Testify for State," *DN*, Nov. 15, 1954, Ex. G.

29. "Thrill Kill Boy Granted Own Trial," *NYJA*, Nov. 22, 1954, Ex. G.

30. Motion by defendant Koslow, *People v. Koslow* (tr. at 333). That he "raised his voice" was reported in the *Brooklyn Eagle*, see Clarence Greenbaum and I. Kaufman, "'Thrill-Kill' Gang Split Up," *BE*, Nov. 22, 1954, final edition, *WNY*.

31. Moritt had gone over Barshay's head and applied for a change of venue directly through the appellate division, which was denied by Justice Frank F. Adel. See motion by defendant Koslow, *People v. Koslow* (tr. at 328–330).

32. Motion by defendant Koslow, *People v. Koslow* (tr. at 338–342).

33. Richard J. H. Johnston, "Brother of Victim Made Long Inquiry: Tells of Investigating Cloak-and-dagger Slaying," *NYT*, Aug. 16, 1951; "Inquiry in Slaying Spanned 18 Months: Magazine Editor Credits Rome," *NYT*, Aug. 16, 1951; and Jay Walz, "Holohan Mystery: A New Chapter," *NYT*, Aug. 21, 1955.

34. Tseder, "Youngest of the Accused Boys."

35. Ibid.

36. Ibid.; Clarence Greenbaum, "Lone 'Thrill-Kill' Juror Still Alone as Trial Drags On," *BE*, Nov. 23, 1954, final edition, *WNY*.

37. M. Tseder, "Demand for Mistrial of 3 Boys Rejected," *Forverts*, Nov. 24, 1954; "Speedup May Fill Jury Box in 'Thrill-Kill' Trial by Night," *BE*, Nov. 24, 1954, final edition, *WNY*; "Half of Jury Ok'd for Thrill Kids," *NYWT*, Nov. 24, 1954, Ex. G; "Only 6 Jurors Picked for Thrill-Kill Trial," *DM*, Nov. 24, 1954, Ex. G; "'Thrill Trial' Gets Five More Jurors," *NYHT*, Nov. 24, 1954, Ex. G; "Court in Night Session," *NYT*, Nov. 24, 1954; and "Night Session Adds Only Two to Thrill Jury," *DN*, Nov. 24, 1954, Ex. G.

38. Kopper's Coke was a fuel company that sold coke fuel.

39. M. Tseder, "Images and Impressions from the Courtroom Where the Three Brooklyn Boys Are on Trial," *Forverts*, Nov. 29, 1954.

40. Ibid.

41. Ibid.

42. M. Tseder, "The Four Brooklyn Jewish Youth that Stand under the Shadow of the Electric Chair," *Forverts*, Nov. 22, 1954.

43. M. Tseder, "Last Act of the Tragedy with the Brooklyn Jewish Boys," *Forverts*, Dec. 13, 1954.

44. Tseder, "Images and Impressions."

45. M. Tseder, "Murder Trial of the 4 Brooklyn Boys Officially Begun and Recessed for a Week," *Forverts*, Nov. 16, 1954.

46. Fred Morgan, "Melvin Mittman, Jerome Lieberman and Jack Koslow (left to right) leave courtroom at recess," photo, *DN*, Nov. 30, 1954, Wertham papers.

47. "Brooklyn Youths Face Murder Jury," *NYT*, Nov. 30, 1954.

48. "Today's Profile," *BE*, May 9, 1945, *WNY*; and "McCabe Named Chief Assistant in D.A.'s Office," *BE*, Dec. 23, 1953, *WNY*.

49. Opening statement for the people (tr. at 384–386), *People v. Koslow et al.* (N.Y. App. Div. 1958); and transcript of *The Barry Gray Show*, November 29, 1954, Fredric Wertham papers, box 22, folder 11, Library of Congress.

50. Procedure at the time dictated that the defense attorneys open in the order in which the defendants were listed on the indictment: first would be the melodramatic Moritt, followed by the more staid Healy, and then Murray. This is no longer standard procedure in New York courts.

51. Opening statement for defendant Koslow, *People v. Koslow* (tr. at 397–402).

52. Ibid. (tr. at 408–409).

53. Ibid. (tr. at 410).

54. Ibid. (tr. at 412–414).

55. Ibid. (tr. at 416–418).

56. Ibid. (tr. at 420–421).

57. Ibid. (tr. at 425–6). That it was said "crisply," see "Attack on D.A. Stirs 'Thrill-Killing' Trial," *BE*, Nov. 29, 1954, final edition, *WNY*.

58. Ibid. (tr. at 428).

59. Opening statement for defendant Mittman, *People v. Koslow* (tr. at 433–434).

60. Ibid. (tr. at 442).

61. Ibid. (tr. at 436–444).

62. Opening statement for defendant Lieberman, *People v. Koslow* (tr. at 446).

63. Ibid.

64. Ibid. (tr. at 446–449).

65. People's Exhibit 4 read into record, *People v. Koslow* (tr. at 686). The exact statement in the report reads as follows: "The feet show some incrustation with dirt. Some wrinkling of the skin about the ankles is present. There is no evidence of laceration, abrasion, or burns."

CHAPTER 8

1. Testimony of Raymond E. Duggan, *People v. Koslow* (tr. at 1433–1818); testimony of William Elliott, *People v. Koslow* (tr. at 1856 to 2033) (tr. at 770–800).

2. Marya Mannes, "The 'Night of Horror' in Brooklyn," *The Reporter*, Jan. 27, 1955; and "Mercury Drops to 26.5, Autumn's Low to Date," *NYT*, Dec. 4, 1954.

3. Robert Walsh, "Youngest of Thrill Kids Throws Blame on Koslow as Murder," *DN*, Dec. 4, 1954, Wertham papers.

4. Testimony of Robert Trachtenberg, *People v. Koslow* (tr. at 2058–2096).

5. Testimony of Robert Trachtenberg, *People v. Koslow* (tr. at 2518–2519).

6. Marya Mannes, "The 'Night of Horror' in Brooklyn," *The Reporter*, Jan. 27, 1955.

7. Statement of Jack Koslow, people's Exhibit 24, *People v. Koslow* (tr. at 2848). Newspapers that published the quote (or a paraphrase thereof) include the following:

Max Lerner, "New Confessions to Close State's 'Thrill-Kill' Case," *NYP*, Dec. 8, 1954, Wertham papers; "Boys' Stories Told in Murder Trial," *NYT*, Dec. 8, 1954; Erwin Savelson, "Allow 'Thrill' Confessions," *DM*, Dec. 8, 1954; "'Thrill-Kill' Statements Read in Court," *BE*, Dec. 8, 1954, final edition, *WNY*; and Robert Walsh, "Hear Thrill Kids' Words on Victim," *DN*, Dec. 9, 1954, Wertham papers.

8. "Mr. Moritt said, 'I am suspicious that the written records were 'fixed' by the District Attorney." M. Tseder, "Prosecution Ends Case Today against Brooklyn Boys; Defenders Will Demand to Void the Trial," *Forverts*, Dec. 8, 1954.

9. Testimony of Charles Menter, *People v. Koslow* (tr. at 770–800).

10. Milton Bracker, "Teen-age Killers Identify Body of 2d Victim, Taken from River," *NYT*, Aug. 20, 1954; John Ferris, "Thrill Victim Found in River," *NYWT*, Aug. 19, 1954, Ex. G; and "Thrill-Killer's Victim Found in East River," *NYJA*, Aug. 19, 1954, Ex. G.

11. Testimony of Arthur Drucker, *People v. Koslow* (tr. at 3221 to 3222).

12. Colloquy, *People v. Koslow* (tr. at 3763 to 3792).

13. Testimony of Francis Sheridan, *People v. Koslow* (tr. at 1062 to1287).

14. Summation on behalf of defendant Koslow, *People v. Koslow* (tr. at 3854).

15. Testimony of Harold Neyer, *People v. Koslow* (tr. at 986–1042).

16. *People v. Koslow, et al.*, 6 A.D.2d713, 174 N.Y.S.2d 709 (N.Y. App. Div. 1958).

17. "Thrill Teen's Father Faints in Courtroom," *NYWT*, Dec. 1, 1954, Wertham papers; "Accused 'Thrill-Killer' Quoted by Sleuth: 'The Police! Oh, My God, the River!'" *BE*, Dec. 1, 1954, final edition, *WNY*; Murray Schumach, "Alleged Slayer Linked to Sadism," *NYT*, Dec. 2, 1954; Elihu Hicks, "Youth's Father Faints at Trial of 3 for Murder," *Daily Worker*, Dec. 2, 1954, Wertham papers; "Thrill-Killer Had 'Supreme Adventure,'" *NYWT*, Dec. 2, 1954, Wertham papers; and Robert Walsh and Henry Lee, "Cop Tells Thriller Confession: A 'Bum-Hunt'—Then Murder," *DN*, Dec. 2, 1954, Wertham papers.

18. The successful photographer was Nick Sorrentino, whose picture of the collapsed, elderly woman ran on the front page of the *Daily News*. Nick Sorrentino, "Fear and Relief," photo, *DN*, Dec. 10, 1954, Wertham papers; "'Kill-for-thrill' Case Goes to Jury Tuesday," *BE*, Dec. 10, 1954, final edition, *WNY*; and "One Youth Clear in Dock Murder," *NYT*, Dec. 10, 1954.

19. Barbara Brent was best known for introducing *The Jackie Gleason Show*, on which she starred as one of the "Away We Go" girls before breaking her contract to become a member of the "Goldwyn Girls"—a musical stock company of female dancers employed by Samuel Goldwyn. John Cashmore, weekly column, *BE*, Dec. 10, 1954, final edition, *WNY*.

20. Motion for directed verdict of acquittal on behalf of defendant Lieberman, *People v. Koslow* (tr. at 3513–3522).

21. Ibid. (tr. at 3531).

22. People's Argument against the motion for directed verdict of acquittal on behalf of defendant Jerome Lieberman, *People v. Koslow* (tr. at 3540).

23. *The People of the State of New York, Respondent, v. Giro Ligouri and William Panaro, Appellants*, Court of Appeals of New York, 284 N.Y. 309; 31 N.E.2d 37; 1940 N.Y. LEXIS 830.

24. *The People of the State of New York, Respondent, v. Jacob Weiss, Jacob Simmons and Harry Epstein, Appellants*, Court of Appeals of New York, 290 N.Y. 160; 48 N.E.2d 306; 1943 N.Y. LEXIS 1126.

25. People's Argument against the motion for directed verdict of acquittal on behalf of defendant Jerome Lieberman, *People v. Koslow* (tr. at 3579).

26. The judge dismissed the case with "no comment" as he would preside at the trial of the same defendant for the manslaughter indictment (tr. at 3710).

27. "One Youth Clear in Dock Murder," *NYT*, Dec. 10, 1954; and M. Tseder, "Youngest of Three Brooklyn Boys Freed," *Forverts*, Dec. 10, 1954.

28. Ibid.

29. Irving Lieberman and Nancy Seely, "Call Koslow's Ex-counsel in Thrill-Killing," *NYP*, Dec. 10, 1954, Wertham papers.

30. Testimony of Murray Cutler, *People v. Koslow* (tr. at 3717 to 3756).

31. Summation on behalf of defendant Koslow, *People v. Koslow* (tr. at 3794 to 3996). Any adjectives used to describe Moritt's summation, such as "thundered," "pleaded," "lowered his voice," etc., were derived from the following article: "Koslow Not Thrill Gang Boss," *BE*, Dec. 13, 1954, final edition, *WNY*.

32. The original title of Agatha Christie's 1939 book was also *Ten Little Niggers*, which then became *Ten Little Indians* for both the book and film released in the United States. By 1954, both the book and film had been retitled again, becoming *And Then There Were None*. Summation on behalf of defendant Koslow, *People v. Koslow* (tr. at 3794 to 3996); and Marya Mannes, "The 'Night of Horror' in Brooklyn," *The Reporter*, Jan. 27, 1955.

33. Summation on behalf of defendant Mittman, *People v. Koslow* (tr. at 3999 to 4062).

34. Clarence Greenbaum and Sid Frigand, "'Thrill' Case Heads to Jury," *BE*, Dec. 14, 1954, final edition, *WNY*; and summation on behalf of defendant Mittman, *People v. Koslow* (tr. at 4011).

35. Summation on behalf of defendant Mittman, *People v. Koslow* (tr. at 4000).

36. Ibid. (tr. at 4055).

37. Ibid. (tr. at 4045–4046).

38. Ibid. (tr. at 4046–4050).

39. Ibid. (tr. at 4052).

40. Summation on behalf of People, *People v. Koslow* (min at 4064–4069).

41. Ibid.

42. Summation on behalf of People, *People v. Koslow* (min at 4102–4136).

43. Ibid.

44. Summation on behalf of People, *People v. Koslow* (min at 4180).

45. I. Kaufman, "2 Thrill Killers Get Life or Chair—Decision in a Month," *BE*, Dec. 15, 1954, final edition, *WNY*; "2 Thrill Kids Guilty; Life Asked," *DN*, Dec. 15, 1954, Wertham papers; Judd Mehlman, "Mittman (left) and Koslow (right) are taken away after conviction," photo, *DN*, Dec. 15, 1954, Wertham papers.

46. Verdict, *People v. Koslow* (min at 4473); Lieberman, Irving, "'The End for Us, Too,' Sob Thrill Kids' Parents," *NYP*, Dec. 15, 1954, Wertham papers; Paul Meskil, "What Makes a Boy Turn into a Sadistic Killer?" *NYWT*, Dec. 15, 1954, Wertham papers; Robert Walsh and James Davis, "2 Thrill Kids Guilty; Beat Chair, Get Life," *DN*, Dec. 15, 1954, Wertham papers; Peter Kihss, "Teen-age Killers Guilty, Face Life," *NYT*, Dec. 15, 1954; and Kaufman, "2 Thrill Killers Get Life or Chair."

47. *Williams v. New York*, 337 U.S. 241 (1949).

48. Interestingly, the legal counsel involved in setting the legal precedent in 1948 that gave Judge Barshay sole discretion to decide the boys' fate were none other than

Assistant District Attorney Kenneth McCabe and defense attorney Leo Healy. "1948 Case Gives Judges Discretion on Jury Plea," *NYT*, Dec. 15, 1954.

49. Sentence, *People v. Koslow* (min at 4500).

50. "Two Thrill Killers Calmly Hear Life Sentences Passed," *BE*, Jan. 24, 1955, final edition, *WNY*.

51. Ibid.

52. "Boy, 16, Committed in Thrill Killing," *NYT*, Jan. 19, 1955.

53. Meskil, "What Makes a Boy."

54. Max Lerner, "The Verdict and the Guilt," *NYP*, Dec. 15, 1954, Wertham papers.

55. "What's Behind the Thrill Trial?," advertisement, *BE*, Dec. 19, 1954, final edition, *WNY*.

56. "Problem Youngsters Require Psychiatric Aid, Parents Told," *BE*, Dec. 15, 1954, final edition, *WNY*.

57. Edith C. Jackson, "2 Thrill Killers Steeped in Horror Books," *NYWT*, Dec. 15, 1954, Wertham papers.

58. Edith C. Jackson, "Thrill Killer Needed Long Mental Care," *NYWT*, Dec. 16, 1954, Wertham papers.

CHAPTER 9

1. "Thaw in City Ends 3-Day Cold Spell; 37.7 High Brings Relief, but Turns Snow to Slush—Fair Weather Forecast," *NYT*, Feb. 5, 1955.

2. "Our Historic Building," website of the New York City Bar Association, www.nycbar.org/index.php/about-us/our-historic-building, accessed August 6, 2013; and "Lawyers' New Building," *NYT*, Sept. 20, 1896.

3. Amy Kiste Nyberg, *Seal of Approval: The History of the Comics Code* (Jackson, MS: University Press of Mississippi, 1998), 43.

4. New York State Legislature, *Joint Legislative Committee to Study the Publication of Comics—Interim Report* (Albany, NY: Williams Press Inc., 1950).

5. Ibid. However, it should be noted that none of the witnesses had any complaints concerning either Walt Disney comics or "classic" comics. See Nyberg, *Seal of Approval*, 45.

6. New York State Legislature, *Joint Legislative Committee to Study the Publication of Comics Report*, Legislative Document No. 15 (Albany, NY: Williams Press Inc., 1951).

7. David Hajdu, *The Ten-Cent Plague: The Great Comic-Book Scare and How It Changed America* (New York: Farrar, Straus and Giroux, 2008), chapter 4.

8. Ibid., 93.

9. *Winters v. New York*, 333 U.S. 507 (1948).

10. Ibid.

11. See Laura Wittern-Keller, *Freedom of the Screen: Legal Challenges to State Film Censorship, 1915–1981* (Lexington, KY: University Press of Kentucky, 2008), chapter 8.

12. Ibid., 142.

13. Ibid.

14. Author's summary of the production code as reprinted in Nyberg, *Seal of Approval*, 165.

15. Hajdu, *The Ten-Cent Plague*, 129–130.

16. Nyberg, *Seal of Approval*, 43.

17. Ibid., 42.

18. Hajdu, *The Ten-Cent Plague*, chapter 8.

19. Ibid., 190.

20. Nyberg, 48.

21. One of the inherent issues with the bill was the lack of definition for the terms, such as "lewd," which gave the censors broad discretion. New York State Joint Legislative Committee to Study the Publication of Comics, "Report of the New York State Joint Legislative Committee to Study the Publication of Comics, March 1954" (Albany, NY: Williams Press Inc., 1954), appendix A; Warren Weaver Jr., "Dewey Signs Bills on Obscene Books: Measures Designed to Add Strength to Present Curbs on Sale and Distribution Liquor Laws Tightened Illicit Making and Possession of Alcoholic Beverages Is Made a State Offense," *NYT*, Apr. 16, 1954.

22. Paul Crowell, "Ban on Crime-inciting 'Comics' Ordered Sought in Court by City: Crime Book Fight Opened by Mayor," *NYT*, Sept. 9, 1954.

23. Ibid.

24. For an examination of the banning of the comic book *Nights of Horror*, see Craig Yoe, *Secret Identity: The Fetish Art of Superman's Co-creator Joe Shuster* (New York: Abrams Comic Arts, 2009), 27–34.

25. "Tabs Horror Comics Thrill-Kill Blueprint," *BE*, Aug. 23, 1954, *WNY*.

26. Hajdu, 285–286.

27. Ibid. Interestingly, in the final report of the New York State Joint Legislative Committee to Study the Publication of Comics in 1955, Exhibits 41 to 47 are from *Classics Illustrated*, to demonstrate that even though Gilbertson's comics were based on literature, the comic book versions tended to boil the plot down to its most gruesome and salacious moments.

28. The New York State Legislative Committee to Study the Publication of Comic Books, *Transcript of the Proceedings* (New York: Municipal Stenographic Service, 1955), in *Senate Judiciary Committee: Subcommittee to Investigate Juvenile Delinquency, 1953–61*, the National Archives, box 211, "Comic Books," 10 (hereafter, NYSLC, transcript).

29. NYSLC, transcript, 9–14.

30. Ibid., 27–28.

31. Ibid., 26. Murphy's attitude was reflective of an older standard of moral authority and censorship, which had given way in the 1930s to a more male-centered "democratic" model. See Andrea Friedman, *Prurient Interests: Gender, Democracy, and Obscenity in New York City, 1909–1945* (New York: Columbia University Press, 2000).

32. *Hearings before the Subcommittee to Investigate Juvenile Delinquency of the Committee on the Judiciary United States Senate, 83rd Congress, 2nd Session Pursuant to S. 190, April 21, 22, and June 4, 1954* (Washington DC: United States Government Printing Office, 1954), 212.

33. Ibid., 214.

34. NYSLC, transcript, 20.

35. NYSLC, transcript, 22.

36. Ibid., 55–57.

37. Ibid., 57–58.
38. Ibid., 58–60.
39. Ibid., 62.
40. Ibid.
41. Ibid., 65.
42. Ibid., 67.
43. Ibid., 74.
44. Ibid., 72.
45. Ibid., 83–85. The U.S. Supreme Court cases he is likely referring to include *Burstyn v. Wilson, Gelling v. Texas,* and *Superior Films v. Department of Education of State of Ohio*—recent cases, all of which struck down state or local movie censorship in various ways as violating the First Amendment. See Laura Wittern-Keller, *Freedom of the Screen.*
46. James A. Fitzpatrick, letter to Dr. Fredric Wertham, December 17, 1954, Fredric Wertham papers, box 16, folder 8, Library of Congress.
47. James A. Fitzpatrick, letter to Dr. Fredric Wertham, February 1, 1955, Fredric Wertham papers, box 16, folder 8, Library of Congress.
48. Nyberg, 47.
49. James A. Fitzpatrick, letter to Dr. Fredric Wertham, January 6, 1955, Fredric Wertham papers, box 16, folder 8, Library of Congress.
50. Nyberg, 45 and 47.
51. Dr. Fredric Wertham, letter to Senator Kefauver, September 21, 1954, Fredric Wertham papers, box 16, folder 8, Library of Congress.
52. NYSLC, transcript, 116–117.
53. Ibid., 118.
54. Ibid., 117.
55. Ibid., 121, 126.
56. Ibid., 132–135.
57. Ibid., 142.
58. Ibid., 122–123.
59. Ibid., 147–150.
60. Dr. Fredric Wertham, letter to James Fitzpatrick, January 18, 1955, Fredric Wertham papers, box 16, folder 8, Library of Congress. On pages 52 and 58 of the *Report of the New York State Joint Legislative Committee to Study the Publication of Comics, March 1955,* it is reported that Wertham did forward the aforementioned examples to the committee and that, further, forty-seven books bearing the seal contained advertisements for various illicit weapons, despite Charles Murphy's assurances to the committee otherwise. See State of New York, *Report of the New York State Joint Legislative Committee to Study the Publication of Comics, March 1955* (Albany, NY: Williams Press Inc., 1955), 52, 58.
61. NYSLC, transcript, 102, 160–164.
62. Ibid., 181.
63. Ibid., 176.
64. Ibid., 182–185.
65. Ibid., 191.
66. State of New York, *Report of the New York State Joint Legislative Committee to Study the Publication of Comics, March 1955* (Albany, NY: Williams Press Inc., 1955), 14.

67. Ibid.
68. Ibid.
69. Ibid.
70. Ibid., 15.
71. Ibid.
72. Ibid., 16.
73. Ibid., 22.
74. Ibid., 52, 113.
75. Ibid., 17.
76. Ibid., 82. David Hajdu has a very different take on the effectiveness of Murphy's enforcement of the code, arguing that Murphy and his censors enforced the code "fastidiously." See Hajdu, *The Ten-Cent Plague*, chapter 15.
77. State of New York, *Report of the New York State Joint Legislative Committee to Study the Publication of Comics, March 1955* (Albany, NY: Williams Press Inc., 1955), 82.
78. Ibid., 56–58.
79. Ibid., 95–96.
80. Ibid., 141.
81. State of New York, *Report of the New York State Joint Legislative Committee Studying the Publication and Dissemination of Objectionable and Obscene Materials, March 1956* (Albany, NY: Williams Press Inc., 1956), 117–118. The statute was ultimately found to be unconstitutional for failing the *Winters* test, see "The New York Law Controlling the Dissemination of Obscene Materials to Minors," *Fordham L. Rev.* 34, no. 692 (1966) 699.
82. Hajdu, *Ten-Cent Plague*, 312, 326.

EPILOGUE

1. Letter to Joseph Lonardo, June 18, 1958, Indictment 1917/1954, District Attorney Records, Municipal Archives, New York City; and letter to Edward H. Levine, June 18, 1958, Indictment 1917/1954, District Attorney Records, Municipal Archives, New York City.
2. Motion for writ of error, coram nobis, September 14, 1961, Indictment 1917/1954, District Attorney Records, Municipal Archives, New York City.
3. Hearing on motion for inspection of grand jury minutes and dismissal of indictment, *People v. Lieberman* (N.Y. App. Div. 1956), 25.
4. Ibid., 24.
5. *People v. Lieberman* (3 N.Y, 2d 649; 148 N.E. 2d 293; 171 N.Y.S. 2d 73; 1958 N.Y. Lexis 1242).
6. Motion for bench trial, June 29, 1959, Indictment 1916/1954, District Attorney Records, Municipal Archives, New York City.
7. "UA Graduate Freed in 'Thrill Killing,'" *Tucson Daily Citizen* (Tucson, AZ), July 1, 1959.
8. Notes, folder jacket cover, Indictment 1916/1954, District Attorney Records, Municipal Archives, New York City.
9. *Adrian P. Burke, as Corporation Counsel of the City of New York, Plaintiff, v. Kingsley Books, Inc., et al., Defendants*, 208 Misc. 150; 142 N.Y.S.2d 735; 1955 N.Y.

10. Levy quotes here from Judge Curtis Bok, "If We Are to Act like Free Men," *Saturday Review*, Feb. 13, 1954, 9–10, col. 3.

11. There is only one scholarly article on the Brooklyn Thrill Killers, in which the author foils a cursory examination of six *New York Times* articles concerning the Brooklyn Thrill Killers against two *New York Times* articles covering a murder committed by a black youth gang a decade later. In the article, the author concludes that "a majority white city looked sympathetically on a crime committed by 'bookish' white youth . . ." (1369)—a completely erroneous conclusion as evidenced by the more extensive treatment given the gang and the subsequent trial in this book. Otherwise, the gang was briefly discussed by Craig Yoe in his book on *The Nights of Horror* comic books. See Anders Walker, "When Gangs Were White: Race, Rights, and Youth Crime in New York City, 1954–1964," in *Saint Louis University Law Journal* 55 (2011): 1369–1378; and Craig Yoe, *Secret Identity*.

12. This included the *Utica Daily Press* (Utica, NY), "2 Youths Win New Trials," May 20, 1958; the *Schenectady Gazette* (Schenectady, NY), "Thrill Killers to Be Retried," May 20, 1958; the *Niagara Falls Gazette* (Niagara Falls, NY), "2 Youthful Killers Get New Trial," May 20, 1958; *Citizen-Advertiser* (Auburn, NY), "Young Thrill Killers Win New Trial," May 20, 1958; *Kingston Daily Freeman* (Kingston, NY), "New Trials Are Ordered for Two 'Thrill Killers,'" May 20, 1958; and the *Binghamton Press*,(Binghamton, NY), "Thrill Killers Get New Trial," May 20, 1958.

13. Ibid.

14. Grand jury testimony of Casimir Czarnowski (tr. at 160), *People v. Lieberman* (N.Y. App. Div. 1957).

Index

About the Author

Mariah Adin, Ph.D., is a Fulbright Scholar, historian, and writer specializing in juvenile delinquency and modern American history. She holds a Ph.D. in American history from the University at Albany, State University of New York, and is currently the coordinator for the Pathways in Technology program for SUNY Orange.